To Mum,
with love,
Keith + Eleonore
xx

£7.50

ll

A
PEOPLE'S WAR

Peter Lewis

Thames Methuen

To my mother who, like other mothers,
coped with it

By the same author
Churchill: The Finest Hours
The Fifties
Syria, Land of Contrasts
George Orwell, The Road to 1984

First published in Great Britain 1986
by Methuen London Ltd
11 New Fetter Lane, London EC4P 4EE
in association with Thames Television International Ltd
149 Tottenham Court Road, London W1P 9LL

British Library Cataloguing in Publication Data

Lewis, Peter
  A people's war.
  1. World War, 1939–1945—Social aspects—Great Britain
  2. Great Britain—Social life and customs—20th century
  I. Title
  941.084   DA566.4
ISBN 0–423–01950–3

Contents

ILLUSTRATIONS

ACKNOWLEDGEMENTS

THIS BOOK was written as a companion to the Channel Four television series, *A People's War*, made by Thames Television. The series was produced by Richard Broad and his team under the aegis of the then Controller of Documentaries and Features, Catherine Freeman, all of whom I would like to thank. In particular, I would like to thank Alex Sumner and Joyce Jeal for their help with the illustration research, and Andrew Dickson, who suggested the idea for the series.

I would like to thank all those who were interviewed by Thames Television for allowing the use of their interviews and memories in the text. I am also indebted to the Tom Harrisson Mass Observation Archive at Sussex University, who allowed me access to their files and granted permission for me to use some of their material.

There is, of course, an immense literature on the Second World War but all writers on the Home Front are particularly indebted to the detailed, balanced and epic survey by Angus Calder, *The People's War* (Jonathan Cape, 1969). I have also drawn on and quoted from a number of other works, a list of which appears at the end of this book. I would like to thank the following for permission to quote extracts from various publications: the Estate of the late Sonia Brownell Orwell and Secker and Warburg Ltd for George Orwell's *Collected Essays, Letters and Journalism*; Hodder and Stoughton Ltd for John Wadsworth's *Counter Defensive* and William Beveridge's *Power and Influence*; Hodder and Stoughton Ltd and David Higham Associates Ltd for R. A. Butler's *The Art of Memory*; William Heinemann Ltd for J. B. Priestley's *Postscripts, Margin Released* and *Three Men in New Suits*; Cassell Ltd for Sir Winston Churchill's *The Second World War* and *The War Speeches*, edited by Charles Eade; Curtis Brown Ltd on behalf of Winston Churchill, MP for extracts from Sir Winston Churchill's papers (Copyright the Estate of Sir Winston Churchill); and the Peter Maurice Music Co Ltd for permission to reproduce lines from 'A Nightingale Sang in Berkeley Square' and Noel Gay Music Co Ltd for permission to reproduce lines from 'Hey Little Hen', words and music by Ralph Butler and Noel Gay.

PREFACE

AS THE SECOND WORLD WAR retreats further into the past, the number of people who do not remember it increasingly outnumbers those who do. People now in their forties can scarcely recall living during the war; they depend on the memories of people still older for a picture of what daily life was like under such conditions. Apart from that, there are the books and films of the time which deliberately encouraged confidence in victory and exaggerated the morale and endurance of the British under stress. Once the atmosphere of war had faded, their propagandist tone of voice seemed to ring false. As well as an aftermath, the war had an aftermyth. Later generations wearied of tales of unalloyed heroism, undaunted defiance, unfailing cheerfulness and community spirit, undismayed whatever the odds. So there came a sceptical reaction which belittled these things.

The balance is hard to strike. This book attempts to avoid as far as possible the distortions of hindsight by telling the story of the Home Front through the eyes of ordinary people (and a few extraordinary ones), wherever possible using diaries, descriptions, letters, broadcasts and quotations written at the time. The present-day memories quoted are largely those of nearly a hundred people ranging from government officials to evacuees who were interviewed for the television series *A People's War*.

The Tom Harrisson Mass Observation archive has been extensively drawn upon. Although it was not, and did not claim to be, a scientific sampling of opinion from which valid generalisations could be made about the nation as a whole, it was used at the time by the Ministry of Information as a litmus paper to test public reaction to many of the trials of war and it is a rich, unrivalled store of anecdotal oral history.

It is worth trying to recapture the quality of the experience of living in wartime Britain while enough of those who did so are close enough to remember it accurately. The Second World War was the most powerful experience of their lives for those who lived through it. The myths of the war were founded on experiences like those recounted here. Those experiences should help readers to decide for themselves what it was that enabled the people to endure, survive and triumph in a people's war.

CHAPTER ONE

A BRACING DEFEAT

THE BBC RADIO NEWSREADER made the announcement at six o'clock on 31 May 1940: 'Men of the undefeated British Expeditionary Force have been coming home from France.... Their morale is as high as ever. They are anxious only to be back soon – "to have a real crack at Jerry".'

What was this? If our Army was undefeated, why was it coming home? Why hadn't it had a real crack at Jerry when Jerry advanced? And why, above all, did nobody mention the evacuation until it was nearly over? Three-quarters of the British troops at Dunkirk had already been transported by railway to reception camps and hospitals without a word being said publicly. And then this news bulletin announced, with blithe unconcern, a colossal military disaster.

For most people in Britain the war really began that evening. Of course they had realised that something was wrong. Confused reports from France had indicated that the Germans had disposed of the Maginot Line, supposedly impregnable, by simply coming round the end of it, that the French army was in confusion and that the British could be cut off. But to be sent packing across the Channel.... Until that moment, the war had been something that was happening 'over there', in France or Belgium; now the front line had suddenly moved to Britain itself. It concentrated the mind wonderfully.

And all the time the sun was shining. Many things are hard to believe about 1940, the year when according to the odds Britain should have lost the war. All the traumatic events of that year took place against the background of Nature at her most genial. Brilliant cloudless spring weather accompanied the BEF on its retreat to the French beaches and across the still sea. Invasion was hourly awaited in the deep green peace of a perfect English June. The dogfights of the Battle of Britain were fought high in August's breathtakingly blue skies scored with vapour trails, and in September the barrage balloons over London glowed russet in the sunset as they awaited the black formations of bombers returning at dusk like flights of wild duck. At least we had nice weather for it. Perhaps that had something to do with the way these dangers were endured – perhaps not.

There was nothing glorious, even to the men who were rescued from it, about Dunkirk. They were angry. Most of them had not yet fought a battle, not even fired a shot at the German Army, except in retreat; they felt let down, by the French Army from whom they had been cut off, and by the authorities who had not equipped or trained them to withstand a German *Blitzkrieg*. All of them had lost their weapons. But now they were home they could let their feelings be known. There were no journalists at Dunkirk to report what had happened, and those who were told of the evacuation were sworn to silence, as were the Southern Railway drivers and guards who shifted the exhausted men – someone reported passing a trainload 'almost every man of them sunk in a stupor of sleep'. 'The railway line, from Dover more than halfway to London, is strewn with cigarette packets, ice cream cartons, bottles and squashed drinking vessels and everywhere orange peel and bits of equipment – a belt, a rainsheet, even a bayonet,' reported an eye-witness. At stations in Kent, when the news spread of the troops coming home, women and children stood alongside the railway tracks with picnic baskets full of bottles and jugs and jamjars of lemonade, with fruit and cigarettes and postcards stamped and ready to post. Collecting-boxes were set up at stations for refreshments and cigarettes for the troops, and many people would stick a handful of cigarettes from their own packet into the opening of a large cardboard carton supplied for the purpose. Cigarettes were still the currency of comfort in those days.

People remarked how brown the troops were, from the sun and exposure on the beaches, or how dirty they were – 'and did they smell!' observed a nurse at a reception hospital for the wounded. Men who had been shelled night and day, dive-bombed and machine-gunned by low-flying aircraft – or, having waded out up to their necks in the water, had to be rescued from it again when the ship they boarded was sunk – were not likely to have a high state of morale. Above all they had been given no explanation of their sudden and ignominious ejection from the Battle of France. Leon Atkins, in 'Dunkirk', put their feelings into incoherent but vivid lines of verse:

> Backs to the sea!
> O bitter the word 'Retreat'
> And bitterer yet 'Evacuate'
> – And nobody told the soldier why.
>
> Pointing speechless guns
> At contemptuous Huns
> And five dud rounds in our pouches . . .
> And nobody told us why!

Neither was the evacuation always the orderly British queue it has been represented as. 'I couldn't stop laughing,' said one Coldstream guardsman surprisingly. 'I was scared stiff all right but when I saw the lads who'd talked

so big pushing me aside on the beach in their hurry to get into the boats, I just couldn't stop laughing.' A staff officer greeted the Grenadiers at Folkestone with 'You're in England now, not a bloody rabble on the seashore.'

Basil Dean, director of ENSA (the entertainments organisation) was shocked by the state of mind of the troops he found in a Dorset pub – 'the seething soldiery (yes, that is the only adjective to use) expressing blasphemous resentment at what had happened to them ... dismayed men, savagely wounded in their pride, seeking relief in bitter criticism of those set over them.' John Lehmann, the left-wing editor of *Penguin New Writing*, noted in his diary: 'The soldiers from Dunkirk seem to be stirring up a violence of opinion in the country against the Old Men of Munich that must burst soon: a more effective army of revolutionary agitators, penetrating to the furthest village, could not have been organised by the cleverest political party.'

There were now 225,000 such British troops in the country – the rest of the total of 338,000 evacuated were French, who were repatriated only to surrender a fortnight later when France capitulated. The impact of all this

1 Men of the British Expeditionary Force return home from Dunkirk by third-class railway carriage. Civilians lined the tracks to offer the troops fruit and cigarettes

ought to have produced defeatism. Indeed a Home Morale Emergency Committee was formed in May to advise how to combat defeatism. It proved unnecessary, but there was plenty of depression about as the completeness of Hitler's victory on mainland Europe sank in. Denmark, Norway, Holland, Belgium, Luxembourg and France had fallen to his Panzers in an incredibly short two months. It was a mesmerising run of success. Britain still stood, like the last ninepin in the row, but for how long?

Mass Observation was the name of an organisation of volunteer observers – 2000 of them part-time and unpaid, supplemented by 22 full-time investigators – which had been started before the war by Charles Madge, a poet, and Tom Harrisson, an anthropologist. They referred to Mass Observation as 'the anthropology of ourselves' and used the same techniques as anthropologists use when observing 'primitive peoples'. The task of the observers was to find out what people were saying on a given topic arising from the war – partly through interview, but also through overheard conversations and remarks; some were also asked to keep diaries. From their fieldwork, reports on public opinion and morale were compiled. It was not a balanced sampling of opinion (it should be weighed with caution) but it is the only sampling for the period that we have got.

The immediate reactions to the Fall of France quoted by Mass Observers were mixed but gloomy: 'There's no doubt we shall be exterminated. We fight alone now, they've all deserted us. But they haven't won yet.' . . . 'If France and England can't do it together, I don't see what we can do alone.' . . . 'It looks as though all we can do is give up. It's no use throwing away lives when there's no hope.' . . . 'I felt bloody awful when I first heard the news but I'm getting over the shock now. They've not won yet, a miracle might turn up and save us.' . . . 'He's had so much luck so far that it must break.' . . . 'Now they've got France they can do what they like.' . . . 'I think we're losing the war.' . . . 'This country should have kept out of it from the start.' The general report on morale summed it up: 'There is great restlessness, great depression at the fall of France. Home morale is still being bungled. The appeals of the leadership are failing to register. The reasons are partly that persons responsible for morale and propaganda have no sympathy with the majority of the masses.'

This is hardly the state of mind celebrated in national myth, in which Britain stood alone, united and unflinching in its darkest hour. These particular people may not have been typical, even of others in the same class and the same street. Perhaps the Mass Observers tended to record them because what they said was different from the general reaction. And yet their feelings were quite natural. They had had a tremendous shock, the rudest of awakenings from the unreality of the war up till then, the so-called 'Phoney War' which they had so often been assured they were bound to win.

For nine months the land war had been a stalemate – while the Home Front had been a dreary catalogue of restrictions, regulations, frustrations and aggravations, all of which had achieved absolutely nothing. The German *Blitzkrieg* arrived at just the time when the 'Bore War', as it was dubbed, had reduced most of the civilian population to apathy. Home Intelligence Reports, prepared for the Ministry of Information each month from various sources, including Mass Observation, again and again reported apathy, boredom and irritation with the civil defence preparations that seemed in the early months disproportionate to any attack that was likely to come.

Sir John Reith, the BBC's first director-general, who was Minister of Information in the early months of 1940, reported to the government that a 'passive, negative feeling of apathy and boredom is apparent. . . . There is a general feeling that individuals do not count in the conduct of the war, and that the only thing to do is to live as normal a life as possible.' People were apathetic about appeals to evacuate their children, to take air-raid precautions at home, to go back to carrying the detested gas masks, which they had long ago given up bothering with. 'People are apathetic, because they do not know what they ought to do,' concluded one intelligence report in the first week of June, but added: 'Events of the last month [up to Dunkirk] have actually improved morale. At least the period of wishful thinking is over.' On 28 May, when the French and British Armies were in full retreat and, although no one at home knew it yet, the Dunkirk evacuation had already begun, George Orwell noted in his diary: 'People talk a little more of the war, but very little. As always, it is impossible to overhear any comments on it in pubs. Last night, Eileen and I went to the pub to hear the nine o'clock news. The barmaid was not going to have it turned on if we had not asked her. To all appearances, nobody listened.' When a war has become a matter of such indifference to the ordinary pub-goer, nothing is likely to be so bracing as a major, catastrophic defeat. Dunkirk provided it. People certainly wanted to listen to the news after that.

Until then they had not trusted what they were told. So complete was the censorship insisted on by the three service ministries that it appeared that absolutely nothing was happening for most of the time. Hence the growing audience for 'Lord Haw-Haw', the inspired nickname bestowed by the *Daily Express* on the voice of the newsreader on Radio Hamburg, whose news bulletins began with the call-sign: 'Germany calling!' – only the German intonation made it sound like 'Jairmany calling!' All over the country, schoolboys could be heard imitating this voice with glee. By January 1940, BBC audience research found that 6 million people – one out of every six adults – were regular listeners to German radio news and propaganda, and 18 million more listened sometimes. Mass Observation tried to find out why: 'We nearly always turn him on at nine fifteen to try and glean some news that the Ministry of Information withholds from us,' was one revealing comment. Most people enjoyed ridiculing the Haw-Haw broadcasts and said they only listened to have a good laugh – one of the early jokes was that Haw-Haw had claimed that bombs had been dropped at 'Random'.

There was such a hunger for some real news that credibility was given to Haw-Haw's mocking tones. 'There's a lot in what he says. It's no use calling it rubbish because there's no smoke without fire.' . . . 'There's something vaguely likable about him and his witty sayings.' . . . 'He makes me chuckle and, true or not true, he's a great psychologist.' In fact, 'Lord Haw-Haw' was more than one person. The superior, contemptuous tones which first earned him his nick-name belonged to Norman Baillie-Stewart, a former officer in the Seaforth Highlanders, who had been imprisoned under the Official Secrets Act in the Thirties and then gone to Nazi Germany. The audience in Britain seized on his affected upper-class tone as the voice you love to hate. But Baillie-Stewart was soon eased out by William Joyce, Irish by family but an American citizen, who had worked for Sir Oswald Mosley's British Union of Fascists. He then founded an extreme, pro-Hitler party of his own, the National Socialist League. He had great talent for invective and sarcasm and, having been caught in Germany when war was declared, offered his services as propagandist. He was skilled at undermining his listeners' confidence. 'Where is the *Ark Royal*?' he would ask, 'It was hit in a German attack – there was a terrific explosion. Where is the *Ark Royal*? Britain, ask your Admiralty.' The ship had not been sunk but the Silent Service remained characteristically silent, leaving many people wondering just how much they were not being told. During the Blitz, Haw-Haw was to be credited with almost clairvoyant powers of knowing what was going on in England, as we shall see.

In March 1940, one person in ten was in favour of stopping the war immediately, according to the admittedly rough soundings taken by Mass Observation. Why? The answer could be encapsulated in one name, Neville Chamberlain. It was Chamberlain who had tried for so long to appease 'Herr Hitler', who had boasted of 'peace in our time' on the strength of Hitler's signature on a piece of paper during the Munich crisis, who had been so transparently eager to compromise and who had been so easily fooled. Lloyd George's estimate of Chamberlain's abilities – 'a good Lord Mayor of Birmingham in a bad year' he called him – was over-contemptuous. But he was not made of the stuff to unite the nation when at last he was reluctantly compelled to declare war.

The reason for going to war was ostensibly to defend Poland, which Britain could not do. Now that Poland was crushed there had to be another reason for going on with it, but Chamberlain's government never gave one. Although often asked for them, it refused to declare its war aims and showed a far from wholehearted desire to wage total war, seeming to prefer a minimal war which would disturb life little and cost as little as possible. Government propaganda stressed that 'time is on our side' and that the economic blockade of Europe 'will bring Hitler to his knees'. It was as if we only had to wait around, doing nothing in particular in a defensive posture, for Hitler to crack up while we were digging for victory. 'We do not have to defeat the Nazis on

2 *Anxiety and uncertainty is written on the faces of these London boys arriving in a strange town bearing the badges of evacuees – luggage labels and gas-masks in cardboard boxes*

land, but only to prevent them from defeating us,' concluded one of the stirring pamphlets issued by the Ministry of Information. The height of complacency was reached when Chamberlain announced in April, 'Hitler has missed the bus.' He implied that Britain and France were now ready to defeat any attack he might launch. Just a month later came the *Blitzkrieg* that knocked out Western Europe.

Defensive measures at home – the black-out, shelter drill, gas-mask carrying, evacuation – had by this time made everyone fed up, or 'browned off' as the service slang then put it. During the Thirties, and especially after the Spanish Civil War, when Hitler's pilots got their bombing practice, people had been mesmerised by Stanley Baldwin's prophecy, 'The bomber will always get through.' When the war came, people feared instant annihilation just as today we expect instant nuclear incineration. When the sirens wailed for the first air-raid warning just after Chamberlain's broadcast announcing that 'this country is at war with Germany', people thought the prophesied moment had come. Even Winston Churchill, looking down Whitehall at that moment, had a vision of fearful destruction: 'My imagination drew pictures of ruin and carnage and vast explosions shaking the ground; of buildings clattering down in dust and rubble, of fire brigades and ambulances scurrying through the smoke. . . . For had we not all been taught how terrible air raids would be?'

Official calculations of what sort of casualties to expect anticipated 100,000 tons of bombs to rain on London in the first fourteen days – more than London received in the entire war. Mistakenly, using First World War figures, the government calculated that there would be fifty casualties per ton. As a result it cleared the hospitals, making hundreds of thousands of beds empty in readiness, and provided millions of cardboard coffins, burial forms and lime-pits to dispose of the corpses. Those were pardonable errors, as was the assumption that the Germans would use gas – it was safer to provide gas-masks for the population than to take a chance. So 38 million gas masks had been issued in 1938. Bewildered schoolchildren were given practice in spitting on the inside of the mica window to stop it misting up, and told to put their chins in first. Many of them sat in classrooms wearing the things, plunged into a foggy gloom that smelt pungently of disinfectant and rubber, making foggy replies and rude noises. People were told to get used to wearing their masks every day and to carry them everywhere – 'If the gas rattles sound, put on your gas-mask at once wherever you are, even in bed,' said the leaflets. For a time people meekly obeyed instructions, lumping the unsightly cardboard boxes, on strings that were always breaking, through the streets. After two months of war – and no gas – the gas-mask carriers were a distinct minority. By the spring, nobody bothered any longer.

ARP (Air Raid Precautions) had been begun in 1938. Shelters were dug or built, while 100,000 air-raid wardens and 60,000 auxiliary firemen had been recruited. Every home had been urged to equip itself with a stirrup pump, buckets of water and sand and a long-handled shovel to put out incendiaries. But as the months passed and there was a negligible amount of bombing, public sentiment turned against the air-raid wardens, who had nothing much to do for their £3 a week except play cards in their sector posts. Wardens were disliked because of their bossy enforcement of the black-out, which for the first weeks of war was total (no street lighting) and lethal (road deaths doubled). Although sharp corners, kerbs, steps and car running-boards were painted white, by order, and tree-trunks were circled with three painted white rings, people still barged into them or fell over them, or toppled off them. By January 1940, one person in five had had some sort of an accident, and Winston Churchill was moved to take time off from directing the Admiralty to suggest that modified street lighting would save lives, remove general depression and allay anxieties about rape. Very dim street lighting was restored at crossroads and other places, and torches were allowed, providing you covered the lighted end with two thicknesses of tissue paper and pointed it downwards. Soon there was a vexing shortage of torches and, especially, of 'No. 8' batteries to fit them. Railway carriages were steeped in gloom after dark, with faint blue shafts of light down the centre of them, leaving the

passengers' faces floating in the darkness like ghostly luminous fish in an aquarium. Passengers leaned forward in their seats in the hope of being able to read a line here and there of the evening paper or the crossword.

For all this, the nights resounded with the cry of the air-raid warden, 'Put that light out!' It might have been a chink in the corner of a heavily curtained window, it might have been a match lighting a cigarette, it might have been a garden bonfire flaring up unexpectedly – but however innocuous and unlikely to guide a bomber thousands of feet up, prosecution and fines frequently followed, adding to people's irritation.

Car headlamps were at first blotted out, with cardboard or old socks, but after more than 4000 people had been killed on the roads a speed limit of 20 m.p.h. in built-up areas was introduced, along with headlamp covers which had horizontal slits in them, directing what light they emitted downwards. Dashboard lights were not allowed: you were meant to judge your speed from the engine note.

The only compensation for the black-out restrictions was the introduction of 'summertime' all the year round, with 'double' summertime in the

3 From 1938 onwards, people were being urged to take air-raid precautions and to expect an immediate onslaught of bombs on the cities as soon as war began

SHINE YOUR TORCH **DOWNWARDS**
WHEN CROSSING THE ROAD

4 *The black-out was the worst hazard of the 1939 winter. Road casualties doubled when street lighting disappeared. 'Wear something white', people were urged*

summer months. But Guy Fawkes celebrations, neon signs, camp fires and fairground lights disappeared for 'the duration'.

The main air-raid precaution at the beginning of the war was, of course, evacuation. This involved 3.5 million people altogether, the biggest shift in population England had ever seen, comparable to the exodus caused by the Plague in 1665. About 2 million out of the total were people evacuating themselves to bolt-holes in the countryside, thanks to having either the means to rent them or the friends to lend them. The other 1.5 million were schoolchildren (800,000), mothers with children under school age (550,000), expectant mothers and chronic invalids evacuated under the official scheme. The children were labelled and marshalled by their teachers in school parties at the railway stations and despatched, often without knowing where they were bound.

Many of the children were agog with excitement, but not many of them remained so for long. In some places they were received by billeting officers who had more willing foster-parents than evacuees, but in others the children were herded into a village hall for local people to look over and choose from, as if they were cattle up for auction. (The billeting allowance for an evacuee was 8s 6d (42p) a week, or 10s 6d (52p) for a single child or one who was over sixteen.) Some bewildered children found themselves in big houses, being waited on by servants. Winifred Selby was a maid in a big house outside Cambridge, and she remembers four East End children arriving looking spick and span – until their top-coats were removed 'and they had nothing but dirty rags on underneath'. The children lived in the kitchen with her and she, aged nineteen, was made responsible for their well-being.

> Looking back on it now I can see how tragic those children were. They couldn't get used to the open space and the quietness, particularly at night. They also couldn't understand why I never went to the pub. When their family came down to see them, carrying a baby, they spent a little while with the children, then dumped the baby with me and departed to the local pub till closing time. The children didn't seem to mind. It must have been what they were used to.

Children from overcrowded homes in the slums, who found themselves the unwanted guests of the middle-classes, took an instant dislike to 'posh' people with posh houses – and the dislike was mutual. Where class, manners and habits were not the cause of friction, town and country soon found their differences rubbed each other up the wrong way. Town children were rough and rude and blasphemous in language to country ears. On the other hand, privies at the end of a dark garden path were a terrifying ordeal to children like eight-year-old William Bush, transported from Liverpool to a small Welsh-speaking village:

Mrs Roberts told her son to take me to the toilet, through the garden up the path, and I'd never seen anything like it in my life. A scrubbed wooden toilet seat and a shadowy black hole. And when I looked up, the roof in the toilet was festooned with cobwebs and spiders and I thought, if there are spiders over my head, what in the name of God is beneath me? And when I came back from the toilet, an animal came running out of a doorway towards a gate where I stood looking over the wall. I gave a scream and ran to tell these people that there were wild animals in their garden. Well, they laughed – in fact it was a pig-sty. They kept pigs. I'd seen lions and tigers at the circus but I'd never been that close to an uncontrolled, I thought wild animal, a pig.

In this confrontation with how the other half lived, what caused the most public outcry was vermin, dirt and skin diseases. Evacuation took place at the end of a long summer holiday, when schools had not held their de-lousing parades for a long time. In some places people estimated as many as half the evacuees were verminous; while others put it at 10 or 20 per cent. Hosts were also shocked at the condition of their clothes – some children had never worn night-clothes and some had no change of underwear. Many foster-parents set about making good these deficiencies at their own expense. 'The WVS gave my mother a load of clothes for us,' said a Stepney boy, Kenny Micallef, evacuated to share a Guildford mansion, 'I remember going round telling the kids, "Oh, I wear underpants, do you?" It was such a novelty.'

Many children missed the sort of food they got at home, however unsuitable it seemed to their new hosts. Some wanted bread and margarine, fish and chips, tinned milk or even beer for supper. Many were used to sharing the bed with the whole family and nearly all were disturbed and homesick in their strange surroundings. The result was a countrywide outbreak of bedwetting, which made relations worse, as Tony Collins recalled: 'The first morning after it happened we went to school as usual, but when we returned the door flew open and I was whisked into the front room where the mattress was drying in front of the fire. The lady of the house thrust my nose into the mattress and said, "How do you like that, you little pig?"'

Women's Institutes, 1700 of them, spread over the reception areas, put together a shocked report called *Town Children Through Country Eyes* on the evacuees' 'condition and habits', which was sent to the health and education officers of the towns from which the children came. Women's Institute members naturally had little idea of the insanitary conditions which slum-dwelling mothers had to fight against, as will be seen by their comments:

In practically every batch of children there were some who suffered from head lice, skin diseases and bed-wetting ... some children [from Manchester] had never slept in beds. ... One boy [from Salford] had

never had a bath before; his ribs looked as black as if black-leaded. . . . The state of the children [from Liverpool] was such that the school had to be fumigated after reception; we have never seen so many verminous children – it appeared they were unbathed for months; the majority had scabies in their hair and septic sores all over their bodies. . . . It is hard to exaggerate the state of the [Bethnal Green] children's heads when they came; their habits were disgusting. . . . The habits of most of the [Fulham and Hammersmith] children were unspeakable and have caused great distress and expense to those who gave them billets . . . the children relieve themselves any time and anywhere.

As for food:

Bread and lard are a usual breakfast for a number of [Walthamstow] children when at home. . . . A number of the [Leeds] children were surprised that we had 'Sunday dinner' every day . . . some of the [Grimsby] children did not even know what a pudding was! . . . Few [Manchester] children would eat food that demanded the use of teeth – could only eat with a teaspoon. . . . One little girl of five [from Liverpool] remarked she would like to have beer and cheese for supper. Children had been used to receiving a penny at home to buy their own dinners. One used to buy broken biscuits, the other Oxo cubes. . . . One [Newcastle]

5 The evacuees poured out of the cities, especially from the poorer inner-city areas, to be faced with the unfamiliar sights and pursuits of the countryside. Some adapted and loved it, others longed for home

[13]

mother admitted they never had soup, while two boys attempted it with a knife and fork ... some [Gosport] children had never used a knife and fork.... The [Finsbury] children did not understand sitting down for a meal but seemed to like the food in the hand ... most of the [Fulham] children had never sat down to a cooked meal.

Some children, said the Women's Institute members, had been sewn into their clothes, which were in such a state that they had to be burnt at once. Clothing sent by their parents was often sent dirty and in need of repair. As for behaviour – they used bad language, 'had no idea of telling the truth', stole from their hosts' households, were uncouth and lacking in table manners.

In spite of the affronted tone, the report mentioned the 'real affection' between hosts and children. Almost all of them spoke with satisfaction of how greatly the children had improved in health, weight, cleanliness and manners and how they would miss them when they went home. 'Most of the children wept bitterly when taken home to Manchester. Those who stayed have improved wonderfully in appearance and in their manners.' The children's interest in country life had come on by leaps and bounds, but their ignorance had been sublime. Some were amazed to learn that eggs were laid by hens and one, seeing horses and fowls sharing a field, asked anxiously: 'Won't the horses eat the chickens?'

But although the children could be forgiven for rudeness and dirty habits, homesickness and bedwetting, their mothers, who had let them get that way, could not. Some of the town mothers who were evacuated with children under five attracted feelings of outrage from the country mothers who had the dubious pleasure of sharing their homes and kitchens with them. Women's Institute members reported that they 'found it hard to be sympathetic to women who could neither cook, sew, nor conform to the ordinary standards of human decency. And whose idea of enjoyment was to visit the public house or cinema.' They were 'horrified and disgusted' at the state of filth in which some mothers left their billets and at the reflection that 'this type of mother exists in every one of our big towns.' 'The poorest cottagers were shocked at their ignorance of managing, at their lack of ordinary cleanliness.' Some places put the proportion of bad mothers as high as 40 per cent. 'The general feeling was one of shame that such people are being bred in our big cities.' There was a strong nannyish flavour about the attitudes of the Women's Institutes, though plenty of evidence of compassion for the children, who obviously responded in many cases to being close to country sights and sounds. But evacuee horror stories swamped the country. The issue was raised in Parliament, and stories appeared in the newspapers and novels of the time, notably Evelyn Waugh's *Put Out More Flags*. Some believed that nothing but good could come of the shock, as slum poverty was exposed at close quarters before the eyes of people more comfortably off. Something should clearly be done – but it would have to wait until after the war.

Meanwhile, where were the bombs? Where was the justification for the whole traumatic exercise? Months went by and no bombs came. Children went on missing their parents and parents, perhaps to their surprise, found out how much they missed their children. The result was inevitable – a widespread desire to call the whole thing off. Many of the evacuees were only too anxious to say goodbye to their hosts, whatever the Women's Institute thought. 'We were scruffy kids, city kids, they didn't really want us,' said Liverpool evacuee Patricia McCann who was six at the time. 'I'm sure we were only taken because of the money. We were watched all the time we were writing home to make sure we couldn't complain. In the end we saved our bus money by walking to school and bought a stamp, so we could write and ask Mum to bring us home.' Isobel Murphy and her brother and sister didn't dislike the family that looked after them in Ormskirk, but they missed home.

My dad said it was going to be bad in Liverpool and we'd better stay. But by the time he came to see us a second time we were in a terrible state. I was so determined he wouldn't get away, I waited outside the toilet door and, as he walked out, I took hold of his trouser leg and there I stayed until he said, 'Obviously I'll have to take them home. If we are going to be killed, I'm afraid we'll all have to go together.'

For some children the departure was more traumatic. Jo Spence, evacu-ated from London to Cornwall at the age of six with her school, remembers: 'I was sent to an isolation hospital with scabies. We used to sit in the bath and the nurse would eternally scrub the sores off and then put gentian violet on the open wounds. My mother came to visit me and was so appalled by my condition that she took me back to London. I hated my mother because she sent me away.' Sometimes children came up against intolerance that they did not know existed, like Abigail Sabel, teenage child of Jewish immigrants in Whitechapel, who was sent to a Berkshire village outside Windsor. 'Every Sunday we were asked if we would like to go with them to church and we said no. Eventually the woman insisted and my sister told her we went to a synagogue, not a church. She was absolutely horrified. She said to us, get out! In the East End no one had ever said anything like that.'

Tony Collins, one of a Stepney family of children, was moved to four different billets before his father took him home. 'The last straw was when a boy who had bought a pen for threepence sold it to me for sixpence. When I found out, I called him a fucking swindler. My guardians sent for my father and complained but said they were prepared to give me another chance. My dad, who hated their condescending manner, said no they fucking wouldn't and I went home.'

By January 1940, nine out of ten mothers with young children had gone back home and nearly half of the schoolchildren were back too; the great majority followed them soon afterwards. In other words, evacuation was a

6 By January 1940, most mothers evacuated with young children and nearly half the schoolchildren had given up and gone back home, because no bombs were falling. This poster was part of a campaign to persuade them to stay in the countryside. It didn't work

flop – unless viewed as an exercise in finding out how the other half lived. It was a flop chiefly because it proved to be premature, and it made it all the harder to persuade parents to send their children away a second time when the bombs really did start falling.

When the children returned home, they often found there were no schools to go to. The education system was in chaos. In the 'danger areas', local authority schools had been closed wholesale at the outbreak of war and many of them requisitioned for civil defence (two-thirds of London's schools, for instance). Schools were not allowed to reopen until sufficient shelter space for their pupils had been provided; meanwhile a million children who had not been evacuated were running wild in the streets. Sheffield's city fathers had not seen fit to provide shelters before war began and only 15 per cent of its schoolchildren were evacuated. William Alexander (later Lord Alexander of Potterhill) had just been appointed as education officer:

> I knew I had 55,000 children and no schools open. I heard an announcer on the radio say 'This is the BBC Home Service [its new name]'. Home service – that was the answer. We appealed for 5000 school rooms in private houses, for which we paid 2s 6d a week, and we moved the desks and furniture from the schools into these houses. The children were divided into groups of twelve and each group was taught for an hour and a half a day. Sheffield was, I think, the first place to institute home tuition and many of the children went on receiving it for four months, often in people's kitchens or bedrooms. They spent another one and a half hours a day in the local library.

It wasn't until April 1940 that compulsory education was once more the rule and local authorities were struggling to reopen enough schools to provide it.

By April 1940, Chamberlain's government did not look the sort of team that wars are won by. The war was costing £6 million a day. What was the country getting for it? The *Graf Spee*, trapped and then scuttled by its own captain in Montevideo harbour, was the chief success to date – not much to put against our own heavy losses at sea. The land war was bogged down well short of the Siegfried Line, on which the most popular song of the winter had promised we would 'hang out our washing'. The RAF was mainly occupied in dropping leaflets, not bombs, on the Germans and when it was suggested in Parliament that an incendiary raid could set fire to the Black Forest, the Air Minister, Sir Kingsley Wood, sounded scandalised: 'It is private property! You will be asking me to bomb Essen next!' Essen, of course, was the site of the Krupp armament works. Herr Krupp's millions were the kind of private property the Chamberlain government apparently respected.

What it had succeeded all too well in catering for was the streak in British officialdom which loves to play Nanny to the nation. Those fines for lighting a cigarette in the black-out were one symptom. Another was the cascade of leaflets that came through every letterbox, like so many wagging fingers from the Nanny state: 'What To Do About Gas', 'Make Your Home Safe Now' ('If you have a garden you can dig a trench. Don't dig a *deep* trench unless you know how to make one properly. Deep trenches are apt to fall in'), 'Masking Your Windows' ('If your blinds do not fit closely, paint the edges of the window panes with dark paint'), 'Always Carry Your Identity Card – you must produce it on demand'. A classic of the finger-wagging genre was a leaflet entitled 'When you go to shelter – what you should know':

> Bedding should be aired daily. . . . Try not to lie on your back – you are less likely to snore. . . . Make your family gargle before they start for the shelter: Make them gargle again when they return. *Don't spit: it is a dirty habit.* If you see anyone spitting, it is your duty to tell the warden at once. . . . Keep your feet dry. One of the easiest ways of catching cold is by sitting with wet feet. . . . Entertainment : a certain amount of entertainment is good for us all, but don't let it become a nuisance. . . . Try to find a home for your pets. If you can't, take them to a vet. You cannot take them to the shelter. . . . Pay No Attention to Rumours.

Most of the communications from the government to its people adopted this testy tone of voice, the tone of Nanny, who does not want any trouble but expects tears before bedtime. Charles Ritchie, a Canadian diplomat serving at his embassy, summed up the early months like this: 'Living in London is like being an inmate of a reformatory school. Everywhere you turn, you run into some regulation designed for your protection. The government is like the School Matron.'

Bureaucracy was outdoing itself. Stately homes, public schools, Oxford and Cambridge colleges, and many of the best hotels in spa towns such as Bath, Cheltenham and Buxton had been requisitioned at a few hours' notice to accommodate ministries evacuated from Whitehall. Their civil service mandarins settled down at these prestigious addresses to an orgy of directive-writing; the Home Office alone produced 500 of them in the first few months. Local authorities despaired of keeping abreast. The London *Evening News* complained in October 1939 about 'the barbed wire of bureaucracy, the tin Hitlers of Bumbledom'. It was a sitting target for cartoonists and comedians. Tommy Handley began *ITMA*'s first series in the winter of 1939–40 in the character of a lunatic bureaucrat, the 'Minister of Aggravation' ('I have the power to seize anything on sight') whose ministry performed in the 'Office of Twerps' (the Office of Works was notorious for being the agency which commandeered houses and hotels and then, often, left them empty).

Most of the public ticking-offs and warnings were written for the various ministries by the Ministry of Information, whose 999 civil servants were housed in the Senate House of London University, then the tallest tower block in London. One of the Ministry's jobs was to compile the Home Intelligence

7 (Facing page) There were government leaflets and posters about everything from painting the edges of window-panes to stopping people snoring in shelters. It was, wrote a Canadian visitor, 'like living in a reformatory school'

"*If only they'd tell us all what to do.*"

Reports, based partly on the censorship of letters abroad passing through the Post Office. Another was to produce morale-building propaganda which covered poster sites all over the country. They adopted the same remote and condescending tone of the leaflets: FREEDOM IS IN PERIL – DEFEND IT WITH ALL YOUR MIGHT . . . WE'RE GOING TO SEE IT THROUGH . . . IT ALL DEPENDS ON ME. Such were the vacuous exhortations which the Ministry felt would inspire the man and woman in the street. They were widely ignored or disliked, and the notorious slogan pictured below provoked especial hostility and suspicion. When Mass Observation tested public reactions it found that a substantial proportion asked who was this 'us' which 'your' efforts are going to make victorious? It sounded all too familiar to many of them – they were being exhorted to help keep the bosses, the Establishment, in business.

Life for the better-off was indeed very much as it always had been. As in the Depression of the 1930s, the well-off were not sacrificing much. The first wartime Budget, introduced by Sir John Simon, put up income tax by only 2 shillings (10p) in the pound – to 7s 6d (37p), and to prevent manufacturers making extra money out of wartime demands and shortages an Excess Profits Tax of 60 per cent was introduced. Prices of food, clothing and household goods had shot up, but in effect their suppliers were still being allowed to keep 40 per cent of the extra profits for themselves. Meanwhile, government

8 This was one of the slogans devised by the Ministry of Information which appeared on hoardings all over the country. It was widely disliked. Who, people asked, do they mean by 'us'? The bosses?

meanness reached new levels with the allowances paid to servicemen's wives: 17 shillings (85p a week), plus 5 shillings for the first child, 3 shillings for the second, and 2 shillings for subsequent children. The basic allowance was only sixpence more than it had been in the First World War, and there were already over 1.5 million newly enlisted men whose wives were having to live on it.

Most people favoured rationing and fair shares, instead of the unfair advantage that the rich had in stocking up with durable foods such as sugar and tinned meat, which were in short supply. Ration books, which had been printed back in 1938, were at last doled out in January 1940 and meat rationing on a fairly generous scale began in March. But this did not noticeably cramp the style of Loelia, Duchess of Westminster. On 11 May, the night of the German attack on Holland and Belgium, Cecil Beaton was asked to a party to celebrate the fact that she had reopened her drawing-room, which had been under dustcovers since the war began. 'We all felt the dinner to be so excellent that we wanted to keep the menu as an archaeological specimen, showing that this was the meal that we in England were fortunate enough to enjoy, even after six months of war effort. Anyhow, while we could, we would be as gay as possible. We went out to night clubs and danced all night.' This was not an exceptionally frivolous evening. Advertisements for butlers and housemaids appeared regularly, often adding 'eight other staff kept'.

In May 1940, the French National Tourist Office advertised holidays in what they described as The Briton's Second Home. 'Casinos reopened – big-game shooting at small expense in French Africa.' In the English shires hunting was still going on, though with reduced numbers, and so was racing. Perfectly fit men were still in uniform as commissionaires or chauffeurs, not soldiers, and despite petrol rationing there were still twenty makes of car on the market. Most extraordinary of all, there were still a million unemployed men on the labour market – a legacy of the Thirties – for whom the government had not yet found any use. People were singing 'There'll Always Be An England', and it looked as though this was the sort of England there would always be. Unemployed miners could be found singing to West End queues with their caps held out and, observing this, the *Times* remarked also on the number of young able-bodied men 'hanging about amusement arcades', the long queues for the cinemas, the overcrowdedness of hotels. Its headline asked (this was 24 May) 'Are We Really At War?'

The widespread belief that we would never really be at war while Neville Chamberlain was Prime Minister had brought about his downfall two weeks earlier. Ostensibly the occasion was the bungling of the expedition to Norway, where a British force had been 'forestalled and outwitted' by the speed of the German conquest of the country. Britain's intervention was a fiasco and ended in a speedy withdrawal, but the famous House of Commons debate on it raised wider issues. It put Chamberlain in the dock as an

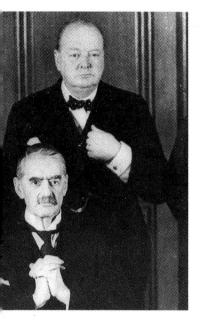

9 *In a photograph of the cabinet Winston Churchill stands behind Neville Chamberlain, the man whom he was to succeed as Prime Minister in May 1940 – the man who had tried to stop the war and who proved an inadequate leader when he failed*

irresolute and inadequate war leader; 41 Conservatives voted against their own party and 60 abstained. 'Go, go, go!' shouted members when the figures were announced, although the government still had a majority of 81. But if Chamberlain went, who was to take his place? Lord Halifax, the likely choice of the Conservative party, dodged the task with the excuse that he could sit only in the House of Lords. The Labour Party, which was to join the Conservatives in a coalition government, put matters on the knife-edge by voting unanimously that Labour would not serve under Chamberlain.

That left only one possible leader, Winston Churchill, a man deeply disliked and distrusted on the Conservative benches. For seven weeks after his appointment they sat in silence behind him, while the Labour benches opposite cheered his speeches, the speeches that are now seen as a crucial influence on Britain's survival. Churchill took power as Holland and Belgium were being invaded. 'I felt as if I were walking with destiny,' he wrote, but for the next month it looked to him as though it was his destiny 'to announce the greatest military disaster in our long history' – defeat at Dunkirk, followed by the loss of the entire British army in France. But against all expectations, the British Expeditionary Force, nearly a quarter of a million men, had been saved to fight another day. That was the inspiration of 'the Dunkirk spirit', that beloved British folk-memory, which has been appealed to, unsuccessfully, on so many occasions in peacetime.

It is worth analysing what the 'spirit of Dunkirk' really meant. It meant, first of all, that the nation suddenly found unity. Despite all its deeply entrenched class divisions, there was for a time, for perhaps a year after Dunkirk, a feeling of everyone belonging to one tribe. Patriotism is perhaps too simple a word for it because Britain at such moments is very conscious of being an island, a right little, tight little island, which cannot take foreigners beyond the seas entirely seriously, even if they have just won a big victory. George Orwell wrote in his 1940 pamphlet 'The Lion and the Unicorn':

> There can be moments when the whole nation suddenly swings together and does the same thing, like a herd of cattle facing a wolf. There was such a moment, unmistakably, at the time of the disaster in France. After eight months of vaguely wondering what the war was about, the people suddenly knew what they had got to do. It was like the awakening of a giant. . . . England is a land of snobbery and privilege, ruled largely by the old and silly. But one has got to take into account its emotional unity, the tendency of nearly all its inhabitants to feel alike and act together in moments of supreme crisis.

It takes a crisis of awesome proportions to awaken this giant – that is why appeals to the Dunkirk spirit fall on deaf ears at less challenging times. The shock of defeat referred to above was overtaken by relief that it had come at last. People had been unconsciously longing for the real war to start. 'Thank

God we are now alone,' said Air Marshal Sir Hugh Dowding, head of Fighter
Command – the man who had defied Churchill's orders to send more fighter
squadrons to help France in its death throes. 'There was more than a touch of
the address before Agincourt in the air,' wrote Margery Allingham, describing the reaction of her Essex village. Britain now was last man in. Its
European allies had snapped like dry reeds. Were the British surprised at this?
Not really. Deep down they had always suspected foreigners would let you
down. Along with their patriotism, all the latent chauvinism and xenophobia
in the British came to the surface: 'No more bloody Allies!' shouted a tug
skipper on the Thames to A. P. Herbert's passing boat, 'Now we know where
we are!'

Soldiers with bitter memories of the French Army's chaotic retreat were
heard to declare, 'You're better off without the French!' And the King himself
echoed the other ranks when he wrote to his mother, Queen Mary,
'Personally I feel happier now that we have no allies to be polite to and to
pamper.' It was now a straight contest, just as it had been before, in a long
history of keeping invaders at bay. 'We're in the biggest mess since the Battle
of Hastings,' said a Welsh MP to Vera Brittain at the House of Commons. It
was an encouraging thought: the last time an invader had won was that long
ago. A. P. Herbert put the same idea into one of his doggerel verses that
appeared in popular newspapers. It was addressed to Hitler:

> Napoleon tried. The Dutch were on the way.
> A Norman did it and a Dane or two.
> Some sailor-king may follow one fine day
> But not, I think, a low land rat like you.

Hitler had won every match, but he had not yet played a really serious
side. When he received news of the capitulation of France, he did a smirking
little jig of triumph. When it was seen on the newsreels it did as much as
anything to stiffen the resolve that he would do no smirking here. The
national adrenalin started to flow all the better for the sight of an enemy so
patently and leeringly evil. The impossible alternative was rubbed in all the
more by the sight of the refugees from continental Europe – 30,000 Dutch,
Belgian, French and as many more from the Channel Islands. John Lehmann
met them in almost every street during the post-Dunkirk days. 'They are
pouring across in fishing smacks, row-boats, any kind of boat. To most
people the Channel is a magic barrier and makes everything beyond it
infinitely distant.' Yet here they were, giving their reasons for fleeing to Mass
Observation: 'I wasn't going to stay and work for the Germans. I'll be a slave
to nobody.' . . .'The Nazis are not human, death is kinder.' . . . 'My father
died for France and I will fight for her.' . . . 'Everything was burning. We just
ran and kept running. People were like terrified animals.' . . . 'I didn't want to
live with beasts. I felt angry, not afraid.'

The old faith in the protection of the sea welled up – the sea that had stood Britain in good stead against the Spanish, against the Dutch, against Napoleon. These feelings, vague and half-conscious in most people, needed public voices to make them articulate. Fortunately they were there. One was the voice of J. B. Priestley, whose comforting, gravelly, pipe-laden north-countryman's tones came on compulsively on Sunday nights after the nine o'clock news, delivering his fifteen-minute *Postscripts*. They sounded like the spontaneous saloon-bar reflections of an ordinary drinking Englishman. He began on the Sunday after the Dunkirk evacuation by pointing out how English it was – 'When apparently all was lost, so much was gloriously retrieved. What began as a miserable blunder ... ended as an epic of gallantry, another English epic, and what was most English about it was the part played by the little pleasure steamers ...' He played on the positive satisfaction that the British obtain from bad news, from the knowledge that the situation is desperate, and there was also the strong appeal of the idea of the amateur coming to the rescue. In fact, gallant as the 'little ships' with civilian skippers were, amateurs played a smaller role in lifting the troops than they were credited with. Many of the pleasure steamers and small craft had been requisitioned and were manned by the Royal Navy, every bit as professionally as the destroyers. And luckily the sea and the weather had been on the side of an exploit so natural to an island race.

10 J.B. Priestley's Yorkshire voice broadcasting Postscripts *after the news on Sunday nights rallied the nation. He was second only to Churchill in his ability to raise people's patriotic spirit*

One final fillip was given to the post-Dunkirk spirit of defiance by the declaration of war on 11 June by Italy. Mussolini had shown no urgent desire to be in the fighting, but he wanted to be in at the death of France and, as he calculated, of Britain and to divide the spoils. Churchill used only the lightest of banter to deflate the menace of the Italian Duce: 'We shall be delighted to offer Signor Mussolini a free and safeguarded passage through the Straits of Gibraltar in order that he may play the part to which he aspires.' Here were combined a number of well-aimed pinpricks. 'Signor' Mussolini, not important enough to be referred to by his surname alone; the 'safeguarded passage' implying that the Italian navy, though large, could not break out of the Mediterranean without the Royal Navy's leave; 'the part to which he aspires' – that of greedy victor – classed him as an actor not up to his role.

A few Italian ice-cream parlours and fried fish shops in England were damaged. George Orwell walked round Soho and found three shops with smashed windows and several with notices proclaiming 'This establishment is entirely British', one of them displayed by a French restaurant. 'The low-down, cold-blooded meanness of Mussolini's declaration of war at that moment must have made an impression,' he noted.

11 In the beautiful summer of 1940 the English beaches basked untrodden behind a forest of barbed-wire entanglements, awaiting the invader. You could not go within ten miles of them without a permit

The Ministry of Information was soon asking the newsreels not to refer to the Italians as 'ice-cream merchants'. It was causing offence in the ice-cream trade. A. P. Herbert did not miss the opportunity for a verse entitled 'Top Wop':

> One cannot quite ignore the way
> That Hitler sees things through,
> But when I think of Hitler's mate
> I really must expectorate,
> There's nothing else to do.

Unfortunately, it was not the Italians but the Germans who were expected at any moment. When their Panzers rolled on to occupy the whole of Northern France, Britain gained an unexpected breathing space in which to turn the island into a fortress. Sea-borne invasion was the obvious danger but parachute troops, a new phenomenon of war, had been effectively used in Holland and Belgium. Places within ten miles of the south and east coasts were cleared of visitors, evacuated of children and declared 'defence areas' which could not be entered without a permit. Seafronts basked in temperatures of 90 degrees with their sands bare of holidaymakers. Instead, barbed-wire entanglements were being unrolled across the beaches, piers were half demolished or mined ready for blowing up, the dunes and cliffs were planted with sandbagged or concreted gun emplacements, and the hotels and big seafront houses were being requisitioned. Laurie Lee caught the melancholy of the scene in a poem called 'Seafront':

> Here the maze of our bewilderment,
> The thorn-crowned wire spreads high along the shore
> And flowers with rust, and tears our common sun;
> And where no paths of love may reach the sea,
> The shut sands wait, deserted, for the drowned.

Sir Brian Horrocks, whose brigade was charged with defending a ten-mile stretch of coast centred on Brighton with only 3000 men, reflected: 'We wouldn't have stood much of a chance against a well-organised invasion. Even so this was probably one of the most strongly defended parts of Britain. Fortunately, few people realised quite how thin was the shield protecting them.' His divisional commander was a Major General, Bernard Law Montgomery. 'Monty used to pay constant visits. "Who lives in that house?" he would say, pointing to some building which partly masked the fire from one of our machine-gun positions. "Have them out, Horrocks. Blow up the house. Defence must come first."'

The possibilities of an airborne invasion were more perplexing to deal with. 'Remember that if parachutists come down near your home they will

not be feeling at all brave,' ran one particularly fatuous government pamphlet issued in June. 'They will not know where they are, they will have no food. *Do not give any German anything*. Do not tell him anything. Hide your food and your bicycles. Hide your maps. See that the enemy gets no petrol. . . . If you keep your head you can tell whether a military officer is actually British or only pretending to be.' It was Nanny speaking again from an imaginary nursery where badly behaved German children could be sent to bed without their supper, and not allowed to play with English bicycles, or play charades with funny English accents. That would show them. The Ministry of Information was absolutely brimming with good advice that summer, some of it in Nanny's voice, some of it in the manner of a bluff scoutmaster: 'WHAT DO I DO . . . if I hear news that Germans are trying to land or have landed? I do *not* get panicky. I *stay put*. I say to myself: Our chaps will deal with them. I do not say: I must get out of here.'

Staying put was emphasised, prompted by memories of the collapse of France, when refugee civilians clogged the roads fleeing from the German advance and made it impossible for the army to manoeuvre. Nevertheless, it was not by staying put in the fields, the streets or in the hills that the natives intended to beat back the invaders. By June, our chaps who were planning to deal with them included nearly 1½ million Local Defence Volunteers, soon to be renamed at Churchill's suggestion Home Guards. The LDVs had sprung into existence within hours of a broadcast by Anthony Eden as War Minister

12 Inland, gun emplacements and 'pill-boxes' sprang up to keep any wide-open spaces under cover of their fire. This 'haystack' was a new addition to the fields behind Folkestone

on 14 May, as the German advance struck through Holland and Belgium into France. He spoke of the German parachute drops that had been made behind the lines and went on: 'We want large numbers of men who are not at present engaged in military service between the ages of seventeen and sixty-five to come forward and offer their services to make assurance doubly sure. . . . You will not be paid but you will receive uniform and will be armed.' It was vague enough, but it was what large numbers of veterans of the fighting in 1914–18 had been waiting for. Within a week, 250,000 men had enrolled and been given armbands, for want of uniforms. For want of rifles a motley collection of privately owned weapons were donated or scrounged by the men themselves.

This is where the legends of the Home Guard as a comic institution took root. It is true that they sometimes drilled with broom handles – so, in that summer, did some recruits to the regular army. It is also true that a Manchester museum lent rifles displayed for historical interest which had seen service in the Indian Mutiny and the Crimea. Drury Lane Theatre

13 This is the image of the Home Guard that has come down to us: ageing veterans of the First World War drilling with broomsticks. But this genial Home Guard sergeant at least had a tommy gun under his arm in December 1940. The Americans sent them over

contributed four dozen Lee Enfield rifles which were used in patriotic stage tableaux. Norwich City Museum lent guns and a sentry box, naval cutlasses were rounded up to arm a cutlass platoon, and one Lancashire battalion was armed with six-foot spears. It was a time for homely improvisation, though most of these 'weapons' were used for drill. For shooting, the Home Guard relied on their own shot-guns.

There were, in the early days, a large proportion – perhaps half – of First World War veterans, some of them high-ranking officers (whose survival rate was, in 1916 or 1917, higher than that of lower ranks). Some of them paraded in their old service dress, with Sam Browne belts and insignia, and one company in East Sussex boasted six former generals as privates. Two bishops, of Chelmsford and Truro, also enrolled, though whether they paraded in purple vestments is unknown. The oldest Home Guard was identified as one Alexander Taylor, of Perthshire, who had served in the Egyptian campaign of 1884–5 and in the attempt to relieve Gordon at Khartoum. He was eighty. It was ruled that old uniforms and badges of rank must go – indeed, to begin with, the Home Guard was a democratic, people's militia which elected its section leaders. Later, army ranks were introduced and saluting, at first a voluntary matter, became general.

The early musters of local platoons, especially in rural areas, had a picturesque quality that appealed to the sense of history that lurks in literary men. The Wiltshire farmer–author, A. G. Street, described how at the first meeting in the village hall 'owners of great estates rubbed shoulders with tenant farmers and small-holders in a loud buzz of conversation and a cloud of tobacco smoke. The butcher, the baker, the blacksmith, the thatcher, the gamekeeper and the poacher was represented.' J. B. Priestley went on dusk-to-dawn watch with his Isle of Wight village unit, including a parson, a bailiff, a builder, farmers and farm-labourers.

> Even the fast-disappearing trades were represented – we had a hurdle-maker there, and his presence, with that of a woodman, and a shepherd, made me feel sometimes I had wandered into one of those rich chapters of Thomas Hardy's fiction ... there we were, ploughman and parson, shepherd and clerk, turning out at night as our forefathers had done before us, to keep watch and ward over the sleeping English hills and homesteads.

The last time it had happened was in 1803, when half a million men mustered to stand ready to repel Napoleon Bonaparte's threatened invasion, but there had been Trained Bands and Musters raised as far back as the reign of Elizabeth I, in the year of the Armada.

The first function of the Home Guard was to stand-to at dusk and watch for landings by airborne troops until dawn – evoked by Cecil Day-Lewis in the poem, 'Stand-To':

Last night a Stand-To was ordered, thirty men of us here
Came out to guard the starlit village – my men who wear
Unwitting the season's beauty, the received truth of the spade,
Roadmen, farm labourers, masons, turned to another trade.
A dog barked over the fields, the candle stars put a sheen
On the rifles ready, the sandbags fronded with evergreen.
The dawn wind blew, the stars winked out on the posts where we lay,
The order came, Stand-Down, and thirty went away.

They went away to their daily work, having lost a night's sleep. Not all kept watch over the star-lit countryside: factories formed units, so did the railways, the Bank of England, the big offices, the Houses of Parliament and the staff of Buckingham Palace. Each took responsibility for defending their premises from the invader. The LMS railway created a large catapult for throwing lighted petrol cans, the Bank of England's catapult would hurl a Molotov cocktail 100 yards, while a Bolsover colliery invented an 'anti-tank gun' that would fire a broomstick with a grenade attached. Americans left in London formed the American Home Guard, much to the disapproval of US Ambassador Joseph Kennedy, who did not rate Britain's chances of survival at all high and feared that US citizens would be shot. American well-wishers collected and sent arms across the Atlantic, including sporting rifles and gangsters' tommy guns.

George Orwell was a sergeant in the St John's Wood Home Guard, many of whose volunteers were Jewish refugees from Germany, Poland and France. On their first drill parade, 'some officers who had, I think, come to scoff were quite impressed'. Conferences were held in the committee room at Lord's cricket ground and the first full parade of the volunteers from the North-West London zone was in Regent's Park. 'Allowing for the dreadful appearance that men drilling in mufti always make, not a bad lot,' noted Orwell. 'Perhaps 25 per cent are working class. The general inspecting us was the usual senile imbecile.' Orwell, with his experience of fighting with militias in the Spanish Civil War, was infuriated by the officers of this citizen defence force – 'an astonishing phenomenon, a sort of People's Army officered by Blimps. The rank and file are predominantly working class with a strong middle-class seasoning but practically all the commands are held by wealthy, elderly men, a lot of whom are utterly incompetent . . . retired generals and admirals and titled dug-outs, sometimes as old as seventy.'

The role of the Home Guard, as a back-up to regular troops, was to defend their home ground and to die on it. 'Should the invader come, there will be no placid lying-down in submission before him as we have seen, alas, in other countries,' declared Churchill in a broadcast on 14 July. 'The vast mass of London itself, fought street by street, could easily devour an entire hostile army and we would rather see London laid in ashes and ruins than that it should be tamely and abjectly enslaved.' To this the German radio

sarcastically replied: 'Churchill has spoken about the Home Guard under arms. We ask – under what arms? Broomsticks? Or the arms of the local pub, with pots of beer and darts in their hands?'

It had a point. The supply of rifles and especially of ammunition was desperately short all summer. After three months' waiting, Orwell noted in his diary that his platoon had about one rifle for six men and no other weapons except incendiary bombs. Without weapons, how was London or any other town or village to be fought street by street? The commander of the British battalion of the International Brigade in the Spanish Civil War, Tom Wintringham, aroused keen public response by describing in *Picture Post* how civilians could resist an invasion if they knew how to make amateur grenades and Molotov cocktails, or to decapitate enemy motor-cyclists with wire stretched across the road, or even to stop them by scattering enough broken glass on it. The upshot was a privately run Home Guard school, financed by *Picture Post*'s publisher Sir Edward Hulton, at Osterley Park in Middlesex, whose grounds were made available by its owner, the Earl of Jersey. Wintringham taught guerilla tactics, learned in Spain, with the help of other British veterans and Spanish refugees. 'The response was fantastic. We could have filled the school three times over. What it taught us was simply do-it-yourself war,' wrote *Picture Post*'s editor, Tom Hopkinson. Nearly 5000

14 Home Guard exercises took place in view of the public – in this case strollers with prams in a London park, who watch with idle curiosity as a patrol flings itself into a defensive position during an exercise

[33]

men passed through the school, including parties from regular regiments, until the Army set up its own official schools of street warfare. It was Wintringham who coined the phrase 'The People's War'.

By August the Home Guard was making an impression in exercises where they were pitted against the Army. 'Their greatest asset was local knowledge,' wrote Sir Brian Horrocks, 'We could make a dent but, like a cushion, they always bobbed up somewhere else.' And for all his scorn, Lord Haw-Haw sounded rattled:

> Suicide academies have apparently been set up all over Britain. The headmasters are cunning blackguards who teach their inmates how to make bombs at the modest cost of two shillings each, how to poison water supplies by throwing dead dogs into streams and how to kill sentries noiselessly from behind. . . . Truly the Lord has afflicted these people with blindness! So bombs at two shillings a time are to be used against the German Stukas! The people of England will curse themselves for having preferred ruin from Churchill to peace from Hitler.

The Ministry of Information's counter to this sort of things was another piece of look-here-you-slackers finger-wagging:

> WHAT DO I DO . . . if I come across German or Italian broadcasts when tuning my wireless? I say to myself: Now this blighter wants me to listen to him. Am I going to do what he wants? I remember that German lies over the air are like parachute troops dropping on Britain – they are all part of a plan to get us down, *which they won't*. I remember nobody can trust a word the Haw-Haws say. I switch 'em off or tune 'em out!

The Home Guard took over the job of guarding 'vulnerable points', thus releasing thousands of regular troops for regular duty. Many of them were stationed at road blocks, improvised from all kinds of obstacles – broken-down motor vehicles or even farm carts, reapers and steam ploughs – surrounded by barbed wire. Here motorists were halted and required to show their identity cards. Quite a number chose not to obey and some paid a heavy price. 'The man who refused to show his identity card found his car key abstracted, his car pushed to the side of the road and held. The man who drove on when challenged, thinking those yokels won't dare to shoot, was shot at and usually hit,' wrote A. G. Street. One officer, who decided to hold up the Home Guard sentry with his revolver, had not noticed there was a second sentry covering him from the shadows. Shotgun pellets in the backside enlightened him. A village drunk was lying senseless on a neighbouring grassy bank when a motorist expostulated at the barrier, 'Shoot me? You wouldn't dare!' The sentry indicated his apparently lifeless fellow villager. 'Arr,' he said in broad Wiltshire, 'That's what 'ee thought.' The motorist found his identity

card very, very quickly. (Some people actually *were* shot dead for failing to stop.) Couples in parked cars were sometimes embarrassed by the demand for their identity cards. One pair was held up when returning from the fields to their car. 'You've been in a prohibited area,' they were told. 'No, he hasn't,' said the girl huffily.

The Home Guard was never called upon to fight for its territory, so the jibe of 'Dad's Army' was easy to make. In the earliest months it could hardly have caused much delay to properly armed and armoured German troops, which could have swept its obstacles aside. But as the months passed, its average age decreased and its weaponry – including tommy guns – increased. By 1941, thought George Orwell, it was a serious force capable of strong resistance for a short period. By 1942 it was undergoing battle training with the regular army and learning how to fire anti-tank and anti-aircraft guns. At its peak it was nearly 2 million strong. Churchill told these part-time soldiers, 'If the Nazi villains drop on us from the skies, you will have to make clear to them that they have not alighted in the poultry run, or the rabbit farm, but in the lions' den.'

If the Home Guard looked amateurish, so did the anti-invasion obstacles that soon disfigured any open space flat enough to tempt gliders carrying airborne troops to land. Fields and commons were scattered with derelict lorries and buses, farm implements, even kitchen ranges or iron bedsteads.

15 Men of the London GPO Home Guard with fixed bayonets prepare to engage the 'enemy' in the rubble around St Paul's Cathedral

16 *An airborne landing by paratroops was a new threat. It had been successful in Belgium and Holland, so every open space wide enough for gliders to land on it was obstructed by whatever obstacle could be found – even kitchen ranges and iron bedsteads*

Sports grounds and golf courses were festooned with rollers and criss-crossed with newly dug ditches. 'No golfer could possibly object to the hazards of the course being increased,' ran a reader's letter to *Picture Post*. But German radio, misunderstanding these activities, reported that there had been a destruction of playing fields 'in a revolt against plutocratic cricketers'.

Other anti-invasion measures involved the removal of all signposts and the painting out of street-names, the destination signs on buses and trams, and the replacement of the names of railway stations with miniature name boards in letters only three inches high. This was to confuse the enemy on arrival. No doubt it would have done, for it caused such confusion to the natives that a certain number of signs saying vaguely 'To the North' were restored. The ringing of church bells was banned until further notice as this was to be the signal that the invasion had begun. One seventy-year-old rector in Lincolnshire who did not know of the order was sentenced to a month's jail for ringing his church bell. He won his appeal, but only after twelve days inside. Car radios were banned and many motorists were fined (or had their tyres let down) for not obeying another emergency order – to immobilise their parked cars by removing the rotor arm. This was to prevent a newly arrived enemy from helping himself to transport (presumably having landed with duplicate ignition keys). Radio announcers started announcing their names, in case the BBC microphones were captured and Nazis with suave English accents gave the listeners false information. Several more desperate measures were contemplated and experimented with. Churchill was prepared to drench the beaches with mustard gas if the Germans got ashore. Experiments were made to surprise the invaders by setting fire to the sea by pumping oil into it through pipes off-shore; this only worked on calm days, so the ambitious fantasy of ringing the coasts with a wall of fire had to be abandoned.

But what was the ordinary citizen to do if the storm troops were actually descending on his street or village? 'Staying put', as he had so often been instructed, was a counsel of frustration. It was certainly not Churchillian thinking, but he too wondered what would have happened if 200,000 troops had established themselves ashore. 'I intended to use the slogan, "You can always take one with you."' He had a rifle range near Chequers where he used to practise not only with a rifle but a revolver, which he could fire with considerable accuracy, noted his private secretary Sir John Colville, 'while smoking a cigar'. King George VI also set up a rifle range in the garden of Buckingham Palace, where he used to practise, as did Queen Elizabeth. 'I shall not go down like the others,' she announced, thinking of the continental queens who had fled to England. No doubt the royal example would have been followed more readily than the advice of the Ministry of Information to stay put, though all private weapons had officially been surrendered for the use of the Home Guard. Nevertheless, some people decided to commit suicide if the Germans came. Most people of prominence were on the 'Nazi black list' for immediate capture and, presumably, execution. It was a curious list. Within two pages it contained such names as Churchill, Noel Coward, Richard Crossman and society hostess Nancy Cunard (it also included the name 'Sigmund Freud', who was dead). Some of the people on the list decided to take their own lives before the Nazis could. Sir Harold Nicolson, MP and junior minister, provided himself with lethal pills, as so did the editor of the left wing *New Statesman*, Kingsley Martin. The miners of South Wales, on the other hand, planned to blow up their pits and take to the hills with picks and shovels.

Obviously, children had no place in the areas most vulnerable to invasion. There was a second evacuation during the summer of 1940 of some 200,000 children from London and the south-east. People were urged to leave the south-east coastal towns 'while the going was good', and about 300,000 did so. The population of Essex and Kent coast towns was reduced by a quarter, while the population of Buckinghamshire, Berkshire and Cornwall increased correspondingly. In July the government offered free passage for children to Canada and the United States and received 211,000 applications. Only 2600 had gone when one of the ships, carrying 73 of them, went down in the Atlantic and the scheme was wound up. Churchill had never been in favour of it and, asked by the Home Secretary to send a message to the Canadian prime minister through 'the senior child' on the next boatload, he minuted: 'I certainly do not propose to send a message by the senior child, or by the junior child either. If I send any message to anyone it would be that I entirely deprecate any stampede from this country at the present time.'

However, 11,000 children were sent by private arrangements to friends or contacts in North America who were offering to take them. Two of these were the children of Vera Brittain, Shirley Williams and her brother. Their mother agonised like many other mothers about being parted from them. 'Going to bed that night, I feel I cannot face this separation; cannot endure to submit them for one terrible week to the dangers of torpedoes in order that they may be removed from the long-drawn risk of bombs. ... The sudden wail of the midnight air-raid siren comes as an unexpected relief. The threat pulls me together with its reminder of the ordeal ahead.' Although her children went cheerfully, others who were offered the chance by no means wanted to go. One of these, David Wedgwood-Benn, a younger brother of Anthony Wedgwood-Benn, wrote angrily to *The Times* about his feelings: 'I would rather be bombed to fragments than leave England.' Churchill approvingly sent the boy a signed copy of his own youthful adventure story, *My Early Life*. It was naturally assumed that the two princesses, Elizabeth and Margaret, would also be sent to Canada, but this idea was rejected by their mother in forthright terms: 'The children could not possibly leave without me. I would not go without the King. And, of course, the King will never leave.' Most families who considered the matter preferred to stick together, come what may.

The other people who were removed from the scene were the 70,000 aliens from Germany. As early as May, some 2000 male 'enemy aliens' living within twenty miles of the coast had been rounded up, and when France fell in June there was a reaction against foreigners of every kind. Anyone with a foreign name or accent, even with a beard, was suspect and the press demanded that we 'Intern the Lot'. The majority of them, of course, had come to Britain as refugees from Hitler in Germany, Austria and Czechoslovakia and six out of seven of them were Jews. Now Nazi-sympathisers and passionate anti-Nazis were swept up indiscriminately – scientists like Max Born, Rudolf Peierls, Hermann Bondi and Otto Frisch; doctors like Ludwig Gutmann; scholars like Ernst Gombrich, Niklaus Pevsner and Hilde Himmelweit; psychologists like Hans Eysenck; bankers like Sigmund Warburg; future publishers like George Weidenfeld and Paul Hamlyn; musicians like opera conductor Rudolf Bing and three members of the (future) Amadeus string quartet. This formidable collection of brains, which was to enrich British science and culture, was herded into camps or barracks under guard. Many were held in the Tote building at Kempton Park racecourse, others at the winter quarters of Bertram Mills' circus at Ascot. Some suffered worse hardships and some committed suicide. Arthur Koestler, recently escaped from France by devious means, found himself put in Pentonville prison for a few weeks before he was allowed out to join the Pioneer Corps as a uniformed manual labourer.

Most internees were moved to the Isle of Man, where conditions improved and they were handed a leaflet asking them in gruff British fashion not to take offence: 'A man's internment is not regarded here as a reflection on his character. He is credited with being a man of good intent until he proves himself otherwise ... you are assured of justice.' Hundreds were shipped overseas to Canada and Australia; one ship, the *Arandora Star*, was torpedoed in the Atlantic and went down with 1500 German and Italian refugees. Britain's treatment of its aliens has been called shameful, but in daily expectation of a German assault it was difficult for the government to do anything else but intern first and ask questions afterwards. An aliens' tribunal was set up and, bit by bit, the great majority were released, many of them to resume valuable work for the country which had put them behind barbed wire. However, life in the Isle of Man camps had its compensations. The internees set up their own university and there was no lack of talent to provide culture and entertainment; some of them did not even want to come back.

Even with all aliens out of the way, the British spent much of 1940 wondering whether there was a Fifth Column in their midst, preparing to welcome the Wehrmacht. The phrase had been coined in the Spanish Civil War, when Franco's general claimed that besides four columns of troops besieging Madrid, he had a 'Fifth Column' of sympathisers within the city. In April came the sudden collapse of Norway followed by the rule of the Norwegian collaborator, Vidkun Quisling. Was this not the work of the Fifth Column? And the collapse of Holland the following month suggested that the Germans were helped by traitors among the Dutch population. Who, people wondered, were the pro-Nazi traitors in Britain?

The most obvious candidates were supporters of Sir Oswald Mosley and his British Union of Fascists, of the black-shirted pre-war rallies, though Mosley himself had been arrested even before Dunkirk, the BUF was dissolved and his henchmen imprisoned (Mosley and George Pitt-Rivers, an anti-Semitic racist, were both cousins by marriage of Mrs Churchill). No offence was alleged or charge made against Mosley – he and some 1600 others found themselves in Brixton prison under Regulation 18B, which allowed imprisonment without trial of those sympathisers with 'any Power with which his Majesty is at war'. 'Naturally I feel distressed at having to be responsible for an action so utterly at variance with all the fundamental principles of British liberty,' minuted Churchill to the Home Secretary later in the year, and went on to inquire whether Mosley and his wife, who was imprisoned after she had had a baby, were allowed hot baths, exercise, books and the wireless. 'What arrangements have been made for Mosley's wife to see her baby, from whom she was taken before it was weaned?' he added.

This concern in the middle of a crisis for Britain's leading Fascist was not shared by the bulk of ordinary citizens, and Mass Observation found unanimous approval of Mosley's detention. Many of the Fascist sympathisers detained were released fairly quickly; the Mosleys, later given a flat in Holloway prison with the right to employ servants, were kept inside until 1943. One other notable detainee was a Conservative MP, Captain A. H. M.

Ramsay, a product of Eton, Sandhurst and the Coldstream Guards, who organised cricket in the prison yard. Communist party members – who, in obedience to Moscow, were urging working-class men not to join the Home Guard – were not detained. Members of the IRA were.

Even with the obvious suspects out of the way, 'Fifth Column Fever' infected many of the populace and cast suspicion on such innocents as ramblers, photographers, campers, water-colour painters and anglers. It was forbidden to photograph or sketch any military installation (that attractive woodland scene might conceal a gun-site) or landmarks, such as gasometers. The Ramblers' Association advised its members not to ramble after nightfall – and they must not use a map of a scale larger than one inch to a mile. Angling was banned in the reservoirs of Edinburgh and Dundee by their city councils, on the grounds that an angler might be a Fifth Columnist in disguise with the object of poisoning the water supply.

Despite the fact that no hard evidence of Fifth Column plots came to light, people in high places continued to believe devoutly that the Fifth Column existed. The Commander-in-Chief of the Home Forces, General Sir Edmund Ironside, made a speech to the Home Guard in which he wrestled with this hypothetical enemy none too convincingly. 'We have examples of people definitely preparing aerodromes. We want to know from you, is anything peculiar going on? Are there any peculiar people? I am not going to have any more of these people, the Fifth Column, making trouble. If there are people who should not be here, if you tell me, they will not be there long.' These people were peculiar indeed in their ability to prepare aerodromes without anybody knowing who they were. Soon after this, Ironside was replaced by the less fanciful General Sir Alan Brooke.

But the whole keyed-up population was liable to 'see' things that summer, or to believe any rumour that got into circulation about the wiliness of the enemy. Perhaps, once again, the hot weather had something to do with it, for reports that parachutists had been seen landing in this place or that came in daily. Anti-aircraft shell-bursts were mistaken for enemy parachutes, as were RAF pilots baling out, a barrage balloon being wound to earth, or even swans flying low by moonlight. Much credence was given to the story that in Holland parachutists had descended disguised as nuns. Nuns got some very strange looks that summer. The tale was told of one seen in a railway carriage who, when reading a book, carelessly revealed hairy wrists . . . or was it legs?

The nun stories were the equivalent of the First World War story that Russian troops had passed through the country with snow on their boots, some of which had been spotted next morning on the trains they used. No one seems to have wondered why German parachutists should operate in such inconvenient dress, or whether their habits did not blow up above their heads during the drop – presumably revealing jack-boots underneath. A government poster campaign under the slogan CARELESS TALK COSTS LIVES, showing Hitler eavesdropping on unwary citizens on buses, in telephone booths or even in stately homes, possibly added fuel to the ubiquitous spy myths. Such German spies as were caught seemed to have been poorly trained and equipped. One walked out of the sea wearing a Homburg hat and carrying a green suitcase; another aroused suspicion by going into a pub at breakfast time and asking for a glass of cider, and we have it on the authority of

A FEW
CARELESS WORDS
MAY END IN THIS—

Many lives were lost in the last war through careless talk
Be on your guard ! Don't discuss movements of ships or troops

17 'Careless Talk Costs Lives' was the theme of a memorable poster campaign. This poster brought the risk home to people very graphically

Malcolm Muggeridge that a German spy, educated in English customs by reading the works of P. G. Wodehouse, was apprehended in the Fen country actually wearing spats.

The truth of any story was hard to verify because of the censorship clampdown and the fact that the hot summer ripened as fine a crop of wild rumour as the country had ever harvested. There were tales of secret rays in use on roads, which, as if by magic, could stop car engines; of secret messages given over the radio by the popular pianist Charlie Kunz playing notes in a prearranged code; suspicions that spies were passing messages through the Personal Column of *The Times*. Imaginations became so fevered that it was made a chargeable offence to cause 'alarm and despondency' by circulating depressing rumours or defeatist opinions. Ill-conceived appeals were made by the Ministry of Information to inform on 'defeatists', and Ministry investigators who eavesdropped in pubs and public places were denounced as 'Cooper's Snoopers' after Duff Cooper, the Minister. Some seventy prosecutions were brought for 'defeatist' remarks, such as 'Hitler will soon be here' or 'I bet we shall lose by March', until Churchill put a stop to the foolish, unpopular campaign.

'I am so glad we have got the government down about the Silence Column and rumour-mongers and the sentences will be remitted or revised', wrote Rose Macaulay, the novelist, to her sister. 'It really does make one feel we have a democracy.' But she reported some defeatist talk in late June: 'I hear it is very common to hear people say it would be as good under the Nazis as it is now, so why not let them come quietly instead of bombing us first?'

One of the most popular subjects for rumour was the sayings of Lord Haw-Haw, who was credited with virtual omniscience about petty details, especially the state of public clocks. It began with Banstead, of which he was alleged to have said, 'We all know all about Banstead, even that the clock is a quarter of an hour slow today.' And in fact it was. The same story was told about many places, that clocks in East Ham, or Cambridge, or Wolverhampton, were so many minutes slow or had stopped and Lord Haw-Haw, thanks to his underground contacts, had broadcast the fact. The odd thing was that Lord Haw-Haw never made detailed observations of this kind. Yet it was universally believed that he had.

That summer William Joyce lent his propagandist talents to writing news bulletins for a new short-wave transmission – the 'New British Broadcasting Station', NBBS. This purported to be an underground radio station in England, run by disaffected English patriots who believed that Britain was fighting the wrong enemy. The NBBS played on the belief that invasion was imminent. In August it announced that parachutists equipped with maps and plans had landed near Birmingham, Manchester and Glasgow and had now gone to ground, being hidden by the Fifth Columnists in their homes. That night the Luftwaffe had indeed dropped unmanned parachutes in those places, with radio transmitters, maps and photographs of local sabotage targets. The NBBS kept up its story and added that the parachutists were equipped with a mysterious 'death ray' weapon but, unfortunately, the parachutes found in the middle of cornfields had no human tracks leading away from them.

Perhaps the most persistent rumour was the story that an invasion had already been launched and had failed, and that the bodies of the German troops involved had been washed up on various beaches along the south coast. According to some versions, those bodies were badly charred because the sea had been set on fire. Churchill, in his history of the war, attributed these bodies to an invasion practice by the Germans on the French side of the Channel. Had some of their barges sunk? Peter Fleming in his *Invasion, 1940* discounts this explanation, since the bodies would have had to float 100 miles from the embarkation point of Le Havre and no records of German dead were reported by the Red Cross or through any of the usual channels. Nor are any graves known. It is just possible that the corpses could have been dumped by British Intelligence deliberately to foster the rumours of a failed invasion, which circulated in occupied countries of Europe and gave comfort to many people. But nobody knows the truth – or has ever revealed it.

When all the emergencies were over, it was generally admitted that there had been no Fifth Column worth the name in Britain – certainly nothing more than isolated, disaffected individuals, and nothing like an effective organisation. The one person who might have deserved the title of Fifth Columnist was a woman called Anna Wolkoff, the daughter of an Imperial Russian admiral and an admirer of William Joyce. She wrote Joyce what was intended to be a helpful letter about the Haw-Haw broadcasts, which was intercepted by the security service. 'Stick to plutocracy. Avoid King,' she advised Joyce. 'Churchill not popular. Keep on at him. . . . Stress his conceit and repeated failures.' She asked for an acknowledgement by a reference on the radio to the name 'Carlyle' – and one duly came. Soon afterwards, she was sentenced to ten years.

German intelligence on Britain was notably poor and inaccurate. The Abwehr over-estimated the strength of the defending army and under-estimated the RAF fighter strength. German propaganda for home consumption painted a lurid picture of London in panic: riots every night, the rich providing themselves with private machine-gun nests, a million people leaving the country, Jews having their hair dyed and their noses straightened. 'The British nation has taken to drink.' Quoting this in a broadcast to America, J. B. Priestley commented, 'We had – long before the Nazis.'

The summer of 1940 was also remarkable for its displays of British sang-froid, encouraged by the beautiful weather. In Hyde Park on 4 August – Bank Holiday weekend, although the holiday Monday had been cancelled – Vera Brittain found the grass crowded and the orators at Speaker's Corner numerous. They included the pacifist Peace Pledge Union and a new body, the Anti-Fifth Column League. The centre of the park was a fenced military area.

I notice several mothers and fathers, their shoes kicked comfortably off, resting their backs against the anti-aeroplane sand-heaps while they eat their sandwiches. Despite repeated exhortations to evacuation, they have brought their families to town for the day. At the bottom of a trench several boys and girls are making pies with discarded tins. One baby plays blithely with piles of sandbags. Only a few yards from the barbed wire entanglements, a laughing throng drinks its cups of tea beneath orange umbrellas. On the Serpentine, hundreds of holiday-makers are boating and bathing . . . I cannot help wishing that Herr Hitler and Dr Goebbels could be transported here to inspect the vast London population which they have so often described as panic-stricken.

The daylight air attacks on South-East England had already begun two or three weeks before, and Londoners were used to seeing the barrage ballons go up on the signal of 'yellow alert' – raiders approaching. 'These balloons resemble huge oxydised fish, or swollen pigs with large, distended ears,' noted Vera Brittain. 'When they soar higher, they take on the more romantic appearance of pearl beads floating beneath the clouds.' Their purpose was not, as some thought, to bring down enemy planes with their cables, but to keep them from making low-level and more accurate attacks.

One of the young men in Hyde Park whom Vera Brittain had noticed was reading a yellow-jacketed best-seller of the time called *Guilty Men* which bitterly attacked Chamberlain (who was still in Churchill's government) and 'the old gang' for the humiliation of Dunkirk and our unpreparedness after it. It was the work of three journalists, most notably Michael Foot, who concealed themselves behind the pseudonym of the ancient Roman denouncer 'Cato'. Many people wanted Chamberlain removed from the government altogether. Churchill would not do it, but cancer did, later that summer: he died six months to the day after his fall from office as Prime Minister. George Orwell, who loathed his policy, nevertheless admitted that he had represented the wishes of the British people in his attempts to stave off war. 'Like the mass of the people, he did not want to pay the price either of peace or of war. And the public opinion was behind him all the while.' Well, it was a different story now.

The Battle of Britain officially began on 10 July. A BBC reporter called Charles Gardner, who was broadcasting from Dover, saw a dog-fight develop before his eyes. He turned his prepared script into a running commentary with a sporting flavour: 'Somebody's hit a German and he's coming down . . . he's coming down completely out of control, a long streak of smoke . . . ah, the man's baled out by parachute . . . he's a Junkers 87 and he's going slap into the sea and there he goes – smash! . . . Oh boy, I've never seen anything so good as this!'

All that month and the next, the British looked up at the blue sky –

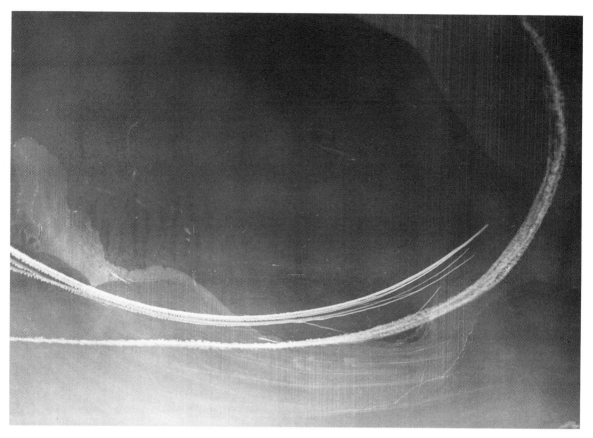

sometimes while they were picnicking on a beautiful afternoon – straining to see a Spitfire, a Hurricane or a Messerschmitt at their deadly acrobatics, listening for the distant sputtering sound of the machine-gun fire and sometimes watching a plume of smoke streaking down to earth. The sensation of being spectators at a sporting event persisted – no one could conceive of the real terrors of the pilots overhead. 'They were just like butterflies – lovely to watch,' Vita Sackville-West reported someone saying to her in Kent, adding, 'We had just counted a third wave of bombers and fighters roaring past. "Please, madam," said a quiet voice, "Would you like luncheon out of doors? Then you could watch the fights better."'

At first the German raiders concentrated their attacks on the Channel convoys and the coastal defences. 'Rumours would sweep through Folkestone that a convoy of ships was going through and we'd all rush to the front to watch,' remembered Donald Steel, a chemist who was living there at the time. 'The atmosphere was just like a football match. We would cheer every time a German plane went down. Of course, we didn't feel so pleased when one of ours was hit.'

18 All through the late summer people strained their eyes at the blue skies, watching the vapour trails as Spitfires, Hurricanes and German Messerschmitts performed a deadly aerial circus to the faint sputtering of machine guns

Every day as the battle developed people wanted, above all, to know the score. And the headlines in the evening papers announced them: so did the placards chalked up by the paper-sellers:

BIGGEST RAID EVER
SCORE 78 TO 26
ENGLAND STILL BATTING

The battle was more deadly than any of the spectators knew. Hitler, who had been toying with invasion preparations since the beginning of July, issued his invasion directive on 16 July: 'I have decided to begin to prepare for, and if necessary carry out, an invasion of England.' The reason for his hesitance was two-fold: his navy and army chiefs were far from enthusiastic about making a seaborne attack under the guns of the British navy, and Hitler was still hoping that an invasion would not be necessary because Britain would make peace without one. Three days later, on 19 July, Hitler addressed his 'last appeal to reason' to the British people, in a speech to the German parliament, the Reichstag. After attacking Churchill as a warmonger – when the final blow fell, 'Mr Churchill no doubt, will already be in Canada' – he prophesied that the war would end in the destruction of 'a great empire which it was never my intention to destroy or even to harm'. He ended: 'I feel it my duty to appeal once more to reason and common sense in Great Britain . . . I can see no reason why this war must go on.'

According to William Shirer, an American journalist then in Berlin, the Germans 'had not the slightest doubt that the British would accept what they believed was a very generous, even magnanimous offer by the Führer. They were dumbfounded when the offer was rejected.' The British government hardly bothered to reply, Churchill remarking, 'I do not propose to say anything in reply to Herr Hitler's speech, not being on speaking terms with him.' But three days afterwards the Foreign Secretary, Lord Halifax – often classed as an appeaser and one of the 'guilty men' – made a broadcast in which he dismissed Hitler's offer as 'a summons to Great Britain to capitulate to his will'. He said he would not waste his audience's time dealing with all Hitler's distortions of events. Copies of the speech were dropped over England by German planes, but they were generally treated as a grim joke and in some places auctioned to raise money for the Red Cross.

A few days earlier, on 14 July, Churchill had told his radio listeners: 'Perhaps it will come tonight. Perhaps it will come next week. Perhaps it will never come.' No one could have believed then that it would never come. Reconnaissance reports were coming in of special craft being assembled in Kiel harbour, of parachute regiments moving to Belgium, of stores being concentrated in northern France. All depended on the Germans winning control of the air. On 1 August Hitler issued another directive ordering the Luftwaffe to 'overpower the English Air Force with all its forces in the

shortest possible time' – by attacking the RAF units and air-fields, and also the aircraft factories that supplied them. 'Eagle Day' was to be 13 August, by which time the Luftwaffe was to achieve mastery of the air as a prelude to invasion about a month later. One of the biggest daylight attacks came on 15 August, when the Germans flew 1800 sorties. Their formations were quickly dispersed, however, before they could do much damage. The RAF claimed a record number of 182 brought down, but the true figure, which could only be verified from German documents afterwards, was 75. On average, the RAF shot down two German planes for each one it lost.

There was little that the civilians could do to help the battle, but they could demonstrate their support by offering their money to Spitfire funds and Hurricane funds, which sprang up in city, factory and sporting clubs. It was announced that £5000 would pay for a fighter and it would be named by those who raised the money. After one battle over the Channel, in which sixteen RAF fighters were lost, Garfield Weston the biscuit king contributed £100,000 to replace them. Altogether £13 million was raised.

19 As the Battle of Britain brought waves of German planes towards the coast, RAF pilots at fighter stations would 'scramble' to their planes, like this squadron of Hurricanes, and go up to intercept them

[47]

On 20 August Churchill paid his tribute to 'the Few'. Their numbers were getting dangerously few; by 6 September Fighter Command had lost nearly a quarter of its thousand pilots, and to replace them there were only new inexperienced pilots, whose training had often not yet been completed. Attacks on their airfields had also put several of them out of action, the runways ruined by craters. At this stage the advantage had tilted to the Germans and there was great anxiety that they could have delivered a knock-out blow. This was a time when even Churchill had to face doubts as to whether Britain could withstand the assault. News of the build-up of invasion barges across the Channel was coming in daily, and on 4 September Hitler made his last invasion threat in a speech at the Berlin Palace of Sport: 'In England they keep asking, Why doesn't he come? Calm down, calm down. He's coming! He's coming!' And he promised that 'We will raze their cities to the ground.'

Months later Churchill was to admit to Anthony Eden that there were days that summer 'when I awoke with dread in my heart'. The likely dates for invasion in August had passed safely, but now September's favourable weather, moon and tides, from the 8th to the 10th, looked likelier. In fact, the first D-Day set by Hitler was 15 September but because of the bombing of the fleet of invasion barges this was postponed twice. However, that was not known to Churchill, even though some German signals were already being decoded through the Enigma machine at Bletchley Park.

On 7 September barges and small ships were converging southwards on the Channel ports and bombers were massing on Channel airfields. On that September afternoon, wave after wave of German bombers crossed South-East England heading for London, and began incendiary raids on the docks, heavier than anything seen before. By eight o'clock that evening, Home Forces headquarters issued the codeword 'Cromwell', which meant 'invasion imminent'. It was intended to put the Home Front on full alert, at action stations. But it was misinterpreted in many areas to mean that invasion had already begun, and in some places church bells were rung to call out the Home Guard. Even in the islands of the Outer Hebrides their men stood guard on the beaches. The alert remained in force for twelve days for the invasion that never came. For, on 17 September, Hitler postponed Operation Sea-lion indefinitely, much to the relief of the German navy. Meanwhile the Luftwaffe, under Goering, was attempting to bring Britain to the point of surrender without invasion, by intensive bombing of cities and civilians.

The Blitz had begun.

CHAPTER THREE

LONDON UNDER FIRE

SATURDAY, 7 September 1940 was another nice summer's day and Hermann Goering, commander of the Luftwaffe, was by the sea – at Cap Gris Nez, watching 300 German bombers, escorted by 600 fighters, roaring northwards overhead. For the first time the destination of a large-scale bombing raid was to be London. There had been sporadic bombs on London's outskirts, which had been dropped more or less by accident. Now the entire weight of the largest air force in the world was attempting to knock out the largest target in the world, covering as it did 800 square miles. They could at least not miss it.

This was the decisive blow, Goering had promised Hitler. London would be reduced to uninhabitable chaos. Its citizens would flee in terror, blocking the roads, bringing government to a standstill, and Britain would sue for peace. That was the scenario for the 'Blitz', though of course it was not yet called that. *Blitzkrieg* meant a lightning attack; the bombing of London was repeated for seventy-six nights on end, with one night off for bad weather. By then it was hardly a lightning campaign.

At 5 p.m. that Saturday when the sirens went Cyril Demarne, a mobile fire officer, was strolling in the yard of his London Fire Brigade divisional headquarters in the East End.

> It was a gorgeous afternoon, a few fleecy clouds in the sky. I looked up and there was this great flotilla in V formation, this great black rash, coming over. German fighters were weaving in and out and you could just see a little shining sparkle darting in and out among the bombers. We heard the scream of the bombs and the explosions, nearer and nearer. I darted for the control room, dived for shelter. And within a few seconds out went the lights, the mains had been hit. We had guessed this might happen and we had magnificent secondary lighting – candles in jam jars. So we lit our candles and it started.

By nightfall the eastern sky was lighting up London with near midday brilliance. You could read a newspaper in Shaftesbury Avenue by the light of

20 *The Blitz began on 7 September with an all-out incendiary attack on the London docks which turned miles of dockside warehouses into a choking inferno. This is part of the Surrey Docks*

the fires in dockland, five miles away. Miles of dockside warehouses had gone up in flames; there were torrents of burning rum and molten sugar from warehouses, tallow from candle factories coating the roads, choking clouds of smoke laden with pepper, paint or perfume, and 250 acres of timber yard stacks crackling like a forest fire.

Calls for extra pumps started pouring in to Cyril Demarne's candle-lit control room.

> First Dagenham, then Barking, East Ham, West Ham, Leyton, Leyton-stone and in a matter of minutes, we'd run out of pumps to send them. I remember East Ham asked for 100 pumps and West Ham got up to 500 pumps. We had to call on the London control and I think they must have very nearly fallen off their stools. The Chief Regional Fire Officer sent two officers down to reconnoitre and hours afterwards they came back and said, 'How many pumps did you ask for? 500? You could do with 1000.'

A. P. Herbert, independent member of Parliament and boat-lover, was going down-river in his craft *Water Gipsy*, on duty with the River Emergency Service, taking wire hawsers to Woolwich for towing burning barges. It was a fantastic journey:

[50]

The Pool of London that night was like Piccadilly in the good old days. We rounded Limehouse corner and saw an astounding picture. Half a mile of the Surrey shore was ablaze – warehouses, wharves, piers, barges. There was a wall of smoke and sparks across the river. We did not like the look of it much but we put wet towels round our faces and steamed into the torrid cloud. Inside, the scene was like a lake in hell. Burning barges were drifting everywhere. We could hear the hiss and roar of the conflagration ashore but could not see it, only the burning barges and the crimson water which reflected them. We came out safe but sooty, the White Ensign nearly black.

On the roof of his cathedral, the Dean of St Paul's was watching as from a grandstand. 'The whole of that night was almost as bright as a sunny day. Inside the cathedral the light was such that I have never seen the stained glass windows glow as they did then.' It was about the last time he, or anyone else, would see them glow at all. 'It's the end of the world,' said one of the watchers on the cathedral roof. The awesome spectacle made people feel apocalyptic. George Orwell was watching it with Cyril Connolly from his top-floor flat, gazing out beyond St Paul's. 'This is the end of capitalism. It is a judgement on us,' said Connolly. People who were far enough away to be spectators were almost relieved: the time of anticipation, of tension and apprehension was for many people worse than when the bombing actually started. Celia Fremlin, an air-raid warden who worked throughout the Blitz for Mass Observation, remembered the sense of relief.

Everybody instinctively knew that Hitler was moving in to bomb London. You would hear of a bomb at Dover, or somewhere in Kent, then it would be the outskirts, Croydon and so on. People had their buckets all ready to throw over incendiaries and no incendiaries came. Constantly being worked up to a pitch of facing it, and then not having to face it, is a horrible feeling. When it began and you got the measure of what it was like, terrifying though a lot of it was, it wasn't quite as bad as most of us envisaged.

It was before the days of radio-communication. Once the telephone and power cables beneath the streets were knocked out, the only way to send a message was by messenger. The Fire Service messengers were in many cases boys of sixteen on bikes. 'I think some of them put a bit on their ages. Some of them weren't sixteen but they did a marvellous job. In the explosions the kids would be blown off their bikes. But on they'd go with the messages,' recalled Cyril Demarne.

By midnight there were nine 100-pump fires burning along the Thames to Woolwich. Dockland was full of streets of little houses, built cheaply in the 1850s for dockworkers within short walking distance of the wharves; they

21 *The morning after one of the early raids in East Ham. Dockland's streets of little houses, cheaply built by the Victorian employers for their dock labour, were shattered by blast and fell down*

simply fell down, shattered, flattened or set on fire by the incendiary bombs. In spite of their flimsiness, they were not 'slums' – thousands of them had lace curtains and scrubbed doorsteps. Kitty Murphy lived in one of them in North Woolwich. Her mother and the neighbours were in the brick air-raid shelter outside in the street, drinking and singing to try to drown the noise and their fears, but Kitty, who was sixteen, had stayed indoors with her bed-ridden grandfather. He was asking 'who was it banging about upstairs?'

> As I lay there looking through where the windows had been blown out, I heard the air-raid warden shouting my mother's name: 'Nance, come on, you've copped it girl, come out of there, you've got five incendiary bombs!' I jumped. I thought, oh my God. My first thoughts were getting grandfather out – he'd had both his legs off. I pushed his wheelchair up to the bed and I'm saying, please Grandfather, please get in, we've got the house on fire. 'Who's been playing with matches?' he said. I pushed him through the passage, got him down the steps and across the road. Then I thought, oh, the cat, the cat and the kittens. I ran up the stairs, shushed the cat down and I couldn't reach the kittens. The flames now were coming through the window . . .

In spite of that, Kitty went back again and again, saving clothes and bedding and throwing the bundles out of the windows. She even got the new three-piece suite out of the front-room window, the clean washing out of the copper in the kitchen, and filled the galvanised zinc bath with utensils and dragged it out and across the street.

And all this time my mum's shouting, come out, come out you silly. . . . She was calling me everything. Then she grabbed me. She said, no more, no more, you're not going in there no more, let it burn, she said. And I just went to get away from her when the whole of the house caved in. She saved my life. I would have been in there, picking up the clock and the ornaments off the mantelpiece.

That was only the beginning of the East End's ordeal. That night, Black Saturday, 430 people were killed and 1600 badly injured. Hundreds were, like Kitty's family, made homeless. The next night the fires were still burning, which made it easy for the bombers to find their target again, and another 400 were killed. Every fireman and part-time auxiliary fireman in London was mobilised; some men and pumps were in action for forty hours non-stop, and brigades were sent from as far away as Rugby and Portsmouth. The streets were chaotic. There was no electricity, gas or telephone.

The shock to the inhabitants of the East End was numbing. Nothing in the war – any war – until then had prepared people for living in a city under such an onslaught. Naturally, people fled. Some 5000 East Enders put some things in suitcases, prams, wheelbarrows, and made for Epping Forest, where they slept out. Others went to friends or relatives in other parts of London or the Home Counties and came back to their work – if it still existed – every day. By the end of three weeks, half the population of Stepney had moved out, usually under their own steam. Many just drifted westwards towards Paddington and got on a train – any train – and a great many ended up wandering the streets of Oxford or Reading with no idea what to do next.

On the Monday, after two nights of incendiary raids, East End life was at a standstill, according to Mass Observation reports. 'People talked incessantly about air raids. Nothing was done to organise their interest or to bring some ray of light. People left without anywhere to go to.' The only resentment noted was that of Jews having more relatives ready to take them in other parts of London than 'us Cockneys'. The observers reported people as 'dazed' but saw very little open hysterics and weeping.

Those who did not leave made for the shelters – brick street shelters for the most part. On 8 September, Churchill paid a visit to Bethnal Green accompanied by Sir Harold Scott, the Chief Executive responsible for London's civil defence.

People were already in the early afternoon coming in for the night, carrying their bedding and belongings, but they dropped them to cheer the PM. Putting his hat on the end of his stick, he twirled it round and roared,

'Are we down-hearted?' They shouted back 'No!' with astonishing gusto. 'Hit 'em back, Winston,' the East Enders cried. 'Hit 'em hard!' Pessimists had predicted panic and bitterness in the East End but I saw nothing of the kind.

There was, however, another side to the picture of cheerful defiance which is traditionally put forward. There *were* people who found the raids exhilarating, who watched from windows and roof tops, like Churchill himself when he was allowed to, but there were some who found it unendurably frightening. Celia Fremlin watched an outbreak of panic in a street shelter in Cable Street, Stepney.

At the beginning, when nobody was used to it, the women got absolutely hysterical. They were screaming and saying 'I can't stand it, I can't stand it, I'm going to die, I can't stand it!' And there were usually one or two saying 'Calm down, calm down!' Sometimes the women would be really hysterical, crying and falling on the floor. I only once saw it as bad as that in a shelter. The next time I went there, four nights later, they were all much calmer, they'd brought stools to sit on and there was even a bit of community singing. Because, once you've gone through three nights of bombing and come out alive, you can't help feeling safe the fourth time. So the only real panic I saw was then.

22 *East End mothers and their children queue for admission to one of the few tunnel shelters available in the early days of the Blitz. The queues soon lasted all day*

One thing that the East Enders did not trust were the brick street shelters, which would clearly not protect them from a near miss – nothing would from a direct hit. 'A breath of wind would knock them down.' . . . 'The flat roof makes them such a lovely target.' . . . '£93 a block they cost and they're no damn use at all.' . . . 'A bomb fell near one and blew the five of them and the shelter four yards along the road.' Such were the opinions collected by Mass Observation. People wanted deep shelters and none had been built, so on the second night of the September attack Stepney people took matters into their own hands. Bernard Kops, a boy of thirteen, who was to become a playwright, described it in vivid detail in *The World is a Wedding*.

Thousands upon thousands the next evening pushed their way into Liverpool Street Station and demanded to be let down to shelter. At first the authorities wouldn't agree to it and they called out the soldiers to bar the way. . . . The people would not give up and would not disperse, would not take no for an answer. A great yell went up and the gates were opened and my mother threw her hands together and clutched them towards the sky. 'Thank God! He heard me!' As if He had intervened with the government on behalf of the Kops family. . . . 'It's a great victory for the working class,' a man said.

So began the tube shelterers' saga, the strange nocturnal life of the Underground in which people, paying the minimum fare of a penny-halfpenny for a ticket, travelled from station to station to find a platform on which to squeeze themselves. West End stations were considered the safest and deepest, Oxford Circus and Piccadilly Circus attracting large crowds, as did the deepest of all, at Hampstead. But everywhere the platforms were littered with people, their rugs and their eiderdowns, their sandwiches and thermos flasks, their bags and sometimes an open suitcase with a baby sleeping in it. At the peak in late September there were 177,000 people, mainly women and children, spending the night in this way, but even they constituted only about 4 per cent of Londoners (more than half continued to sleep in their own homes, and the rest either went to public shelters or their own Anderson shelters).

In stations where the current was switched off, such as the Aldwych or the Elephant and Castle, people bedded down on the track or slung hammocks over it. They also slept, after a fashion, on the emergency stairs, on the escalators and in the passages. In the early days the atmosphere was stifling and there were no sanitary facilities other than the odd bucket or the tunnels themselves. But at least it was warm and you were not alone and, most important of all, you could not hear the bombs. 'We're living like bloody moles,' one Cockney remarked to an American reporter, 'but at least you can't 'ear blasted Jerry.'

Queues for the best places on the platforms, at the back, out of the draught, used to form as early as ten o'clock in the morning – the stations did not open to shelterers till 4 p.m. Celia Fremlin knew the scene well:

> If you got in too late you would have to sit up straight with nothing to lean against. Most people somehow found room to lie down for some part of the night but I doubt if anyone got more than two or three hours' sleep. They had to leave one yard clear for genuine travellers to get on and off the trains and they were quite good about that. One trouble with this yard was that it made a little open space where the children could run about – nice for the children but a bit scary when the trains came in.

Among the shelterers in the early weeks moved Henry Moore, who spent each night going from station to station, drawing the 'reclining figures' which were to take over his work as a sculptor and make his name. 'It was a quite extraordinary mess and chaos, but that was just what I wanted, the unexpected, the unorganised – what I was trying to portray was the profound depth of this place, their distance from the war that was raging above, but their awareness of it in their faces, their attitudes. What I was sketching represented an artistic turning point for me.'

The government had not provided deep shelters because it feared that people would go underground and not come up again, a menace to health and good discipline. They turned out, as so often, to have underestimated the self-discipline of ordinary citizens. Soon, each station had its 'regulars' with their accustomed pitches and their conversation with their neighbours – the occasional card game, the chat about last night's damage. At nine o'clock there was a self-imposed curfew, comparative quiet – the trains stopped running at 10 p.m. In the morning, after the all-clear, the platforms would empty and by seven the porters would have swept up the litter. It was an orderly scene. The Germans helped, by the regularity of their raids – so much so that if the sirens had not wailed by 6 p.m. people would ask, 'What's up? What's happened to Jerry?'

There were disasters when tube stations got hit, but not the flooding from the Thames that the authorities had feared. The worst disaster was at Balham, on 15 October, when a direct hit on the station blocked the exits, the road above the station collapsed with a double-decker bus nose-down in it, and the broken water mains caused a landslide of sludge which suffocated many of the 600 people who had been sheltering on the platforms below. Another direct hit, on Bank station, blew an outsize crater in the busy crossroads between the Bank of England and the Mansion House, which wiped out the station booking-hall. Some of the 111 victims were killed by being blown on to the line in front of a train that was coming in. At Marble Arch station a bomb exploded in the underground corridors. The 18 people killed by the blast were unmarked but stripped naked.

When the Blitz began on 7 September, the bombs rained down on an

23 (Facing page) Because of the lack of deep shelters, Londoners took over the tube stations to sleep in at night. A space was left along the edge of the platform for passengers to get on and off the underground trains, which ceased to run at 10 p.m. The deepest stations (this is the Elephant and Castle) were the most popular because you could not hear the bombs

apparently defenceless city, partly because the anti-aircraft guns were dispersed about the country. But on the fifth night the anti-aircraft batteries, now greatly reinforced, opened up with an ear-splitting barrage. The effect upon the morale of those on the ground was greater than on the Luftwaffe's bombing fleet; it was calculated that nearly 2000 shells were fired for every aircraft destroyed. The bombers stayed above the range of the searchlight batteries. Shrapnel from the shell-bursts hurtled down on roofs and streets to join the bomb splinters that were being eagerly collected by small boys. Bernard Kops was told by fellow-scavengers in Stepney Green: 'That bit's no good, it's from an AA gun, but that's all right, it's from a German bomb.' 'The noise is tremendous and continuous but I don't mind it, feeling it to be on my side,' George Orwell noted in his diary. 'On the first night of the barrage they are said to have fired 500,000 shells, i.e. £2,500,000 worth. Well worth it for the effect on morale.'

After a few nights the pattern of Blitz life began to settle down – and within days the City and West End were being bombed as much as the East End and eventually more. People hated the sound of the sirens. There was something menacing about the sound itself; the preliminary rattle in the throat, the first upward swoop to a full-pitched howl, the swerving down and up like a wailing roller coaster, took people's stomachs with it. 'Banshee howlings' Churchill called them. 'As if the darkened countryside, like a vast trapped animal, were screaming at us,' said Priestley. More than a third of Mass Observation's informants hated the sirens' sound, 'the worst part of the whole business'. Some were reminded of the hallucinatory noise that one used to hear going under an ether anaesthetic. Some complained that they mistook the noise of cars accelerating – and especially accelerating trolley buses – for sirens. It was, said one, 'an awful noise to wake up to'.

The other noise, apart from the bombs themselves, that unnerved people was the sound of the planes, the far-off deep vibration of engines growing nearer. People claimed to be able to tell 'one of theirs' from 'one of ours' by ear – 'their' engines throbbed and came and went with a curious moaning sound, like that of a vacuum cleaner. But in the early weeks of the Blitz, at least, all aeroplane engine noise during night raids was likely to be 'one of theirs', or, rather, all too many of theirs.

People became debilitated from going without sleep. Most shelters, indoors or out, had makeshift furnishing and seldom allowed much room for lying down. Even those who boldly stayed in bed slept less well than they liked to claim; half the night could well be spent listening, prepared to make a hurried dash to shelter. Most people slept on the ground floor, in the basement if they had one or under the stairs. A survey which Mass Observation made at the end of September showed that two-thirds of the city's population were getting less than four hours' sleep, usually at the end of the night (the raiders went home before dawn). Women were reported to sleep less than men, partly because of looking after young children. About one

person in three claimed not to have slept at all the previous night. 'I daren't sleep now. I roam around the house and garden and keep going back to the cellar to report to the others.' ... 'I can't sleep but I don't feel terribly tired – living on nerves, I suppose.' ... 'We heard a salvo drop a goodish way off, then there's a crash that's a damn sight too loud to be healthy, so we grab the boy and hustle downstairs, Ellie's teeth chattering like castanets.' ... 'I was not frightened nor worrying, yet go to sleep I could not.' ... 'Sleep! You couldn't sleep! We can't go on like this, can we?' ... 'It's the wife that worries me, a bundle of nerves. Can't sleep well, I feel a bit of a wreck myself. A few more nights of this would put the tin lid on it.' ... 'It's tragic to see people with children pouring out of the shelters, tired, cramped and aching from six hours sitting on hard benches.' These were some of the fruits of a Mass Observation study of how people slept on the night of 15 September. Of course, they got better with practice.

The other thing dragging people down was worry – usually about other members of their families who were away for the night or living in other parts of London. 'I won't admit to myself that I'm as worried as hell, but Dad is not in, those big ones were near him, I fear,' ran one Mass Observer's report. 'Having an elderly mother who worries so much when I'm out, I'm forced to

24 *A corner of Leicester Square the morning after one of the heaviest raids of the Blitz. People are going to work past shattered and smouldering buildings. Just out of sight to the right other people queued daily outside the Odeon to see* Gone with the Wind

return by black-out time.' . . . 'I have parents in south-east London and I know how terrible the raids have been. Tried to telephone but failed to get through. I await every letter with trepidation.' . . . 'My lover expects me not to mind, to make love with complete abandon, having only had phone-calls to comfort me all week. I'm on the verge of saying goodbye to him. I wouldn't mind if he was kept from me by outside agencies but it's his carefulness for his own skin.'

People did not worry – or said they didn't – about themselves. 'You'll go when it's got your number on it.' That, or a variation of it, was reported over and over again. But it was sometimes different while you listened to it and wondered whose number *was* on it. An East End parson, the Rev. H. A. Wilson, asked one of his parishioners if she prayed when she heard a bomb falling nearby. Oh yes, she said, she prayed 'Don't let it fall here.' But it would be a bit rough on other people, he pointed out, if her prayer was answered and it dropped on *them*. 'I can't help that,' replied the devout lady, 'They must say *their* prayers and push it off further.' John Betjeman's lady from Kensington attending a service in *Westminster Abbey* had much the same thought:

> Gracious Lord, oh bomb the Germans.
> Spare their women for Thy Sake,
> And if that is not too easy
> We will pardon Thy Mistake.
> But gracious Lord, whate'er shall be,
> Don't let anyone bomb me.

It was natural to think first of yourself – and of your nearest and dearest – even to be thankful that someone else and not you had 'copped it'. But what was it like to 'cop it'? There were enough amazingly narrow escapes for people to tell that tale.

The unearthly sound of a bomb falling really close by was different from the whistle you heard from more distant bombs. It was like 'the sound of tearing silk', as if someone 'was scratching the sky with a broken fingernail', like 'a great sheet of air being ripped through', 'something between the rustling of a paper and the letting out of the bath water'. So people variously described it. But the effect was more than a tearing sound: one could *sense* the motion of the approaching bomb. 'They rushed at enormous velocity, as though dragged down by some gigantic magnet.' . . . 'It developed into the roar of an express train.' George Orwell noted: 'The commotion made by the mere passage of a bomb through the air is astonishing. The whole house shakes, enough to rattle objects on the table. Why it is that the lights dip when a bomb passes close by, no one seems to know.'

The anti-aircraft barrage, wrote Priestley, made a sound 'as if gigantic doors were being slammed to' in the sky, while the sound of distant bombs was a 'crump' that shook the ground. Near to, it was an elemental shock, in which the blast preceded the sound. Air-raid warden Barbara Nixon, on a bicycle, described in *Raiders Overhead* the order of events as a bomb fell nearby:

Suddenly the shabby, ill-lit five-storey building ahead of me swelled out like a child's balloon. I looked at it in astonishment that bricks and mortar could stretch like rubber. At the point when it must burst, the glass fell out. It did not hurtle, it simply cracked and dropped out, allowing the straining building to deflate and return to normal. Almost instantaneously there was a crash and a double explosion to my right. As the blast of air reached me, I left my saddle and sailed through the air.

The freak effects of blast became a favourite topic when comparing air-raid experiences. There were tales of people being hurled on amazing journeys around corners, of being sucked up chimneys or stripped naked where they sat. Tall buildings fluttered and swayed like aspens, without falling. Posters were ripped from hoardings. Windows buckled inwards but sometimes straightened out, uncracked. Buses were blown into first-storey windows. Front doors, like magic carpets, went flying down the street. One man said that just as he grasped his front-door handle 'a bomb fell and blew the house out of my hand'. 'I remember seeing a roll of material inside a shop window which had rolled underneath the window and come out on the pavement. The blast had bent the glass and sucked out the material before the window snapped back into place intact,' wrote another witness.

Before any bombing had started, somebody – probably a committee of senior civil servants – had met to decide on what word should be used to describe the effect of a bomb. They came up with the perfect unemotive, colourless, civil service word: it was to be called an 'incident'. Again and again during the Blitz the most shattering experiences were sanitised, reduced to something mundane, made discussable by this Whitehall euphemism. 'There has been an incident' – so you could not proceed any further down the street, your train was cancelled, the station was closed, the building was out of bounds. However grave, it was only an 'incident'. Who could really be panicked by an incident? But what was it like to arrive on the scene of an 'incident' immediately afterwards? Celia Fremlin's job as an air-raid warden was to leap on her bicycle as soon as a bomb dropped in her sector, go out to locate the incident and bring back an immediate assessment of the damage and casualties – 'until my bicycle was blown from under me, hurled against a wall and smashed, while I was perfectly okay,' she added. Here is her description:

The biggest problem when you got to a bombed house immediately afterwards was that there was such a cloud of dust that you couldn't see anything. You couldn't see the road even. You pushed your way through a choking cloud, this utter confusion of dust and silence. I would piece together what the people stumbling around told me.

You couldn't know how many were injured because – and this was new to us – people who are badly injured don't make any noise at all. The ones who are screaming are the ones who are just frightened or have grazed their knee or something. Screaming is almost always a sign that a person is basically okay. It was the silent injured that were the problem and there was no way of guessing how many there were. Places are terribly silent after a bomb.

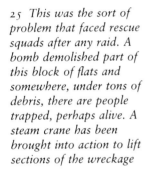

25 This was the sort of problem that faced rescue squads after any raid. A bomb demolished part of this block of flats and somewhere, under tons of debris, there are people trapped, perhaps alive. A steam crane has been brought into action to lift sections of the wreckage

Another characteristic aftermath of a newly fallen bomb was the smell. ARP workers agreed that it was the worst part of the bombing: the harsh, rank, raw smell which came from the dust of dissolved brickwork, masonry and joinery. John Strachey, an air-raid warden (later a minister in the post-war Labour government) wrote of it: 'For several hours there was an acrid overtone from the high explosive which the bomb contained. Almost invariably, too, there was the mean little stink of domestic gas, seeping up from broken pipes. But the whole of the smell was greater than the sum of its parts. It was the smell of violent death itself.'

Then came the problem of helping those who scrambled out of the wreckage of their homes, hurt, shocked and unrecognisable. 'Endless confusion caused by the simple fact that it is usually impossible to recognise anyone without asking who they are,' wrote Strachey. One man dug out unconscious but alive, 'looked like a terracotta statue, his face, his teeth, his hair, were all a uniform brick colour', wrote Barbara Nixon.

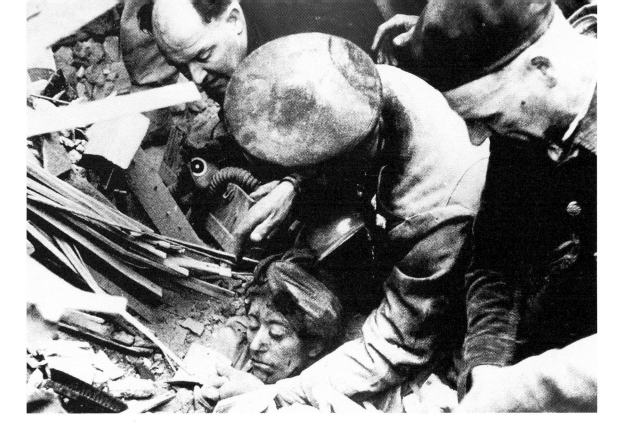

After a bomb, people literally did not know where they were in their own street. The whole geography of streets, which disappeared under mounds of debris, had changed. Under that debris there could well be survivors, buried but able to breathe – to be buried and not found was most people's greatest fear. The rescue squads had a terrible but absorbing task. The only way to tunnel through the compound of rubble, broken furniture, rugs, linoleum, curtaining and crockery, all compressed into a sort of impenetrable pudding, was with their hands; they removed the debris by means of a chain of baskets. Every few minutes digging had to stop while everyone listened intently for the faint sound of voices or of knocking. Local air-raid wardens tried to keep records of where in their houses people spent the night. But the rescue workers, mostly recruited from the building trade, became experts at knowing where to look for likely survivors in spaces under floors or in cellars. Bill Douglas, a structural engineer in the pre-war LCC architects' department, was in charge of St Pancras rescue service. 'There were some patterns known as "V-shape collapse", where the floors had given way at each side and had pushed themselves into a V-shape. You knew you were much more likely to find people alive under the sloping floor. We tried to find places where the debris hadn't fallen and break through into any open space that we could find.'

Rescue workers regarded their work simply as a job – their pay was only £3 to £3.10s a week – and knocked off at the end of their shift, except when they knew a child was buried in the building. Then they would carry on

26 *The crucial moment for a rescue squad when they uncover a survivor, still buried up to the neck. Patiently and by hand they had to free her and lift her clear of several feet of choking rubble. This woman was pulled out alive*

desperately and continuously, no matter what the time. Sometimes they were angry to be relieved when they thought they had nearly reached someone; it was hard to leave before they could discover whether there really was someone at the end of the tunnel – alive. But every day brought hardening experiences, as Bill Douglas explained:

> If we found no survivors, a flag was put up to show the area had been searched. Often what we found were very grim remains, spread all over the place. When you had got enough portions together you would count that as one body. If there were several people trapped, you had to collect all the remains and in conjunction with wardens or a medical officer decide what number of people those portions made.

Sometimes it was too much even for a hardened rescue worker. Bill Douglas remembered being faced with a shelter that had received a direct hit.

> One of the biggest fellows, an ex-regular Army man, looked a bit qualmy, and said, 'I don't feel like going in there. You know what we're going to find, don't you?' And I, knowing what the effect would be on the other men, said 'You've got to go in, you've got to go in.' 'Well, I just can't do it,' he said. So I gave him a last chance to go in or else be dismissed from the service and he said, 'Well, I'd rather do that, guv'nor, than go in.' So he went off. But that was a necessary action to ensure the other men didn't go the same way.

Mercifully, a direct hit was something that could not usually be remembered afterwards, as the survivor was almost invariably knocked unconscious. But people had especially clear memories of what they were doing just before a bomb fell. Dorothy Franklin, sheltering in a neighbour's house in Wimbledon during 15 September's big raid, had just come out from under the stairs during a lull. There were six of them in the kitchen. Someone was making tea. She was standing beside her husband at the kitchen table, reading a letter he had just written. That was the moment when an aerial torpedo struck the row of four houses, blowing them apart into the air. She was the only survivor. Two of the bodies were found six months later – flung to the bottom of the garden and buried under the soil. She described the blank in her life:

> When you get a direct hit, you know nothing. I saw nothing. I heard nothing . . . until I became aware of a voice calling 'Where are you?' I replied, 'I'm in the kitchen.' Only there was no kitchen. I had been buried, unconscious, for six hours. I felt nothing – until they began to move the rubble which was pinning my legs down. Luckily a doctor with morphia was with them.

27 *All too often those dug out of the wreckage of a direct hit were dead. This was the scene after forty-five died when a school was hit, most of them children, and their bodies were collected in the schoolyard. Harrowing pictures like this were, not surprisingly, banned by the censors*

For three days she was left untreated as a hopeless case. She was bristling 'like a hedgehog' with debris and brick dust which had forced itself into her skin. All her hair had to be cut off. The rescue worker who found her alive was himself taken to the same hospital with shock. What she knew only as 'a blank space in my memory' robbed her of her home, her husband and the normal use of the legs for ever afterwards.

That September alone there were 16,000 casualties of the London bombing, nearly 7000 of whom were killed. The poet Ruthven Todd wrote their epitaph in a poem tersely entitled 'These Are Facts':

> Bodies in death are not magnificent or stately,
> Bones are not elegant that blast has shattered;
> This sorry, stained and crumpled rag was lately
> A man whose life was made of little things that mattered;
> Now he is just a nuisance, liable to stink,
> A breeding ground for flies, a test tube for disease;
> Bury him quickly and never pause to think
> What is the future worth to men like these?

The bombed-out, who lost their possessions, but were lucky enough to be uninjured, were not so lucky in other respects. The theoreticians of bombing had not expected survivors and therefore the authorities were not prepared for their needs. A quarter of a million people during the first fifty-seven nights of the London Blitz were homeless for periods as short as one day or as long as one month (many people were bombed out more than once). They needed shelter, food and warmth and there was nothing like enough of any of these.

The 'rest centres' (usually schools) to which the people who had lost their homes were taken were ill-equipped and squalid; they were soon temporarily housing 25,000 people and one of them in Bethnal Green, for instance, had a stock of cutlery that consisted of two spoons and a blunt knife. Food provided consisted of unvarying bread and soup and tea. There were places with only ten pails and coal scuttles to serve as toilets for 200–300 people. There were few wash basins – for people who, like all the bombed, were coated with ingrained dust. There were not enough camp beds or blankets. And – the basic cause of it all – there was not enough money. The parsimonious Chamberlain government, which had organised these bleak arrangements, had decided to put them in the hands of the Poor Law authorities. To be bombed out was to be treated as if you were a pauper in the workhouse – until, amid mounting protests and mutinous feelings, the government threw out the penny-pinching and ordered the Treasury to pay for whatever staff and equipment was necessary.

Compensation in full was ordered by Churchill for all war damage, and applications to the London Assistance Board for payment for lost or damaged furniture and clothing poured in. Re-housing and repair of damage was very slow, hampered by the fact that the raids did not stop for nine months. Building workers had to be released from the army – 5000 of them – to help tackle the huge backlog of repairs. A Londoners' Meal Service was organised, and community feeding places and mobile canteens were run by volunteers.

Notices in the shattered windows of bombed shops announced that 'Looting is punishable by death or penal servitude for life.' These dire punishments were never inflicted, neither was there wholesale looting of the kind that has since become familiar during city riots. But there was wide-spread pocketing of valuables from bombed houses, by demolition squads and even by auxiliary firemen or rescue workers. A blind eye was turned: it was often regarded as a reward for their gruesome task. 'Our sergeant says loot as much as you like as long as you're not found out,' said one auxiliary fireman to Mass Observation. A girl in the AFS was said to bring home something every night, but often it was nothing more valuable than a tin of pineapple. This human failure did not detract from the AFS's public image as heroic, but there were cases of appalling callousness towards people who had been bombed and suffered enough. Kitty Murphy, for instance, whose struggles to save the contents of her burning home were quoted above, found a woman watching her efforts who then offered to look after the salvaged furniture in her shop nearby. Next morning, she and her mother went back to the shop to collect it.

As we neared the shop, my mum said to me, 'Did they have curtains up there, Kitty, last night?' I said, 'Yes, black-out curtains, mum.' 'There's no bloody curtains up there now,' she said. She looked through the letter box. 'My God,' she said, 'they've done a moonlight. They've scarpered,' she said. 'They've robbed us blind.' Oh, the language! Never heard me mum swear like it. 'I'll annihilate them,' she said. 'I'll swing for them. . . . For God's sake don't let people see us crying,' she said. 'Come on.'

Most people rehoused themselves or found friends and relations to put them up, at least temporarily, but the poorest, especially the East Enders, had least choice in the matter. They were the ones who at first trekked with their pramfuls of belongings to sleep out on Hampstead Heath on in Greenwich Park. People even took trains or hitched rides to the hopfields of Kent. Chislehurst Caves, to which 8000 Londoners commuted nightly, were turned into an underground apartment block, equipped with beds, tables, a church, a canteen and even a piano. Some of the small inner caves had been taken over by bombed-out families, with their cooking stoves and beds hidden by curtains. Husbands went to work and returned on the evening train to their suburban cave.

Those who had taken longer journeys away from the inferno in London received a rather more sympathetic welcome than the first wave of evacuees had done when the war began. Several towns made efficient efforts at billeting the evacuees, and most hosts felt they deserved help after their ordeals.

28 After survivors had been rescued came salvage operations. Shop assistants in white coats are sorting out what can be saved from this wrecked shop in South London while firemen and civil defence workers clear debris. A topless table stands forlornly in the road. There were severe penalties for looting, but few prosecutions

Compulsory billeting powers rarely had to be used. When the Blitz began, there were still nearly half a million school-age children in Greater London – about half the usual total – but after an official evacuation of mothers and children in October there were still a quarter of a million children left. It was a far smaller evacuation than that at the beginning of the war. Families preferred to stick together now, even under fire.

One of the chief reception towns was Oxford, where something like 20,000 Londoners took refuge, mostly women with children, and where the mayor started a fund to assist them. Some of them were housed temporarily in the colleges and there were nappies drying in the quad at Christ Church for the first time in its long history. Soon there wasn't a single vacant lodging or hotel room left in town and an overspill of 800 were crowded into a cinema. Oxford, used to visitors of every kind, on the whole ignored them and it wasn't long before many of the East Enders wanted to go back again, preferring the hugger-mugger of their native streets and pubs, even under bombardment, to the aloofness of the dreaming spires.

Vera Brittain, revisiting her old university, was struck by the dense crowds in the High Street, 'which vary from harassed dons in tweeds to weary homeless mothers from Poplar and Plaistow, dragging small bewildered children'. University College was full of evacuees, Somerville full of nurses and the Majestic cinema with East Enders.

> As I enter, a familiar and overpowering stench strikes me in the face like a blow. . . . Beneath the upturned velveteen seats, disorderly piles of mattresses, pillows, rugs and cushions, indicate the 'pitches' staked out by each family. Many of the women lie wearily on the floor though the hour is 11 a.m. and a warm sun is shining cheerfully. The customary collection of soiled newspapers and ancient apple-cores is contributing to the odiferous atmosphere.

Vera Brittain herself knew what it was like to be forced out of her home in Chelsea by that ubiquitous scourge of the Blitz, an unexploded or time bomb – nobody could tell until afterwards whether it had simply failed to go off on impact (one bomb in about ten was a 'dud') or whether it had a delayed action fuse. Before long there were 3000 of these 'UXBs' awaiting attention, causing houses to be evacuated and streets to be closed for 600 yards in all directions. Their nuisance value was far greater than the damage to life that they posed – greater than the Germans realised, or they would have dropped more of them. A third of those rendered homeless were turned out by unexploded bombs, and police guards were placed outside their houses in case they were tempted to step back inside for something they had left behind and badly needed – a bottle of whisky or a change of underclothing could be a great temptation. Meanwhile traffic was hugely disrupted even for walkers. Orwell noted 'little groups of disconsolate-looking people wandering about with suitcases and bundles turned out by unexploded bombs' and found that so many streets around Baker Street had been roped off that making his journey home, of only 300 yards, was like solving a maze. Vera Brittain spent days telephoning her town hall trying to get news. 'No, madam, the delayed action bomb behind your house has not yet exploded,' they said, as if answering a question about the time of refuse collection. 'I do hope your bomb will go off soon and not blow up 254 and that you have got out the things you need, including the wireless,' wrote Rose Macaulay to her sister.

The most famous unexploded bomb in London dug its way twenty-seven feet into the clay subsoil beneath the south-west tower of St Paul's cathedral, right beside the foundations. For three days the cathedral was closed while the men of the Royal Engineers bomb-disposal unit struggled to excavate it; the clay had given it a slippery surface that neither hands nor metal grabs could grip. Traffic was slowed for half a mile around in case the vibration set it off — and brought down most of the cathedral. Twice it was lifted by hawsers and twice they snapped and it fell back, but the third attempt was successful. The bomb, eight feet long, weighed a ton. Lieutenant James Davies decided not to defuse it there and then: 'All the time I've been touching it, I've sort of sensed a voice inside it, shrieking to get out,' he said with the almost psychic insight that bomb disposal men seem to develop. 'I don't think we're going to stop it going off, no matter what we try.' Streets were cleared and closed all the way through the East End to Hackney Marshes, and every house for 100 yards on either side of the route was evacuated. The bomb was lifted aboard a lorry and packed with blocks and cushions. Then Lieutenant Davies, alone — for he refused to take any of his men — got in and drove with red flag flying at top speed through several miles of empty streets and all the red traffic lights in East London. When exploded on the Marshes, the bomb made a crater 100 feet across. The bomb-disposal teams were all volunteers. 'Somehow their faces seemed different from those of ordinary men, however brave and faithful,' wrote Churchill. 'They were gaunt, they were haggard, their faces had a bluish look, with gleaming eyes and exceptional compression of the lips.'

The St Paul's unexploded bomb fell on 12 September. It was on the next day that a lone German bomber dodged below the clouds, flew down the Mall and daringly dropped six bombs on Buckingham Palace. The King and Queen watched two of them burst about eighty yards from their window on the inner quadrangle. Water poured from one of the craters, which burst the mains. So did rats, for days afterwards, the Queen revealed later, for the sewers had also been fractured. This was the time she made her much-quoted remark: 'I'm so glad we've been bombed. It makes me feel I can look the East End in the face.' The Ministry of Information, with its genius for missing propaganda opportunities, was busy suppressing news of the Palace bombing when Churchill heard of it: 'Dolts, idiots, fools!' he is said to have exploded. 'Spread the news at once! Let it be broadcast everywhere. Let the people of

29 *The train now leaning on Platform Two ... The main railway termini were constant targets but train services were restored remarkably quickly, if erratically. This was St Pancras station one morning in October 1940*

London know that the King and Queen are sharing the perils with them.' He was, of course, psychologically correct. Kitty Murphy, herself bombed out in dockland, had the East Londoner's commonplace conviction that the rich West Enders were having a much easier time:

> I mean, they didn't seem to bother about us, the working-class people. If they weren't evacuated to America or wherever they went, they were out in the country where they never saw a bomb. But when the Palace was bombed, we were concerned in case anything happened to our royal family – Queen Elizabeth, King George, we never wanted anything to happen to them. Of course, we thought they were at Windsor, Balmoral or somewhere, away from the bombing. We thought they weren't there.

As luck would have it, they had just arrived from Windsor, where they slept each night with their children. As A. J. P. Taylor wrote, 'There was a difference between the King and his subjects. They had essential work to do, he could have gone through his 'boxes' just as well at Windsor. He attended at Buckingham Palace solely to be bombed.' In this, his sense of duty was rewarded. On one of their earlier visits to the East End, according to Sir Harold Nicolson's diary, 'the King and Queen were booed'. They now received a warm welcome and saw Union Jacks planted pathetically in the ruins of the East Enders' houses.

Buckingham Palace was hit three times by bombs, and many other well-known landmarks were to be damaged. No. 10 Downing Street, Madame Tussaud's, St Thomas's Hospital, County Hall, Broadcasting House, the British Museum – all were early victims. So, on the night of 17 September, were the department stores of Oxford Street: John Lewis, D. H. Evans, Bourne and Hollingsworth, then Peter Robinson. Vera Brittain observed:

> In Oxford Street the fire hoses are still playing on John Lewis's. Like the enormous skeleton of a prehistoric animal, the framework of the great structure still stands, a doorless and windowless erection of stone and steel. From the window ledge of one upper storey, an orange silk vest flutters, to remind passers-by of the elegant prosperity which has vanished.

Outside John Lewis's, George Orwell saw a sight that from a distance he took for a pile of corpses. They were pink plastic dress models heaped beside the empty road, which was bereft of traffic and glittering with fragments of broken glass in the late afternoon sun. Nobody had ever seen a London like it. Many thought of the city as alive, like a great beast, suffering but undestructible. John Strachey wrote:

> The hammer stroke of a heavy bomb plunged into the body of the city. London stirred, quivered and caught her breath, as if wounded. She was wounded again and again. Yet she was so gigantic that her wounds became insignificant, were rendered trivial, were dwarfed till they seemed no more than cuts and sores upon the hide of some great, slow animal.

30 Morning comes to Oxford Street – 18 September 1940. John Lewis's stands gaunt and gutted by bombs. The roadway and pavements are littered with broken glass, plaster and brick dust, water and hoses – some of them still playing. It's sweeping-up time but there will be little shopping today

'Some huge, prehistoric animal' was what Churchill called the capital, and he enjoyed himself describing to the House of Commons what a task the Germans had set themselves in attempting to destroy it. 'It would take ten years, at the present rate, for half the houses of London to be demolished. After that, of course, progress would be much slower.'

All through the residential streets and suburbs, house were knocked out like teeth. Every day it seemed as though there were new gaps in familiar rows. Interior walls were exposed to public view, along with their owner's taste in wallpaper, fireplaces, colour schemes. Privacy had been violated: it seemed almost indecent to stare at these domestic secrets, peeling plaster and rickety landings. One of the worst hazards of the time was the land mine, much heavier than a bomb, which drifted down silently on a parachute. This often entangled itself in overhead wires and trees, from which it would dangle, swaying just above the ground, and all who saw it wondered whether it was going to fall and explode. Rose Macaulay described Marylebone High Street after two land mines had landed on blocks of flats – with a noise and shock like an earthquake. 'The street looked extraordinary next day – chemists shops perfuming the air with smashed bottles, clothes, furniture tossed in heaps among the piles of glass.'

Shops with gaping fronts and shattered windows took pride in their nonchalant notices. 'More open than usual' would appear on a home-made sign-board. 'We've had a close shave – come and get one' announced a blitzed barber's shop, and a police station with blasted windows warned 'Be good – we're still open.'

Carrying on 'normally' became a sort of obsession. After the first weekend of the Blitz, the crowds of commuters arrived as usual on Monday morning. They were not allowed to walk across London Bridge that day because of a burning gas main, the dockland fires were still burning, the streets were full of glass and water – but they came. As the raids went on, their journeys to work became more and more eccentric, making use of diverted buses and those portions of the suburban railway that happened to be running on a particular day. Overnight, telephone cables were cut off, mainline stations closed and tracks torn up; electricity failed and office blocks were turned into windowless shambles – yet the morning after, men and women were struggling to restore services, answer letters, take dictation and deal with orders or accounts, as in John Wadsworth's City bank:

In a night the branch moved back to working conditions of a century earlier. All entries were made by hand in candlelight, their flickering wicks reflected in the pools of water scattered over the banking hall. Letters were handwritten and as far as possible (hand) delivered. No telephones were working, essential messages being sent in the form of brief notes. The staff, delayed by transport difficulties, arrived slowly . . . those arriving early helped deal with the smouldering fire on the upper part of the

31 *Whatever happened last night, today is another day at the office – if it's still there. City workers pick their way over an obstacle course left by the bombers, dressed in normal secretarial attire, attaché cases at their sides, carrying on normally*

premises. . . . Somehow the volume of work was mastered and final figures for the half-year produced . . . the customers of the branch suffered scarcely any inconvenience.

A secretary arriving at Broadcasting House, which was hit several times (on one occasion during the nine o'clock news) wrote in a letter: 'The telephone had been blown right out of the window, hanging down on its cord, and when I rescued it and put the receiver back on, it rang. Still working! It was P. to know if I was all right.'

Celia Fremlin's 'most poignant' memory of one sleepless night was of an East End girl of about twenty, whom she had watched leaning against the wall in a crowded shelter until half past five, when the all-clear sounded. An hour later she happened to see her emerge from a bomb-damaged house nearby.

She was looking absolutely band-box marvellous. She'd got a freshly ironed dress, had obviously found time to put her curlers in, she hadn't got stockings but had gone to the trouble to paint the pretend seam up the back of her legs, just to go to work. I thought it was absolutely terrific. I'll never forget her prancing off down the street, looking as if she'd just come from a party.

The desire for normality is a very powerful thing and it functions in the midst of all kinds of destruction short of total chaos. Fortunately for London, chaos never became total. Parliament met, the law courts and the Stock Exchange functioned, services were held in St Paul's although the altar had been shattered, the newspapers appeared almost on time out of a battered Fleet Street. Londoners as a whole did not lose their nerve, but they lost their reserve. 'As soon as the raids began seriously, people were much readier to talk to strangers in the street,' noted George Orwell in his diary as early as 12 September. What they talked about, of course, were their bomb stories, until there were so many of these that they became rather a bore – 'I'll listen to yours if you'll listen to mine.' By the end of the year Orwell was commenting, 'Everyone in London has had at least one providential escape – these so common it is now considered bad form to talk about them.' But before this stage was reached, there was an understandable and paradoxical exhilaration about the experience of danger, at least for a certain kind of people. J. B. Priestley gave expression to it in a *Postscript* broadcast after the first week of bombing:

> This is a wonderful moment for us who are here in London now in the roaring centre of the battle field. . . . We are not civilians who have happened to stray into a kind of hell on earth, but soldiers who have been flung into a battle, perhaps the most important this war will see. As a kind of civilian life, this is hellish, but as battles go, it is not at all bad.

How different was this attitude to the civilian's role compared with that of the First World War, when a poster showing a Zeppelin over London carried the taunt: 'It is far better to face the bullets than to be killed at home by a bomb (Join the Army at once).' Now, as one wife put it, 'I'm only glad my Jim is in the Army and out of all this.' Indeed, up till September 1942, more civilians than servicemen had been killed and injured.

The Blitz was terrific drama and people with any taste for action enjoyed taking part. Mass Observers noticed that air-raid wardens were far keener to volunteer to go out on patrol, with all its risks, than to stay behind in the post. Celia Fremlin remembered an old man who had been bombed out of his shop, had nowhere to sleep but a shelter, and spent his days hanging about the streets. 'Are you going to evacuate yourself?' she asked him. He replied, 'No, nothing like this has ever happened before and it will never happen again. I wouldn't miss it for all the tea in China.' He was not alone. Vera Brittain confessed that had it not been for anxiety about her evacuated children, 'I should almost have enjoyed the peculiar zest of dodging death. For all their boredom and grimness, I would not for anything have missed the past two months.' One of the 'consolations of war' listed in a broadcast by Rose Macaulay was 'the pleasure of waking up still alive each day'. People came up to London from the country, unnecessarily, to share the risk and see the fun, noted Churchill, who himself much preferred to watch the 'fireworks' from the roof than go to the deep shelter prepared for him. And Priestley himself – twenty years afterwards, admittedly – looked back on the Blitz and wrote:

> I can honestly declare that on the whole I enjoyed that time, those splintered nights, those mornings when the air was the freshest ever tasted. We were all an improvement on our unendangered selves. No longer suspicious of gaiety, we almost sparkled. In 1940–41, the rest of us escaped from the life-haters, felt free, companionable, even – except while waiting for the explosions – light-hearted. It took bombs to deliver us.

In early September during the daylight raids, the pressure on the RAF fighter stations had come near to putting them out of action. When the Luftwaffe switched to night assaults, it gave them a vital breathing space before the crucial daylight battle on 15 September, now commemorated as 'Battle of Britain day', when some 450 bombers came over the Channel. Wave after wave were broken up over Kent and the Thames estuary, and few reached London. One which did, a Dornier bomber, crashed on a roof near Victoria Station, followed down by its destroyer – a sergeant pilot whose parachute landed him in a Chelsea garden a few minutes later. It was claimed that 185 had been shot down. Later the figure was reduced to 52, twice the number of our fighters lost. But it was the turning point. For the rest of the month the German air fleets were suffering losses of more than two to one, and Operation Sea-lion was postponed. By the last big daylight attack on 30 September it was obvious that the RAF had won the air battle, and Hitler turned his thoughts to invading Russia instead.

Nevertheless, the first month of the bombing had caused enough bitterness and resentment at the lack of deep shelters and post-raid preparations to shake the government. Someone had to go and it was Sir John Anderson, the Home Secretary – the man who gave his name to the Anderson shelters of corrugated iron which saved so many of their owners. He was replaced by Herbert Morrison, who had devoted his life to London as the leading personality of the London County Council. On the day he was appointed, 3 October, an Open Letter to Morrison appeared in the *Daily Herald*, written by an angry reporter, Ritchie Calder:

> I have seen tough London workers, of whom you and I are proud, whose homes are gone but whose courage is unflinching, goaded by neglect and seething with resentment and furious reproach. THEY LOOK TO YOU. Much of the breakdown in the last month could have been foreseen and avoided, or mastered by anyone who understood the human problem of the Londoners. GO TO IT, HERBERT.

By then the first shock of the raids was past. People were adjusting to the nightly ordeal to a remarkable degree – perhaps it was a mistake on the part of the methodical Germans to bomb so regularly. Morrison acted with energy and ordered the construction of deep shelters for 70,000 people; they were too late, of course, and were only used for the flying bomb attacks of 1944. Meanwhile, the existing tube stations were to be equipped with 200,000 bunks by Christmas and with proper sanitation. The 'regulars' spending their nights in the tube stations had become friends by now, keeping places for each other. In mid-November 'food trains' began to run between 7 and 9 p.m. and 5.30 and 7 a.m., providing a mobile canteen service at the stations, and there were parties down below that Christmas. The Swiss Cottage tube shelter brought out its own printed bulletin called *The Swiss Cottager*, subtitled 'De Profundis' – out of the depths. Organisation was applied. Shelter marshals were appointed. The metal bunks were mass-produced and installed. Pumps and plumbing for sanitation were provided – with difficulty, for most stations were below sewer level. Tickets were assigned to registered holders, who were assured of regular places, with the warning that the ticket would be withdrawn if 'the holder or any member of his family commits any offence in the shelter or fails to do his share in keeping the shelter tidy and clean'. Remarkably, there were no epidemics, although some stations suffered from plagues of mosquitoes.

It is an intriguing contrast to examine how London Society fared in the Blitz – those members of it who had not moved out, leaving big houses in Belgravia, Mayfair and Kensington standing dark and empty. An advertisement in *Country Life* read: 'REGENT'S LODGE, Regent's Park (near north-west end of lake). Lady Ribblesdale, who is in America, will take any reasonable sum.'

While the poor descended to the tube tunnels, the well-connected and well-off took to the big West End hotels, which had turned their basements into shelters. The Savoy and the Dorchester were the twin hubs of London nightlife and Sir Henry 'Chips' Channon, the American millionaire social butterfly and diarist, described an evening at the Dorchester on 5 November 1940:

> Half London seemed to be there. The Duff Coopers next to us, Oliver Lyttleton, the new President of the Board of Trade was throwing his weight and wit about. I gave Bob Boothby a champagne cocktail. . . . Our bill must have been immense for we had four magnums of champagne. London lives well: I've never seen more lavishness, more money spent, or more food consumed than tonight and the dance floor was packed. There must have been a thousand people.

Ed Murrow, the American radio commentator, broadcast on 10 September in 'This is London': 'We looked in on a renowned Mayfair hotel tonight and found many old dowagers and retired colonels sitting back on the settees in the lobby. It wasn't the sort of protection I'd seek but you might feel you

32 *After dark, while some sheltered or tried to sleep, others carried on normally by visiting their usual haunts, dressed in their usual style, taking advantage of the fact that an underground nightclub could be as good a shelter as anywhere else*

would at least be bombed with the right sort of people.'

'Chips', one of the more notable snobs of his age, was one of the right sort of people to be bombed with, preferably while dining at his house in Belgrave Square. 'As my guests proceeded from the dining-room with their brandy glasses, there was an immense crash, the sound of breaking glass and the voice of the footman shouting "We've been hit." An air-raid warden appeared – whom I recognised as, of all people, the Archduke Robert of Austria.' (It was very considerate of the ARP to send him a warden of sufficient social rank.) 'Chips' rang the bell to obtain service for his unexpected rescuers, who were carrying pickaxes to dig him out. 'Lambert appeared and I asked if everyone was all right downstairs. He nodded and I told him to fetch more tumblers and drinks. I nearly said "the Krug '20" but just didn't.' Perhaps it wasn't an occasion for the very best champagne.

'Most people have abandoned their houses and taken refuge in big, concrete, modern hotels. The most favoured of them is the Dorchester, where you really see the world and his wife,' wrote the wife of publisher Hamish Hamilton to Compton Mackenzie. 'Duff and Diana Cooper sleep behind a screen in the gymnasium. Everyone you can think of is there, too.' 'Everyone you can think of' included, naturally, Cecil Beaton, who entered in his diary for October:

> Most evenings I have beetled off to the Dorchester. There the noise outside is drowned with wine, music and company – and what a mixed brew! Cabinet Ministers and their respectable wives; hatchet-faced brigadiers; calf-like airmen off duty; tarts on duty, actresses (also), déclassé society people, cheap musicians and motor car agents.

The Savoy had turned its basement into shelters for guests and divided the famous River Room into part restaurant (and cabaret), part dormitory. The hotel was equipped with a doctor and a miniature hospital for first aid, and it too was a favourite port of call for cabinet ministers, Fleet Street editors, the ubiquitous Duff and Lady Diana Cooper and Noel Coward, another assiduous diarist: 'A couple of bombs fell very near during dinner. Wall bulged a bit and door blew in. Orchestra went on playing, no one stopped eating or talking. Blitz continued. Carroll Gibbons played the piano, I sang, so did a couple of drunken Scots Canadians. On the whole a strange and very amusing evening.'

It was at the Savoy that the only protest at the contrast between the ritzy rich and blitzed poor had been made. It turned out to be a very moderate confrontation. On 14 September, about 100 protesters from the Stepney Tenants' Defence League marched up the Strand to the hotel, led by two prominent Stepney Communists, including their MP. The marchers arrived during an air raid and some made for the restaurant, where they sat down and demanded to be taken to the hotel shelter, as was their right. As luck would have it, the all-clear sounded almost immediately, while they were still milling around the hotel foyer; they could then only stay legitimately if they ordered drinks or food, so they left. The newspapers played down the story because the protest was Communist-led, while German papers reported it as an anti-government riot. It is remarkable that there were not more like it.

Only one person in seven used the tubes as shelters. Many preferred the alternative of a pub or cinema. At the Crown, near Paddington station, people carried on drinking during the evening raids, making too much noise to hear the swish of bombs. 'But one night, when we were all sitting up on our stools, we heard the crash before the swish,' wrote Jerome Willis. 'The explosion was terribly near and threw some glass over us. Instinctively we all dived under the counter and when we rose, a starry-eyed girl, who was a teacher, nervous but laughing, called out "Who was down first, the Army or the Navy?" One felt safer inside, though there was no reason in the world for the feeling.' Down in North Woolwich it was the same, according to Kitty Murphy: 'Rather than go in the air-raid shelter, people would go and sit in the pub half the night. The doors would be shut and the windows boarded up and they'd have the piano going and everybody singing and drowning the bombs outside. They waited until the All-Clear went and then they'd gradually go home.'

The cinemas kept open in raids for twice as long. The Granada chain offered a night's shelter, with entertainment thrown in. When the last advertised showing ended, if bombs were falling outside, the full programme would be repeated, plus three stand-by feature films, interludes on the organ, a sing-song and an amateur talent show. One record-breaking programme lasted for nearly eight hours after normal closing time, with the audience sitting (or sleeping) beneath the circle for shelter. Several of the cinemas were hit or near-missed during performances and audiences showed dogged determination not to be cheated of any of their entertainment. At one showing of *The Case of the Frightened Lady* a bomb fell beside the theatre, blowing open the doors and bringing everyone to their feet. At that moment the frightened lady gave out a piercing scream on the screen, people laughed and everyone sat down again to continue watching the film.

As the winter wore on, the Germans turned more to incendiary bombs in an attempt to destroy London by fire. September had been bad enough, but 8 December was eight times worse, with over 3000 baskets of incendiaries raining down. There was still no system of compulsory fire-watching at business premises, nor was there yet a network of emergency water tanks; both were ordered by Morrison after the terrible lesson of the night of 29 December, the night of the second Great Fire of London, when thousands of incendiaries were dropped on the City of London over three hours. The night was chosen to coincide with an abnormally low tide on the Thames, so that when the water mains failed the only water available was out in the centre of the river bed and could only be relayed ashore through fire boats. It was also a Sunday night, between Christmas and New Year, when there was no one in the City and its office buildings were locked. Before long they were a mass of flames which leapt from one side to the other of the narrow City streets between St Paul's and the Tower of London. It generated enormous heat and, with a powerful wind drawn in by the uprush of flames, the conditions were ripe for an uncontrollable fire storm. 'We came as close as London ever came to a fire storm that night,' said Cyril Demarne. 'We never had enough water. It had to be relayed from anywhere you could get to, from London Bridge, Southwark Bridge, and pumped through hose lines by relays of pumps. And all the time you were bringing up the water, the fire was moving on and moving on.'

In the midst of the conflagration stood the most conspicuous target and the greatest fire risk in the whole City of London – the dome and outspread roofs of St Paul's. It was also the best prepared and protected. Even before war was declared, the St Paul's Watch had been formed by the Cathedral's Surveyor of 300 volunteers including architects, university professors, civil servants, artists, students, clerics, choir, vergers and postmen. They kept watch on rota every night and had mastered the intricacies of the passages and staircases leading to the roofs of Wren's masterpiece. That night, showers of incendiaries fell upon them in quick succession. A cascade hit the dome and glanced off. The mains water failed, the fire brigade's pumps were clogged with mud from the river bed, but the Watch had installed tanks, baths and pails of water at vulnerable points about the roof. Small squads with stirrup pumps fought each fire separately as blazing pieces of wood from the surrounding buildings whirled past in the wind. Worst of all, one incendiary had lodged in the skin of the dome and the lead around it was beginning to melt. Churchill, receiving news of the blaze, sent a message – hardly necessary – that St Paul's must be saved at all costs. American reporters had already cabled the news that the Cathedral was in flames and Ed Murrow was waiting to broadcast that St Paul's had gone. The famous photograph of the dome afloat upon the sea of flames was taken, and on a hill in south-east London, H. M. Tomlinson was watching the spectacle:

> It floated but at times it was engulfed and we thought it had gone; then the fiery tide lowered and the Cathedral was above the capital as ever, except that it was red-hot. All Wren's fleet of steeples were ardent and reeking. London was a furnace. Now we knew the emotion of Londoners in 1666 when they saw their immemorial city, the one Shakespeare knew, disappearing street after street. . . . We did not speak. There was nothing to be said.

Ritchie Calder described the scene at 3 a.m. from a seventh-floor office in Fleet Street:

> The typewriter is treading flakes of soot into the paper as this is being written. With the curtaining drawn back and the light turned off it is possible to see to type in a light as bright as an angry sunrise. Fiery confetti spatters the papers on the desks with singe-marks. On the roof I saw such a sight as none has seen since Samuel Pepys took boat at Tower Hill. . . . The rooftops of Fleet Street seemed a stockade of flames. The Middle Temple Library was hopelessly alight, Johnson's London was a flaming acre. Part of the Daily Telegraph Building was burning furiously. The spire of St Bride's was a macabre Christmas tree festooned in fire. . . .

'All we can do now is pray,' said one of the St Paul's vergers. 'Then pray standing up, with your stirrup pump handy,' replied the Dean. Were the prayers answered? Dean Matthews described what happened then:

> Suddenly the crisis passed. The bomb in the dome fell outwards into the Stone Gallery and was easily put out. I have to confess that it is uncertain how the bomb came to fall . . . so far as I know, no member of the Watch claims to have had any part in producing the result. At any rate the

Cathedral was saved, whether by human means or by what we call 'accident'.

But when the All Clear sounded, the City all around the Cathedral lay in ruins. The Guildhall, eight Wren churches, including St Bride's, Dr Johnson's Gough Square, the Temple, the Old Bailey and the whole of Paternoster Row and its publishing houses had been destroyed – or badly scarred.

Next morning, exhausted firemen were sitting on the kerb beside the north end of London Bridge when people started to arrive for work. 'The boys were running water from their fire boots and rubbing their feet,' said Cyril Demarne. 'The City was on fire even then, at eight o'clock in the morning. Some of the girls coming over the bridge cried when they saw that and some opened their attaché cases and offered the firemen their sandwiches.' Cecil Beaton was there with his camera. 'Near St Paul's a shop burned unrecognisably. All that remains is an arch that looks like a vista in the ruins of Rome, through which rise mysteriously from the splintered masonry and smoke the twin towers of the Cathedral.'

War is full of might-have-beens. Great was the symbolic significance of that dome and the fact that – unlike the first St Paul's in the first Great Fire – Wren's St Paul's rode safely above the second. It was an epic night commemorated by Stephen Spender's 'Epilogue to a Human Drama':

> London burned with unsentimental dignity
> Of resigned kingship. Banks and palaces
> Stood near the throne of domed St Paul's
> Like courtiers round a royal sainted martyr . . .
> Who can wonder then that every word
> In burning London stepped out of a play?
> On the stage there were heroes, maidens, fools,
> Victims, a Chorus. The heroes won medals,
> The fools spat quips into the skull of death,
> The wounded waited with the humble patience
> Of animals trapped within a cellar
> For the pick-axes to break with light and water.
> The Chorus assisted, bringing cups of tea.

34 (Facing page) Everyone remembers the way St Paul's floated above the sea of flames – intact, thanks to its well-organised Watch. The next day Cecil Beaton climbed among the still-smouldering mounds of ash and rubble in the precincts of the Cathedral to photograph the romantic ruins, still smoking like the gates of hell, beyond which the Cathedral towers rise mysteriously

CHAPTER FOUR

BOMBS ALL OVER

'THE BLITZ' is usually thought of as the ordeal of London. But although London took the brunt of the Luftwaffe's attack from September 1940 to May 1941 and accounted for half the total deaths and serious casualties, the Blitz was unleashed upon towns and cities all over England, Wales, Scotland and even distant Ulster from November 1940. Their ordeals were briefer, but a night or two of concentrated attack could cause worse disruption than many parts of London knew. The German bombing technique, repeated over and over again, was to pinpoint the centre of a town with flares and a concentrated downpour of incendiaries, so that following waves of bombers could aim at a blazing bull's-eye in the centre of the target with their high explosive bombs and land-mines. So city after city found that its heart, containing its shops, administration and all of its major amenities, had been wiped out, burnt out, levelled to the ground in one blow. This was a traumatic experience to which they had no opportunity to acclimatise by habit, as London had. It is not surprising that, on occasions, chaos and despair overcame the appalled inhabitants.

After two months of continuous attacks on London, the Germans switched targets to include the provinces. The first Blitz on Coventry on 14 November was a copybook example of what was to be meted out to cities up and down the land. Coventry was a compact, prosperous, mediaeval cloth town which had turned to engineering and wartime arms manufacturing. On a brilliant night of full moon an operation which the Germans code-named 'Moonlight Sonata' utterly destroyed the centre through fire, gutting the cathedral and 100 acres around it, demolishing 2294 buildings and damaging 50,000 more. Of Coventry's 250,000 population, 554 were killed that night and 850 more seriously hurt. Although it was November, people arriving at the edge of the city next day noticed that the air was as warm as if it were spring. It also remained almost dark at midday because of the fog – a black fog – that hung over the streets and obscured the sky. It was a fog of soot particles, the residue of a town centre which had been incinerated.

For two days the city was stunned. Everyone knew someone who was a victim or homeless. There were no shops open. There was no water. There

35 *The ruins of Coventry Cathedral, a few weeks after the all-out attack, inspected by Roosevelt's envoy Wendell Wilkie (left), accompanied by the bishop and the mayor*

was no telephone. There were no pubs open. With communications knocked out, people were leaving, as best they could, for all roads were impassable for a mile from the centre. Coventry had no suburbs, unlike London, in which to find a hospitable roof where the services were working, so people trekked out to the surrounding villages and the open fields. The rest centres in the town had been overwhelmed, and thirteen of them, the great majority, had been bomb-damaged. Like the water mains, the drainage system was damaged. Soon there were notices urging: 'BOIL ALL DRINKING WATER AND MILK', as a precaution against typhoid. The day after the raid Herbert Morrison, the recently appointed Home Secretary, arrived with the Ministers of Health and Aircraft Production to see for themselves. The mayor offered them whisky and apologised for the fact that there was no water to put in it; the chief fire officer, unshaven and unwashed, fell asleep during the meeting. Morrison gave orders for troops of the Pioneer Corps to be drafted into the city to help clear up, and soon there were 1000 troops clearing up the devastation and 1200 building workers, especially released from the army, helping to repair houses. There was not enough wood to board up the smashed windows and people nailed up brown paper, which soon became soggy and useless with the rain.

Clearing the streets was soon done, but there was little or no public transport, no communication systems and no information. In these circumstances rumours bred, exaggerating the damage and devastation to even greater proportions and increasing people's feelings of helplessness. Mass Observation's reporters concluded: 'People feel the town itself is dead, finished, the only thing to do is to get out altogether.' They drew an interesting moral from the situation – that it was more important to care for the survivors' mental state than to concentrate on clearing up. 'The whole tempo could have been altered if the authorities had spent 5 per cent of their effort on the survivors, e.g. on mobile canteens, loudspeaker vans to give information, newspapers delivered to the streets, social workers.' Fire engines had been brought from as far as Wigan, police reinforcements from all over the Midlands; Mass Observation felt that social services should have been brought in from outside too. These were lessons that most provincial towns had to learn the hard way when their own time came, but remarkably few learned from each other's experience how to prevent a bombed town coming to a standstill by intelligent anticipation, emergency water supplies and so on.

Curiously enough it was the King who, in the immediate aftermath, did much to help Coventry. He arrived on the second day and was taken to the mayor's parlour which was lit by candles in beer bottles. He found the Emergency Committee 'quite dazed' by what they had been through. 'I walked among the devastation. The people in the streets wondered where they were – nothing could be recognised,' he wrote afterwards in his diary, and to his mother, Queen Mary: 'The old part and centre of the town looks just like Ypres after the last war.' Whether or not his visit actually procured practical aid for the city, it certainly brought it something that it needed just as much – national sympathy. Pictures of George VI among the ruins appeared in all the Sunday papers next day, together with lurid accounts of the state of the city. This was of great psychological importance to people who had been shocked and cut off from communication with the country by a wrecked telephone system and a cordon stopping all traffic from entering. 'We no longer felt that we were alone. If the King was there, the rest of England was behind us,' wrote one of the citizens. 'I think they liked me coming to see them in their adversity,' he wrote in his plain, modest style.

The Germans, boasting of their success, now announced over the radio that other cities would get the same treatment. They would be 'Coventrated'. It began to occur to the citizens of Coventry that they were famous and regarded as heroes by their countrymen.

Recovery, when it started, was businesslike. The object of the raid had been to cripple arms production; twenty-one factories had been hit, and nine more brought to a standstill by disruption, but not for long. The enormous roof of the Morris engine works, producing tank and aero engines, had been blown off, but 80 per cent of the workforce carried on under an open sky despite the weather. Production was back to normal after six weeks.

Jack Jones, the Transport and General Workers' Union organiser in Coventry at the time, believed the bombing stimulated a determination to increase output: 'They worked under pretty bad conditions. Some of the factories were just covered in tarpaulins. The only heating would be from coke braziers. And they stuck at the machines day and night, twelve hours at a time, seven days a week. They knew they were front line troops and stuck it.'

By the time Coventry was beginning to recover, its much larger neighbour, Birmingham, was being hit. Three successive big raids began on 19 November, killing nearly 800 people and injuring 2000. By the end of the Blitz in 1941 Birmingham was the third worst hit of British cities, after London and Liverpool, and had lost 2000 dead. With a population of over a million people spread over a much larger area, its sufferings showed less dramatically than in Coventry, although in both cities the dead were so numerous that they were buried in mass graves.

Bristol, which received its 'Coventration' on 24 November, was used to small-scale daylight raids, but this was described by its Lord Mayor, with a taste for colourful alliteration, as 'a veritable volcanic cataclysm'. The Art Gallery, Museum, University, and many churches were hit, and the city centre was turned into a furnace, the fires raging out of control for lack of water – all this in a city considered safe enough to be crowded with evacuees, including the BBC Variety Department. Many more raids were to follow through December to the following April, killing 1100. Much of the population had evacuated themselves, and 1000 people took over an underground tunnel on the outskirts of the city as a shelter, although it was partly flooded. On 3 January 1941, a bitterly cold night of bombing, houses were set alight, doused with fire hoses and promptly festooned with icicles, while fires still raged in the next building. A WVS worker, taking canteens to the air-raid services, reported: 'The firemen put cups down and they froze. The tea froze. The hose froze. We had the choice of being frozen, burned, blown up or drowned in tea.'

By 11 April, Good Friday, Bristol's defences were well organised. The usual preliminary showers of incendiaries were put out by firewatchers within minutes, and hours later the bombers were still trying to find their targets by dropping flares. The next day Churchill, as Chancellor of the University, arrived by train to confer honorary degrees. One of the recipients, the American ambassador Gilbert Winant, recorded the scene they found in a letter to his President, Franklin Roosevelt:

People were cooking breakfast in half-demolished houses, wherever a stove was functioning. The Prime Minister arrives at a town unannounced, is taken to the most seriously bombed area, leaves his car and starts walking through the streets without guards. Before long, crowds of people flock about him and people call 'Good old Winnie', 'You'll never let us down'. When we reached Bristol, where people were still shaken by the bombing, the whole town was back on its feet again and cheering within two hours of his arrival, although no one had got any sleep during the night.

When they reached the University, the building next to it was still burning. People were arriving in academic robes hastily put on over the clothes they had worn all night. Churchill's daughter Mary noted: 'People kept arriving late, with grime on their faces half washed off. They had ceremonial robes on over their firefighting clothes, which were still wet.' Churchill told them that it was 'a mark of fortitude and phlegm worthy of ancient Rome to gather in this way'. According to General Ismay, he got back on his train with tears in his eyes, and hid behind his newspaper.

Southampton went through the purgatory of fire on the last night of November and the first of December. Again, the centre of the city was set alight and again there was not enough water because of fractured mains (seventy-four of them). The fire was so fierce that the updraught tossed away the wreckage of the shops of the long High Street like a whirlwind. Three-quarters of the old town centre was destroyed, leaving only one building intact, the mediaeval stone Bargate. The fires were still burning where the second night's raid started, and even with fire brigade reinforcements from as far away as Nottingham, there was such a water shortage that many fires had to be left to burn. The two nights took a toll of 137 lives (some 500 were killed by the end of 1940).

After a direct hit on a shelter outside a big store, it was reported, 'the carnage was so dreadful that it was decided not to try to sort it out. Instead the crater, debris, bodies and all was sealed'. Bombs demolished the main telephone exchange along with eight churches, all the large department stores and a thousand properties. The Bishop of Winchester, Dr Cyril Garbett, arrived on the morning after the second raid to find 'the people broken in spirit after the sleepless and awful nights. Everyone who can do so is leaving the town . . . struggling to get anywhere out of Southampton. For the time, morale has collapsed.' Mass Observers reported inhabitants saying, 'People who have lived here all their lives don't know the way outside their own doorstep.' . . . 'I've never seen a place so beat – there's not a thing working.' . . . 'The spirit of Southampton is dead.' There was no gas and no hot meals for most people, and many criticisms were made of inadequate leadership. The Regional Commissioner reported to the Minister of Home Security, Herbert Morrison, that the local authority was unable to deal with the situation. An inspector-general of ARP, sent to investigate, reported the authorities as 'incompetent' and ten days later most of the population was still sleeping out of town, some as far out as Salisbury, twenty-two miles

away. However, most came back every morning.

Clara Moore, who rescued her children from under the stairs when their house received a direct hit, was sent at first to a workhouse, then to a big house converted into a rest centre:

> We were there for weeks because you just couldn't get anywhere to live. We had no clothes, only what we stood up in. Somebody had rifled the wardrobe in our bombed flat. I couldn't go in there to pack the things up. They wouldn't let me. One day we were going to have a visitor, because they got red carpets laid down and white bedspreads laid out and toys for my two children to play with. And when the visitor came it was the King and he shook hands and asked, 'Are you quite comfortable here?' I said, 'Yes, thank you.' And after he went they took all the bedspreads, the carpet and the toys away.

The next target singled out for concentrated attack was the steel arsenal at Sheffield, on the moonlit nights of 12 and 15 December. The High Street was set ablaze, its stores burnt out, and cellars and basements became uninhabitable through fire. In one road the inhabitants were incinerated in their cellars; in others they were led through the lines of fires by air-raid wardens. Bombed-out and burned-out victims crowded the wardens' posts for lack of anywhere else to take refuge, and when ambulances could not get through the choked streets, their drivers and first-aid parties got out and walked, carrying their stretchers. Next day a pall of tons of black soot, such as even Sheffield had not seen before, hung over the city. There were heavy casualties – 624 killed, 2000 injured, 85,000 houses damaged, 36,000 people homeless.

36 'Trekking' became a feature of the Blitz in provincial cities. These people took their children, their prams and wheelchairs and walked out of Southampton, whose centre had been devastated, to find safety and rest in the countryside

[89]

37 *Sheffield prided itself on its trams. One stands silhouetted against a blazing city-centre department store during the nine-hour Blitz of 12 December 1940*

Arthur Marshall, a policeman in charge of a city mortuary that night, remembers how the dead were brought in:

> Most of the people employed to do the job were not used to seeing the sort of sights we saw. They were usually undertakers who had only dealt with clean, laid-out bodies and were absolutely useless. I was hardened to it after a while, but when a family came to identify someone, however you tried to hide behind the shell, it was hard.

Ivy Rotheram, a nurse at the Royal Infirmary, remembers how the injured came in next day: 'They brought the dead and the injured to the hospital. They said they had to put the dead somewhere. Those who were brought in injured looked just like miners. They were all covered with a kind of sludge. I'd never seen such injuries.'

After the first raid 60,000 emergency meals were provided in the first twenty-four hours. Chief education officer William Alexander used the hundred surviving schools in the city as rest centres for the homeless, attended by school doctors and nurses and looked after by many of the 3000 regular teachers, who of course knew the children. School attendance officers were turned into billeting officers, using their expert knowledge of many homes. 'The city was bombed for the second time on a Sunday and we had billeted the whole lot by Thursday,' he recalled. 'I was given absolute power and had a very good staff, who between them knew every house in the city. And Sheffield people, poor and rich, behaved marvellously. No single teacher refused emergency duties by night or day. I had the greatest admiration for them.' 'Everyone was dirty and everyone was kind,' wrote the local historian of the raid. 'Reserve not only between neighbours but between strangers broke down completely.' That is saying something in Yorkshire. Remarkably, the bombs missed the steelworks almost entirely and production was scarcely affected.

Manchester had organised its civil defence with businesslike thoroughness, but it was severely tested in the two-night attack of 22 and 23 December. The first of these nights was a Sunday and many commercial buildings were locked and deserted; as a result one side of Piccadilly was soon ablaze and the ruins of its warehouses gaped against the flames 'like the ruins of Ypres'. Deansgate was wrecked, landmarks like the Free Trade Hall and the Royal Exchange left gutted and roofless, Manchester Cathedral damaged and all that was left of the old Shambles was one ancient pub still standing. A thousand people were killed, 75,000 houses damaged and 37,000 made homeless just in time for Christmas. The industrial area of Trafford Park – which turned out Lancasters, tanks and guns – should have been the target, but in fact the city centre and residential Salford and Stretford suffered most. In accordance with the censorship rules, the *Manchester Guardian* was not allowed next day to name the city in its reports of the raids on 'an inland town in North-West England' or state that 'a newspaper office' hit by incendiaries was its own. Only when the Germans boasted of hitting Manchester was Manchester entitled to be told how heavy the raids and the damage were.

38 Manchester was set ablaze just before Christmas on 22 and 23 December 1940. These commercial buildings along one side of Piccadilly were locked and deserted because it was a Sunday night. Firewatching was not yet compulsory

Portsmouth, like Southampton, had suffered frequent daylight raids through the summer of 1940. For a year the sirens went twice a day on average, although the raiders often passed overhead bound for targets inland. On other occasions they harassed the well-protected dockyard. But on 10 January 1941, came the big one. It was the night that old Portsmouth, a townscape of Georgian houses with a maritime air dating from the age of Nelson, ceased, practically speaking, to exist. The big, classical Guildhall and Civic Centre, the Museum and Art Gallery, the shopping centres of both Portsmouth and Southsea, the quiet early nineteenth-century residential squares, the garrison church and others were wrecked or quite demolished. It was another bad night for water. The water main coming into Portsmouth was hit, the hoses ran dry and the spring tide was out by an extra mile. Fire brigades rushed from afar found, as they often did, that one brigade's hose couplings did not fit another's hydrants. Reg Maxwell, an auxiliary fireman, found himself that night firewatching on the flat roof of a brush factory, immediately above the vats of cellulose with which they were sprayed:

If an incendiary had gone through, the cellulose would have gone whoof, you'd have been incinerated. But because I was in charge, I had to choose the roof station for myself – how could I ask somebody else to go up there? And, blow me, one came down just above the cellulose shop. I ran across and covered it with sandbags and to this day I've still got the bomb.

He and his fellow fire-watchers saved their factory but the town, though surrounded by water, was burning street by street. Whole terraces of houses were deserted because their owners were in the habit of going out of town for the sake of a night's sleep, but if some of them had stayed behind many small fires might never have grown into huge ones. Dr Una Mulvany was a GP with responsibility for a First Aid Post in the St George's district, and tried to drive to it in her Jaguar through the thick of the fire:

You couldn't get past the Guildhall, which was well ablaze by then, because a broken gas main was an absolute sheet of flame across the road. There was no question of getting down King Street, ablaze on both sides. In High Street the firemen were standing there with no water, so I bumped over the empty hoses and came to where a basket of incendiaries had started little fires all over the road, going very nicely, thank you. I really regretted having filled up with petrol that morning. I charged through and found the First Aid Post had had a wall blown out. So the Sister and I loaded the car up with dressings, set out for the next post, turned a corner and went straight into a bomb crater. We were just able to crawl out.

While the inferno raged overhead, those in the underground shelters found themselves in danger from the water that was seeping from broken

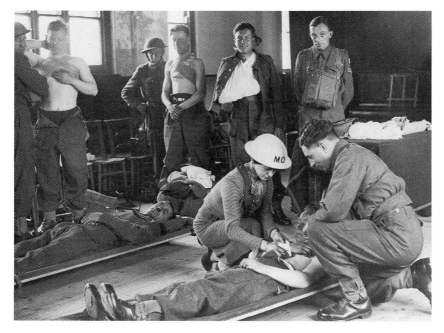

*39 In Portsmouth, Dr
Una Mulvany ran a first-
aid post – here she is
demonstrating how to treat
a casualty – and drove
through blazing streets on
10 January 1941 to reach
it. Portsmouth blazed
while the mains were hit,
the hoses ran dry and the
tide was exceptionally low*

mains. Vi Maxwell found herself trapped in a shelter beneath a shop, but the
door was jammed after a near-miss:

> All of a sudden the water started seeping in and the shelter gradually
> started filling up with water. So of course you picked up your baby and
> you stood up on the bench and it's coming up and up and it's an
> overpowering, terrible feeling. You're just hoping, somebody, please
> God, please God, get me out, somebody. I suppose we were like that about
> an hour. We heard some scratching, we were shouting, 'Please help, please
> help', and a hole appeared and two sailors poked their heads through.
> They were covered in blood from scratches. There were about ten of us
> and they pulled us out.

Dockyard worker Bob Marsh was also trapped in a shelter where the
protecting sandbags were jammed together by the blast to close the entrance.
Having dug themselves out, they found their street had been obliterated.

> All we saw was just one huge heap of rubble. The most fascinating thing
> about it was where the main gas pipes, that led from the road to the
> houses, were sort of standing up on end and all alight, right down the
> street, like a runway on an airport. Of course, our first thought was to get
> them covered up with bits of paving, anything we could find, to keep it
> dark before we got more bombs on top of us.

40 *A common sight after a heavy raid was a cluster of people at the police noticeboard scanning the list of casualties for names they knew. This was the scene outside a sandbagged public library in Portsmouth*

At night Portsmouth used to empty (the city had suffered 750 deaths by late 1941). Many people went to Portsdown Hill, where large shelters had been tunnelled into the chalk and equipped with bunks and canteens; many more went 'over the hill' to the countryside. There was much debate about the rights and wrongs of the mighty trek which jammed the roads out of the town. Dr Mulvany, driving into Portsmouth in the afternoon, would pass them going the other way:

> They were three, four, five abreast. A lot of them had wives and children. A lot of them had homes which had gone and they'd just been in for the day to see what could be done with them. I don't think I envied them. I just thought, well, there'll be fewer people to be bombed. Leaving the city was the most sensible thing to do, unless you had a job of work to do in it.

In the end 65,000 out of Portsmouth's 70,000 houses were damaged or destroyed, and clothing and housing the homeless presented problems on a huge scale. 'Remember this, all we had is what we stood up in – imagine the sight, sand and dirt all over your face, hair all covered in sand, your shirt half torn off your back,' said Bob Marsh. Nevertheless, in that state he presented himself at the dockyard gate at seven o'clock the next morning – 'we were

[94]

doing important work on the warships' armaments and we knew some of these ships were ready to be finished to go out.' He was reclothed by the WVS, with garments sent over by Americans. 'As long as it fitted, that's what they gave you. So we looked a bit posh for a while. My dad, for instance, was given a beautiful suit that was Fifth Avenue, New York. Unfortunately it made him look like a bookie's runner, which was most unlike my dad.'

After being handed on from one relative to the next, Bob Marsh, his wife and son found themselves accommodation, of a sort, at Horndean, twelve miles outside Portsmouth. 'Eventually we got hold of an old wooden hut, planted in the middle of a field. It was an old chicken roost and that was our home for the next five years. There was no water, no sanitation, no light, no gas. It was just a wooden hut stuck in the middle of a field.'

January had also brought the raids to Wales. Cardiff was sharply bombed that month, when the roof was ripped off Llandaff Cathedral, and in February the centre of Swansea was levelled by bomb and fire on three successive savage nights. Both towns suffered over 300 dead. Swansea, on its third successive night, saw the demolition of an estimated 50 per cent of its town centre – where all the underground shelters were. After two nights of attacks on residential districts, most people had taken cover there and were in the thick of the third night's bombing. An abnormally large number of delayed-action bombs caused the roping-off of the town centre, but recovery was well organised and nearby Mumbles opened its doors to the bombed-out. A Mass Observer was impressed by the self-reliance, lack of grumbling and readiness to joke amongst the citizens – 'Swansea people put a good face on things' – and noted that even in bombed districts the pubs stayed open and attendance was average. But there was great resentment of a broadcast by a local newspaper editor, who gave the impression that everyone was going about smiling as though they hadn't even noticed it. 'They couldn't possibly have behaved in that way and resented being made to feel they had fallen short of some ideal standard. Such talks do not benefit morale – people lose confidence because they do not reach this impossible ideal.'

By this time the emergency feeding of Blitz victims had been better organised on a countrywide scale. Mobile feeding convoys, named 'Queen's Messengers', had been provided by the British War Relief Society of America, organised by Americans in London. Lord Woolton, the Minister of Food, received an offer of 'unlimited' help from a Mr Kruger, on behalf of his friends in the United States, and seized it, with the warning, 'Mr Kruger, you and I are both businessmen: your offer was equivalent to drawing a blank cheque. So I ask you again, how much do you want to help?' Mr Kruger did not weaken. There was 'no limit' and he agreed with enthusiasm that the Americans would finance the convoys Woolton had planned – a food ambulance service with tankers, lorries carrying 6000 meals each, mobile kitchens and canteens with soup boilers and a motorcycle escort. The complete fleet consisted of 144 vehicles, manned by the Women's Voluntary

Services and Quakers, and the first went into action at Coventry. Queen Elizabeth gave her name to the convoys on condition that she paid for one convoy herself. They were cheered when they arrived in Swansea.

By now the big attacks were targeted firmly upon the ports, and in March both Clydeside and Plymouth were subjected to intense attacks. Plymouth's ordeal is as well-known as Coventry's. On 20 and 21 March, an area ranging 600 yards in radius from the Guildhall was razed by fire into a brick-pitted desert, scored with broken walls like an archaeological site. The mediaeval buildings, Guildhall, Old Guildhall, Law Courts, Post Office, Library, City Hospital, were wiped out, the shopping centres of Plymouth and Devonport were gutted, 18,000 houses destroyed and 30,000 people made homeless. 'The civic and domestic devastation exceeds anything we have seen elsewhere,' wrote two seasoned Mass Observers. The number of people trekking out of the town at night rose to 50,000, but there was little shelter for them on the moor's edge and many sought out barns, churches, cowsheds – even ditches and quarries – for the night. Post-raid services were elementary, although naval parties were sent in with shovels to clear up. Lord Astor and his American wife Nancy, as Lord Mayor and Lady Mayoress, made characteristic contributions. Lord Astor provided a band for dancing on Plymouth Hoe and Lady Astor, in a steel helmet, walked the streets during the raids from shelter to shelter, where she did cartwheels to cheer people up.

'Lady Astor very breezy, banging people on the back and making jokes,' wrote Noel Coward after walking round the city centre with her. 'The people themselves stoic, sometimes resentful of her but generally affectionately tolerant ... watched the people dancing on the Hoe, several hundred girls

41 *After the two-night Blitz which laid waste the centre of Plymouth, people who had furniture left to salvage piled it in the street outside their uninhabitable houses*

gaily dressed, dancing very well with sailors, soldiers, marines, in the evening sunlight. A sight infinitely touching, not that it was consciously brave, but because it was so ordinary and unexhibitionist.'

Both the Astors criticised their own local authority. He wrote to the Regional Commissioner urging the replacement of elderly councillors, she to *The Times* urging reorganisation of the fire service. 'Everyone knows the first thing a local authority wants to do when a town is blitzed is cover up its mistakes,' she told the House of Commons, 'I was not going to have mistakes covered up in Plymouth.' It hardly increased her popularity with the authorities.

Plymouth was to suffer another series of five severe raids in late April, bringing the total number of its citizens killed to over 1000 – out of a population of only 200,000. When Churchill visited it in May, his secretary, Sir John Colville, noted: 'Scarcely a house seems to be habitable. Far worse than Bristol, the whole city is wrecked . . . I saw a bus which had been carried bodily by the force of an explosion on to the roof of a building.' Churchill, after his visit, was in deep gloom – 'He keeps on repeating, "I've never seen the like."'

Plymouth dockyard, like Portsmouth's, escaped comparatively lightly and never stopped working. It was even more remarkable that the much smaller port of Clydebank, home of the John Brown shipyard, only faltered in production when a force of 460 planes was concentrated on the banks of the Clyde on 13 and 14 March. This was a larger force than had attacked Coventry, and Clydebank, with 47,000 people clustered about the shipyard in only 12,000 houses, took the brunt of it. By the end, only 7 of those houses had escaped damage. Of the 1100 killed on Clydeside, including Glasgow, almost half (528) had died in the holocaust of Clydebank itself – nowhere else in Scotland suffered on this scale. In one short street alone, 80 people were killed; elsewhere, one single family lost 15 of its members. Out of 47,000 people, 35,000 were homeless by the second night, a Friday, and thereafter the nightly population of the town, which was largely uninhabitable, shrank to 2000. And yet, on the following Monday, people reappeared from wherever they had billeted themselves and reported for work. A strike of shipyard apprentices (this being the 'Red Clyde') was called off, perhaps because the strikers had already gone back unasked. The unintended effect of this brutal assault was resolution, not panic; only two weeks afterwards production was normal at John Brown's and at seven out of the town's ten major firms.

This is not to say that people were not traumatised by such experiences. 'We all lost everything. There were very few people who had anything left. There was so much damage it was incredible,' summed up one witness, Ruby Stewart, who survived in an Anderson shelter which caved in. She went away on a coal waggon next day. 'You had to go. There was no water. The police were all in. There was an organisation but it was chaos.' Ambulance driver,

42 *The tall tenements of Clydebank, clustered about its shipyards, took a terrible pasting on 13 and 14 March 1941. Only 7 houses out of 12,000 escaped damage in the worst raid anywhere in Scotland*

John Grindlay, painted the scene: 'Ambulances were hit by incendiaries and caught fire, or they could not get past the damage in the street. We had to pull people out and carry the injured from one ambulance to another. I only saw one woman panic. Somebody thumped her and that shut her up.'

Evacuation was a pretty panicky business. 'Loudspeakers blared out telling everyone to go to the Town Hall as quickly as possible and to take what food and clothing they could carry,' recalled Anne McGuigan Curry (who had been buried in rubble). 'When we got there, masses of people jammed the roadway, trying to get on to the buses, pushing and being pushed, not caring where they were going as long as it was out of Clydebank before the Luftwaffe returned.' Dr J. P. McHutchison, country director of education, wrote at the time, 'Clydebank has had a bad knock, probably severer than Coventry. The gaunt and stark burned-out tenements, the gutted council houses, and overall huge columns of black smoke from the oil tanks made a picture of heartrending tragedy. . . . No praise is too great for the people. Even among those who have lost their home or all their earthly possessions, there has been no complaining.'

The aftermath of the Blitz provided some curious sights; a man sleeping on the floor of a rest centre with his parrot perched on his chest; tramlines blown eighteen feet into the air and tied in knots; a house in which everything had been destroyed except the dog's bowl; a father heating milk for his baby over the glowing end of a spent incendiary bomb.

Cuthbert Douse, then nineteen, helped to dig out his grandmother after a land mine fell: 'We had to dig with our hands but her arm was jammed by the windowsill. I remember my father telling me to turn away because the only way we could get her out was to pull. I'm afraid he pulled three of her fingers off getting her out of the debris.'

Bridy McHard, who was eleven, lost all of her family of eight, except her mother, when their building was hit – they were singing hymns in the shelter at the time:

You came to and you drifted away again and you kept shouting, 'Can anyone hear me?' and eventually I heard a voice saying, 'We're getting to you, don't worry.' I was pulled out by the legs backwards on my face and I actually thought I was in the dustbin. It looked like grey ash that you get out of a coal fire. My brother-in-law came up and kept asking my name. 'Bridy,' I said, 'do you not know me? I'm Bridy.'

Kathleen McConnell, then twelve, was in the same building when it was hit by the land-mine. 'I woke up and to be quite honest I thought I was in bed. I thought the sheets are awful tight somehow and I went to turn and couldn't and then I pulled at the bedclothes, as I thought, and it was stones and rubble that was in my hands and it was very hot.' She shouted for her mother but it was her sister who answered, 'We're buried, shout for help.' They were lifted out while the building still burned and one of her brothers doused her with a stirrup pump. 'It was then I realised that my good school uniform was singed with fire and I was saying, "Oh, how am I going to get this dry for school tomorrow?"'

Strangely enough, even in central Glasgow where the bombing was far less intense, people had no idea of what had happened on the outskirts of the city. Cuthbert Douse remembers getting a lift into Glasgow and being dropped in Hillhead. 'I'll never forget the amazed expression on the faces of the people there. They were only five miles from Clydebank and they had seen the flames, yet they looked at us as if we were a band of tinkers arriving from a holocaust.'

The people of Clydebank had somehow persuaded themselves that the Germans would never find them, so it was all the more of a shock when they did. But the people of Liverpool, the main Atlantic port, and the Merseyside towns of Wallasey, Bootle, and Birkenhead had been targets from the start. In the last week of August 1940, before the London docks were hit, the bombers made a series of attacks on Liverpool docks. More followed through the winter but the worst was to come in 'May week', eight nights of successive raids from 1 to 8 May, which between them killed 1900 people, bringing Merseyside's total to over 4000, easily the largest outside London. Although the city's civil defence had been well tested, there was near-breakdown under such a prolonged onslaught. The port suffered the heaviest attack and twenty

ships were sunk at the dockside. A munitions ship was set ablaze and the flames were fought all night; trucks loaded with shells had to be manhandled away from the flames. Urgent cargoes went on being unloaded even in the thick of the bombing.

Over 40,000 people evacuated themselves to the countryside in Lancashire, Cheshire and North Wales. Special trains and buses were run to take them. In Bootle, only one house in ten escaped damage and by the end of the week half its population of 50,000 had left the town, many of them permanently, the rest trekking out each night for anything up to twenty miles. Even so, the average amount of time lost at work was only eight days.

Mass Observation's reporter found 'almost universal dissatisfaction' with post-blitz administration in Liverpool:

There has been dissatisfaction in other towns but never with such vehemence from so many sources – from working men and businessmen, Conservative and Labour, officials, parsons, servicemen, firewatchers, wardens. An atmosphere of ineptitude seemed to oppress the town, a

general feeling that there was no power and drive left to counter-attack the Luftwaffe. It was being left to the citizens of Liverpool to pick themselves up.

Liverpool was seething with rumours, the most prevalent being that martial law had been declared. This arose from the fact that cars and people without special business were being stopped from entering the city, to reduce congestion in the shattered streets. On top of this, telephone calls could not be made, leaving relatives outside the city unable to get news of their families. There were wild exaggerations: '50,000 deaths', trainloads of corpses sent for mass cremation, food riots, a 'mass demonstration for peace'. 'Never before has the absence of information and explanation been so apparent', according to the Mass Observer. 'Not a single poster or meeting, loudspeaker vans only giving information on transport arrangements.' The city authorities had seemingly lost control of the situation as far as human welfare was concerned and the results were 'unprintably violent comments on local leadership'. There was not so much a breakdown of morale, which was 'on

43 This was the panoramic view of Liverpool, looking towards the Custom House and the cathedral (right and left centre background) after the eight nights of 'May week', 1941

the whole impressive', especially among the young and those who had stayed put, but there was a lot of anger.

For children the ordeal, though terrifying, was in some ways easier to adapt to. William Bush, who was evacuated to a quiet Welsh village at the age of eight, used to pay weekend visits home to a pub his parents ran in Liverpool. He found a way of coping with the strain. 'From the moment the siren went I felt paralysed with fear, all my muscles knotting up with spasm, listening and waiting for them to come. And the relief when they started the bombing. I'd scream my head off and all the tension would be gone.' Isobel Murphy, packed off straight home from school to the shelter, remembers it as a scaring but bearable time:

> If it got really bad, we'd start to sing as loud as we could to drown out the noise. We had the most wonderful ARP warden who'd stand in the doorway and say, 'Listen to all that lot going on, listen – but they won't get us down here, this cellar will keep us all safe even if the house collapses. They'll never get us down here.' Then he'd start us off singing and it really did help. And as soon as the All Clear went we would be out like a shot, collecting shrapnel.

'Bombs were dropped at an East Coast town.' So ran the anonymous announcements of the censored news broadcasts, which did not name bombed towns unless it was sure that the Germans knew what they had hit. The East Coast town, more often than not was Hull and the bombs were mostly left-overs emptied out on the raiders' way home. Although Hull had had forty-nine alerts since the Battle of Britain began, it thought itself the safest town in England when, almost at the very end of the 1940–41 campaign, the Blitz came to Hull with a vengeance on 8 and 9 May, four days after Belfast's only raid. It was the last large town in England to be blitzed, losing over 1000 citizens in the raids, and its shopping centre suffered more, relatively speaking, than the West End of London. The town had 40,000 homeless people out of a population of 330,000, and the fires could be seen in villages fifty miles away. At the height of the fire, blazing warehouses along the River Hull fell apart and disgorged their smouldering grain in torrents into the river. The City Hall, the churches, the flour mills, lay in ruins and the docks were out of action for about three weeks.

Yet Hull took the disruption and damage and dealt with it with notable efficiency. Over 110,000 first-aid repairs were made to damaged houses, many of which were hit more than once, for there were only 92,000 houses in the city. Although twenty-four rest centres were damaged, there were always enough kept open to cope with the homeless, and all of them were billeted within two days. Emergency meals were provided by communal municipal kitchens, thirteen British Restaurants and Queen's Messenger mobile convoys. Hull even ran to a Special Information Centre to answer the questions

44 *One of the most harrowing features of a Blitz – shocked and terrified children, unable to realise what had happened to them. This picture was taken in Liverpool*

45 *The Hull docks were turned into an inferno on 8 and 9 May 1941. The fires could be seen for fifty miles and the warehouses were blown open and discharged an avalanche of smouldering grain into the river Hull*

and solve the immediate problems of the bombed-out, a 'luxury' which many blitzed towns would have done well to have.

Harry Baker, manning an anti-aircraft gun five miles from the city centre, was shocked by what he saw fom his gun-site. 'I never knew what All Hell Let Loose meant until I looked at the bombing of Hull. It looked as if the entire city was disappearing in flames. Buildings were going up in blocks and coming down in pieces. And I thought, Hell's Bells, nobody will live in this. I was thinking of the shelters, there were huge shelters in the centre of the streets.'

Elsie Stephenson was in one of these communal shelters, near the docks. 'It was like being in a ring of fire. When we came out there was just one mass of fire. You could hear the ammunition going off and we kept ducking back inside.' Emma Kitching, who had recently married, remembers that when they did get out of the shelter they were as black as coals:

Everywhere there were piles of rubble and we said – that's Carrington Street, that's the right – no, that's the left side, so we lived there. And then we'd say, oh no, we lived *there*! We made to go to our heaps of rubble but, of course, we were stopped. The only thing I was really interested in was my little yellow canary. I was in a terrible state. I couldn't believe that was my house. And I found my bird. It had flung him across the floor. I picked him up, he was so black he was like a little sparrow.

The morning after the raid was a traumatic time for schoolchildren like Jean Carberry. 'When we went to school, the names would go up on the blackboard – all your friends that had been killed. We used to say a little prayer and hope it would be different the next night, but it wasn't.'

Men came home on leave from the merchant navy and said Hull was worse than being at sea. Herbert Morrison, writing his memoirs, commiserated with its people for hearing day after day their sufferings reported anonymously as 'a North-East town'. 'I would say the town that suffered most was Hull,' he wrote. And Hull's raids, which began later, also ended later than other towns. More heavy attacks occurred in June and July, long after the rest of the country had been left alone. In May a lull began which lasted – and lasted – to everybody's surprise until the reason why the bombers had been withdrawn became clear. They had been sent East. They were waiting for Hitler's attack on Russia on 22 June.

As a parting shot the Luftwaffe made its three heaviest raids on London. There were two on a successive Wednesday and Saturday in April, one of which scored a direct hit on St Paul's which shook the building 'like an earthquake'. The final attack on 10 May, with a 550-bomber force, was the worst night ever. It killed a record number, 1400 people, including the mayors of Westminster and Bermondsey. Every main-line railway terminus was hit, and Westminster Abbey, St Paul's (again), the Temple, Scotland Yard, St Thomas's Hospital and thirteen other hospitals suffered damage. Every bridge in the city was blocked; there were over 2000 fires, and 30 factories and 5000 houses were destroyed. The most notable casualty was the debating chamber of the House of Commons. 'Not one scrap was left of the Chamber except a few of the outer walls,' wrote Churchill to his son Randolph. 'The Huns obligingly chose a time when none of us were there.' The Commons had already stopped night sittings because of the raids. Now they moved into the House of Lords debating chamber, which the Lords vacated for the Robing Room.

May 10 'all but broke the spirit' of the Londoners who had taken so much, and people wept in the streets from despair at so much destruction. It was the culminating blow in nine months of bombing that had already killed 40,000 people, half of them in London, seriously injured 50,000 (half again in London) and made over 2 million people homeless, including one Londoner in six.

So ended 'the Blitz'. There was plenty more bombing to come, but those nine months were the crucial German campaign to defeat the British in one sustained assault on their cities. These cities were the battlegrounds of the Home Front. Their citizens were the front-line troops, whether they were the

active defenders, the wardens, firemen, police and ambulance drivers, or the great numbers of passive endurers who simply sat it out in shelters and cellars, or on watch on their rooftops, and next day went on with their work. Not everyone behaved well – the looting, not only from shops but from bombed houses, was considerable – and despite the exhilaration noted by J. B. Priestley and many others, everyone, sooner or later, who was in the thick of it felt afraid. Great numbers of them trekked their way out of the bombing zone every night. The authorities did not like this – it was considered a sign of low morale, of 'cracking' – and some of their fellow-citizens scorned the trudging army, with their carts or prams, as showing funk. Yet the trekking was, in most cases, a sensible precaution. It occurred where there were no shelters deep enough to protect dwellers near city centres from the onslaughts they received (London, once its tube shelters were operating, did not produce trekkers). The great majority of male adults only went for the night, to get out of the worst danger zone and to get some sleep. Where it was reprehensible was where it left fires to gain hold, unspotted, which could easily have been extinguished by fire-watchers. In some places, like West Ham or Liverpool or Southampton, there was a great loss of confidence in the authorities' ability to cope, but other towns, like Sheffield or Hull, never feared that chaos was about to take over. The difference turned, to a great extent, on the supply of information, which was as important as food and shelter. The authorities who told people what they were doing and where they were doing it, and provided an information service for those who were looking for 'lost' relatives and friends, helped their citizens most.

In the aftermath of a Blitz, the human tendency to invent and believe the incredible reached its height. Martial law was always being alleged to have been declared, in other cities than your own, and Lord Haw-Haw was credited with amazing feats of clairvoyance. 'Don't bother to take up your tramlines,' he was reputed to have told the people of Portsmouth, where trams were being replaced by trolley-buses. 'We'll do that for you. We'll bomb them up.' People would swear that they heard him say, 'You needn't think we can't see the big spire of St Mary's Church. We've left it on purpose as a good landmark for us.' This 'explained' why the church had not been hit. Haw-Haw was so often supposed to have announced what town, or even what building, was to be bombed on a certain day, that the Ministry of Information was driven to deny that he had made any such threats. Orpington was an example. Haw-Haw had 'noticed' that the High Street needed widening – 'we'll do that for you' – and mentioned that the local bakery was serving as a landmark for German bombers. He had 'warned' a certain munitions factory that, when it was bombed, he was sorry that this would break up the pontoon school in the canteen. Another munitions factory was warned that it would be bombed shortly – 'Don't trouble to finish the new paint shed,' he was supposed to have added. No one stopped to ask why German spies or Fifth Columnists would have bothered to send him detailed

46 (Facing page) The last attack of the London Blitz on 10 May was the heaviest raid of all. In nine months, since the previous September, 20,000 Londoners had been killed and this was the view of the City from the dome of St Paul's

[107]

information about tramlines and pontoon schools: he was a legendary character and the essence of his legend was omniscience.

It was not only Haw-Haw about whom the rumours flourished. Ghoulish and supernatural stories circulated about victims of bombing. In Sheffield, for example, there was a widely circulated rumour that the overhead cable of one of the city's trams had been brought down by the bombing, electrocuting the tram driver and conductress and 'shrinking their bodies to the size of dolls'.

Did the breaking of civilian morale, the avowed object of the bombing, ever come near to realisation? It was an American radio correspondent, Quentin Reynolds, who sent home the message 'London can take it'. Many other towns proved they could also take it – in fact some were aggrieved at the

47 The domestic instinct triumphed over terror. Some people managed to make the interior of their Anderson shelter almost homely; the curved, corrugated iron roof was hard to hang pictures on but some managed to decorate the walls and put lino on the floor

inequality of the publicity they received. A typical remark Mass Observers heard in Bristol was: 'We've been told it's been worse here than it was in Coventry or Birmingham, but we haven't had much said about us. Anybody would think Coventry people were the only ones who could take it.'

Celia Fremlin, who as a Mass Observer looked for signs of morale cracking, reflected, 'I would say that there was no possibility that the spirit would have been destroyed. Even a lot more bombing wouldn't have destroyed it.' But nobody can be sure just how much more might have been too much.

George Orwell, at the beginning of the Blitz, supposed that three months of bombing would be enough to break morale. Soon he was writing, for publication in an American journal, 'In London after four months of almost ceaseless bombing morale is far better than a year ago.' This is a mysterious fact about human psychological response and no one found it more baffling than the Germans (in particular the architect of the bombing, Hermann Goering), who expected a British collapse. Some far-fetched explanations for its non-occurrence were put forward in the German press: 'The British masses, exploited by Jews and other monsters, have nothing to live for and meet their deaths wth resignation,' suggested one. The Nazi magazine, *Schwarze Korps*, went further: 'England approaches death with sensual pleasure,' it wrote. 'Psycho-pathologists know of cases where pleasure in destruction parallels delight in self-destruction. Thus is solved the problem of British endurance.' The morbid motives ascribed to the British were later replaced with a much simpler explanation: the British were 'a Germanic race'. That was why, decided the Germans, they could take it. And when their own air-raid experience began on a bigger scale in 1943, they were urged to follow the British example. Dr Goebbels wrote in the party newspaper *Volkischer Beobachter* (People's Observer) on 4 August: 'Just a few of us admired the English when they stuck it out in the autumn of 1940. So we have to stick it out now. I indignantly reject the enemy allegations that we have weaker nerves than the Londoners.'

CHAPTER FIVE

'DAYLIGHT ON SATURDAY'

THERE IS NOT much doubt about who could wield the most power, single-handed, in Britain during the war. It was not Mr Churchill, whose will was at all times subject to the agreement either of the Cabinet or of the Chiefs of Staff, nor was it any service commander, however senior or encrusted with the insignia of rank. It was the massive but dowdy figure of the Minister of Labour, Ernest Bevin. By 1941 he had powers to exercise complete control over Britain's manpower and war production, with authority to decide the jobs of every adult between fourteen and sixty-five. Under the Emergency Powers Act of May 1940, he could 'direct any person in the United Kingdom to perform any service' that he might specify. He could order any worker to work in any industry in any part of the country and could decree what wages, hours and conditions were to apply to any job. Under the Essential Work Order of 1941, he could declare any factory or works 'essential' and no worker could leave such a factory without the consent of his Ministry representative. He could, and did, make strikes illegal and arbitration of disputes by tribunal compulsory. Equally, he could, and did, specify minimum wages and conditions for 'essential' work, which employers had to observe or they would get no labour.

The man with these awesome powers began life as an illegitimate farm boy in Somerset and had never been a Member of Parliament, let alone held office, until Churchill invited him to join his coalition government in May 1940. He had until that moment been the critic and opponent of the government in his capacity as General Secretary of Britain's biggest union, the Transport and General Workers' Union, which he had created. He and Churchill had been bitter opponents in the past, on opposite sides during the 1926 General Strike.

'It will be the greatest godsend to this country if Mr Churchill is out of office for evermore,' he had said afterwards. And in 1939, he castigated the attitude of the Chamberlain government to organised labour: 'The ministers have treated labour with absolute contempt, yet without our people this war cannot be won, nor can the life of the country be carried on.' When invited to join the government, Bevin was at first amazed. 'I didn't know what to say,' he told Hugh Dalton, 'but I thought it would help the prestige of the Trade Union movement and the Ministry of Labour if I went in.'

Bevin boldly took the risk of being regarded by his fellow unionists as 'ratting'. He now had to play the part of the government's spokesman to organised labour. He also boldly assumed the role of spokesman for the working class and the unions within the government, but he was a big enough man, in all senses, to play for both sides with conviction and fair-mindedness. Bevin enjoyed wielding power and was convinced he was the one man in the country capable of doing the job he had undertaken. In the end, manpower was the most vital resource the country had got and he refused to share responsibility for its use with any other ministry or with the armed forces. (As Minister of Labour and National Service he was also responsible for the call-up.)

As final arbiter of the use of manpower, through annual 'manpower budgets', he was in an unchallenged position of authority – and, like Churchill, he admired his own capacities without bashfulness. Clement Attlee wrote of him: 'He did not fear, he embraced, power. And power was given to Ernest. Men recognised in him a national leader, someone to lean on. . . . He would square up to anyone, physically or morally, with relish.' With this went a certain streak of arrogance, irritability (he would hardly tolerate criticism), even ferocity. Even Churchill, with the same streak in himself, took no liberties with him. 'He handled Bevin with kid gloves,' said Anthony Eden, and intervened less in the business of the Ministry of Labour than any other department.

Bevin claimed, with justice, that he instinctively understood the reactions of British working men. Like Moses, he would talk about them as 'my people' and he was fiercely loyal to them. Before he became Minister of Labour he led a union deputation to the Home Office just after the fall of Norway, which had been a result, it was rumoured, of the treachery of Quisling and the Fifth Column. Trade unions, they were told, could not be allowed for civil defence workers for this reason. Bevin flushed with anger. 'Go and tell the Home Secretary that it was not the working class in Norway that sold out to Hitler. Quisling came from *his* class. And, while you're about it, tell the Home Secretary to advise Mr Chamberlain that he'll never win this war without the trade union movement,' he thundered, and walked out. As Minister of Labour he was often under attack in the House of Commons. Once he retorted: 'I have got a rotten job but I am not going to refuse to face it. No one in our movement can accuse me of playing to the gallery. I don't care whether I lose a seat in this House or in the government. I came in with my eyes open to try to win the war.'

This loyalty was, on the whole, returned. Bevin was universally known as

48 *Ernest Bevin, union chief turned Minister of Labour and probably the most powerful man in Churchill's cabinet. 'He would square up to anyone, physically or morally, with relish,' said Clement Attlee*

'Ernie' and his dropped aitches were cherished even by people who did not drop them. This great hulk of a man was described by J. B. Priestley, looking down from the gallery of the House of Commons in July 1940, as 'a fine lump of that England which we all love – one of those men who stand up among the cowardices and treacheries and corruption of this recent world like an oak tree in a swamp.' Bevin and Churchill, sitting side by side on the front bench, appeared to him as the two halves of the English people and its history. The American ambassador Winant wrote that Bevin and Churchill 'had the same fighting stamina for meeting reverses head-on'.

There were many reverses to meet on the labour front. Bevin inherited a desperate situation in spring 1940, when Britain, fighting for its life, still had a million unemployed, despite the fact that over a million men had by then been called up. There was an acute shortage of skilled labour in the vital munitions, aircraft and tank factories and especially in shipbuilding. All through the depression years men had left the coal mines, ship-building yards and engineering workshops that had no jobs to offer them. There had been years of lost industrial capacity which now had to be made up in months. Men who had worked in engineering were now greengrocers, ice-cream salesmen, and milkmen. They had to be persuaded to come back.

For all the dictatorial powers that lay at his command, Bevin was a most reluctant dictator. He believed in what he called, ungrammatically, 'voluntaryism'. Persuasion was to him far better than compulsion; this was after all the main thing the nation was fighting about. Right at the start of his ministry he told a conference of trade union officials from over 150 unions:

> I have to ask you virtually to place yourselves at the disposal of the state. We are socialists and this is the test of our socialism. It is the test whether we have meant the resolutions we have so often passed.... If our movement and our class now rise with all their energy and save the people of this country from disaster, the country will always turn with confidence to the people who saved them.

The delegates were to tell their members that they were all partners in a common enterprise, but after the miseries of the wage-cuts, lay-offs and hunger marches of the Thirties that took some accepting. Perhaps only Bevin, whose whole life had been trade unionism, could have persuaded them to accept it. He offered a square deal in return for union co-operation, insisting there would be no state control of wages – collective bargaining remained sacrosanct. He also set up joint consultation between employers and unions and a factory welfare division of the Ministry of Labour to insist on proper standards of safety, health and living conditions for factory workers.

Jack Jones, who later succeeded to Bevin's old post of General Secretary of the TGWU, put the deal that Bevin won in simple terms:

What he did in effect was to ensure that, on the one hand, the regulations controlled labour, that you could be directed to a job, that you couldn't leave a firm, but to offset that the regulations provided the right to a guaranteed wage and the removal of the power of the foreman to dismiss men. You couldn't be sacked without the right to appeal to an impartial tribunal. The employer knew that if he did not negotiate with the trade union the case could go automatically to arbitration. For the first time trade unions really came into their own.

In return, the craft unions had to accept the breaking-down of skilled jobs into separate operations, some of which could be done by semi-skilled or unskilled workers, many of whom had to be newly trained and, most revolutionary of all, many of whom had to be women.

It was sheer arithmetic that drove Bevin into appealing for woman-power to come to the country's rescue. It was calculated that by the end of 1941, 1.8 million men and women were required for the services and civil defence, over and above those who had already been called up. At the same time the munitions industry had to expand fast enough to equip these enlarged forces, which required another 1.5 million workers. There simply weren't enough men; half the vacancies would have to be filled by women, so, in March 1941, Bevin broadcast an appeal to women, as well as men, to go into the essential war industries: 'We must call for a great response from our women to run the industrial machine. Women made a tremendous contribution to the winning of the last war and will be equally effective in this struggle.' He announced that all women aged twenty and twenty-one would have to register for war work prior to being interviewed to decide what they should do. He promised that women with small children would not be called on, but he also appealed for married women who were working to transfer to war work – managements should offer them half-day shifts or alternate-day working. There were same vague promises of nurseries and child-minders paid partly by the state. 'An average woman should be able to earn good wages,' he said but added, wagging a fatherly finger, 'Now, when you take a job, either in the services or industry, you must stick to it.' Were women to volunteer or would they have no choice? Bevin managed to make it all sound a bit confusing – at one stage he talked about a pamphlet that would explain to factory managers how to handle 'this woman problem'. Women, he implied, were awkward to employ, having inconvenient domestic responsibilities, and they were liable not to stick to a job if they didn't like it. 'You will be dealt with sympathetically,' he promised. If it sounded a bit of a muddle, so it proved. By August, 2 million women had registered but only a quarter of them had been interviewed and jobs in the services or in war factories had been found for only 87,000. The organisation was not ready to cope with them, and many who were eager to do their bit were furious and frustrated.

In 1941 Bevin decided
he would have to solve
the manpower shortage
with womanpower.
But his appeal for
volunteers fell short of
the huge number
required, and Britain
became the first country
to conscript women for
the services or war
work

WOMEN OF BRITAIN

COME INTO
THE FACTORIES

ASK AT ANY EMPLOYMENT EXCHANGE FOR ADVICE AND FULL DETAILS

The appeal for volunteers did not go well. Women gave several reasons for not wanting to do war work: their domestic responsibilities, especially as they feared they would be sent away from home; their fathers, husbands or boy friends who did not want them to go into the women's services or the munitions factories; and their own feelings that factory work would be monotonous, dirty, and would throw them into the company of a 'low type' of girl. There was also the prejudice of many works managers against employing women if they could find a man instead. 'War Work Weeks', with parades and appeals for volunteers, fell flat: they asked for thousands and got only a few hundred volunteers.

Bevin's 'voluntaryism' did not produce adequate results. 'It really was a hopeless muddle,' said Elaine (later Baroness) Burton.

There were no preparations made for women to take on these jobs because there was nobody at the top to look at it from the women's angle. In the entire civil service there were only thirteen women above the grade of principal. Only one was a wartime appointment. So to deal with such problems, the government had called in one woman of responsible rank. It didn't seem to dawn on them that married women had young children and were just hamstrung because they couldn't take the children with them. The plan was to provide 670 nurseries, with accommodation for perhaps 39,000 children, and this after two years of war. Would women have overlooked the nursery problem? I think we all felt, justifiably, that a really good woman administrator would have taken care of it.

So at the end of 1941 conscription of unmarried women began, for those aged nineteen to thirty, and they were given a choice between the women's services, civil defence and industry. Women up to forty had to register at an Employment Exchange for war work, unless they had heavy family responsibilities. Being married was enough to exempt women from conscription and having a child of under fourteen exempted them from being directed away from home. Women with other domestic responsibilities which were held to prevent them doing full-time work could be directed into part-time jobs.

Many women in the exempt categories volunteered to do war work just the same, and by 1943 there were 7.5 million women in paid employment. Nearly half a million of them were in the armed services, while 1.5 million were in 'essential' industries, of which they constituted a third of the workforce. There were, for instance, 600,000 women in engineering, compared with fewer than 100,000 at the beginning of the war. In spite of the drawbacks of domestic responsibilities, over 3 million of the women at work were married and a million had children under fourteen. Britain in 1943 reached a state of full employment with 22 million people in work, a net increase of 2 million in the working population. No other country, not even Nazi Germany, had resorted to the conscription of women and it was perhaps the government's most controversial action of the war. When registration for war work was extended to women up to the age of fifty-one, there was an outcry at the 'direction of grandmothers' in the newspapers and 200 MPs signed a motion of protest. There was far less protest from women themselves. Bevin pointed out in the Commons debate that over 1.5 million women over forty were working already.

What did it mean in human terms? It sent young women far from home for the first time to work at strange, sometimes frightening trades in the unfamiliar atmosphere of masculine machine shops, living in billets or hostels. It gave them wages of which they had never dreamed. For a large proportion it offered an escape from ill-paid domestic service or serving behind a shop counter. On balance most of them, once they got used to the idea, liked the freedom and the money very much. These more than made up for the monotony and the very long hours. Kitty Murphy, at eighteen, volunteered for work in the 'danger buildings' at Woolwich Arsenal:

> It was putting the caps on the detonators of bullets. It was dangerous. You had to wear special clothing and no jewellery, except a wedding ring, because the cordite used to fly about, fly up into your face. It caused a rash, impetigo, and it would come up in big lumps. Your eyes swelled up. We used to work seven till seven on days or seven till seven nights, seven days a week. It was pitch dark going to work. It was very good money, I was earning £10 a week with danger money, but you earned every penny.

Mona Marshall, who changed from being a nursemaid in Lincoln to being a steelworker in Sheffield, cutting shell-cases, soon learned of the dangers:

> The machines we were using were obsolete and really dangerous. My first night shift, a red-hot steel shaving hit me straight across the face. It loosened my teeth and blood just gushed out. I was at a hospital being stitched up for about an hour and I went back to work the next night, black and blue and hardly able to open my mouth. Safety precautions were almost non-existent.

Vi Maxwell, bombed out in Portsmouth, went to work in the naval dockyard as a 'rivet boy'. 'That meant making the rivets hot. You had your rivets in your dolly holder and a big round fire, which you had to make up yourself. You put the rivets in and made them white-hot and the riveter would then rivet them down. I did that on a floating dock and I was the only lady there. I felt that every time I made a rivet hot and the riveter put it in that I was nailing Hitler.'

Barbara Davies had been a weaver in a Yorkshire village before the war. She heard at the local Labour Exchange that Armstrong Whitworth were recruiting workers for their aircraft factory in Coventry at £5 a week, compared with £2. 10s. in weaving. With a friend she volunteered to go – full of anxiety about whether she would be able to manage.

> I was going into a huge aircraft factory and I supposed it would be very skilled and I should not be able to understand the language, even. But there were unskilled men there too – an egg-packer, a painter, a gardener – so that gave me confidence. We were working from drawings to make the very first Lancaster and I was amazed how many men couldn't read a drawing. I could – I was just as skilled as they were at that particular thing.

Barbara also worked six, sometimes seven, twelve-hour shifts and earned up to £10 a week. After staying in various billets she went into a newly-built hostel for women workers, consisting of long wooden buildings.

> The hostels were marvellous. Frugal though it might be, you had a room of your own, very, very small, but it was all yours, where you could sit in your own chair and put curtains up if you wanted. You could have a bath without having to ask permission. There was a main block down the road where all the social activity took place. It seemed like paradise really, it was the beginning of the fun we had during the war.

Attitudes of men to having women working alongside them varied. At a Birmingham factory Mass Observation found foremen slightly bewildered by the experience. One said, 'The men didn't like having the women at first but it's all right now, they're quite happy about it. They're all good workers. If any of them feel bad or a bit faint, I send them to the ambulance room. I believe in letting them sit down and rest for ten minutes – on this heavy work they get tired. Afterwards they get up and work twice as well.' Another foreman admitted: 'I like having women here very much. It surprised me that I do.'

Women liked their work, as a rule, very much. 'I loved it in the factory. It was great. The men thought of us as a big joke to begin with but not later on, because we proved we could do it.' That was how Mickey Lewis remembered her time working a centre lathe, cutting gear wheels for guns. Doris White had been an apprentice dressmaker before she was called up, and chose to work in an aircraft factory. 'At first I was really shy – I had never worked with men before. But I became as interested in mending planes as I had been in dressmaking.'

Because of the uneasiness that some craftsmen felt at seeing women acquiring their skills the Amalgamated Engineering Union would not accept women members until 1943, so most women joined Jack Jones's TGWU.

The men were inclined to think the women could do semi-skilled and unskilled work but they didn't want them to go on to skilled work.

50 Once they got used to it, women often proved the equal of highly skilled men in munitions factories, although many of them had the problem of running a home as well. This painting by Laura Knight is entitled 'Ruby Loftus screwing a breech ring, 1943'

51 Men were often surprised at the adaptability women showed for war work. This woman was a dog-breeder and chicken-farmer retraining on a metal-shaping machine at a government training centre

Gradually, of course, they had to give way. I remember some women going into the holy of holies, the tool room, regarded as the highest of skills, and doing very well indeed. I remember an official of the Amalgamated Engineering Union being trained in welding by a woman welder. I had to remind him that his skill had been provided for him by a woman member of the Transport and General Workers' Union.

Agnes McLean joined Rolls Royce's new engine works at Hillington, Glasgow, to work a milling machine: 'Women's skills were developing the whole time and, in fairness to the management, they gave the women their heads and their attitudes changed. They were doing work to very fine limits, ten-thousandths of an inch. They started using instruments, such as micrometers, and some of them were quite brilliant at it, very neat and tidy engineers. There was one lass who was that good that she trained a lot of the men.'

So what were the arguments that employers used against employing women? Ernie Roberts, later an MP, was a shop steward in Coventry.

The employers would argue that women were slower, that they needed extra supervision, that they did faulty work and made scrap, but this was only at the beginning. After training they became as good as the men. I must admit that many of us thought they weren't capable of it because they hadn't the industrial background we had had all our lives. But it was surprising the adjustments they made, very quickly, to highly skilled work, in a standards room, for instance, checking very precise gauges.

'You could go into the factory and look down the lines of these girls at benches, welding engine mountings, and they were all sloping at the same angle and they just got on with it, from morning to night,' said Arthur Varney, manager of a group of Coventry factories, 'They were really fantastic because they were so disciplined.'

With such acknowledgements of women's skills and discipline it was difficult to understand why they should not be receiving equal pay. Many believed they should have done, including Jack Jones, who tried to negotiate it. 'We were continually up against what I would regard as very unjust opposition from employers, who didn't want to pay the man's rate to women because they didn't want to create a precedent for the post-war period. They wanted to maintain the tradition of cheap labour.' Ernie Roberts believed women were being used as cheap labour in the aero-engine factories. 'The opportunity was being used for the purpose of reducing the prices of jobs. I was in the process of organising a strike of these women to demand they be given the rate for the job. It didn't take place, but women were given the rate for the job on skilled work.' This happened rarely, however.

'We didn't have anywhere near equal pay and we used to argue and complain but it didn't get us anywhere,' said Mickey Lewis. 'Wages were important, but it was more important to get the work done. We were quite patriotic about it really.'

Barbara Davies worked as a riveter in a gang which pooled the earnings of the team and shared out the kitty between them. But the girls were paid about two-thirds of the men's share. 'Nobody seemed to mind because before the war no one had equal pay anyway. You just accepted it, everyone accepted it. It was more money than I'd ever earned and it didn't occur to you to complain.'

But it did occur to Agnes McLean, who was the first woman at her Rolls Royce works to become a shop steward. Although two-thirds of the 24,000 workers there were women, 'it was a tremendous job to get women to join the union'. But the fact that women were getting 43 shillings and men 73 shillings for doing exactly the same work gradually built up resentment until, in 1941, there was a walk-out by the women.

> The issue was not equal pay for equal work. There was a women's rate and a men's rate. The problem was that women weren't even getting as much as the unskilled men's rate. They were working bigger and more complex machines and not being paid as much as men that cleaned the lavatories. Suddenly a group of women said they were not going on working, put on their coats and walked out. Another section did the same, and on it went until all the women were out. Then it was, what the heck do we do now? We hadn't a clue how to conduct a strike.

This particular protest gained little but it gave the employers a fright. In 1943 there was a much bigger strike.

> We were marching along the street, getting eggs and tomatoes thrown at us, and we were in this enormous park, not knowing what to do, fed up, it was pouring with rain and suddenly the men came marching in to support us. Politically they were very sympathetic to the women, once they realised we were being used for cheap labour. And a court of enquiry was set up and the union's case was actually upheld. After that women on the big machines got the male semi-skilled rate, but not the skilled rate.

It was not only pay, but promotion, that was denied to women. Tom Harrisson reported that during six months' investigation by Mass Observation teams in 1942, they never encountered a single woman in a key position in any war factory or as a government representative dealing with these factories. They found that 95 per cent of women were in favour of equal pay, but there were a few women dissidents, like the girl who told them: 'I do feel that equal pay would upset the relations between the sexes. Personally I like a man to have more money than me. It gives me twice as much pleasure to have

52 *A group of workmates at the Rolls Royce aero-engine works at Hillington, Glasgow, where two-thirds of the workforce were women. Agnes McLean (second from left, front row) was the first woman to become a shop steward there and led the women in their struggles for more equal pay*

a dress bought for me by a kindly man than to buy it myself, and this is because I am feminine.' Some women inhabited a very different world from others in the 1940s.

The hours that were worked, week in, week out, now seem almost incredible. Many shifts, day or night, lasted twelve hours and many people, working from 7 a.m. to 7 p.m. only saw daylight on Saturdays, when it was very difficult to persuade anyone to work a twelve-hour shift. As a result women, like men, suffered from exhaustion. 'I got so tired that I became anaemic. I think working twelve-hour shifts, often at night, upset the balance of your body,' said Doris White. 'I had terrible nightmares. You just had to go on and on. No one considered whether you were fit or not.' Mona Marshall used to go home to Doncaster to see her mother on Saturdays. 'I'd say, I'm just going to have a sleep, wake me at four and we'll go to the pictures. When I woke it would be dinner time on Sunday and I'd missed the pictures.' At Agnes McLean's Merlin engine works they worked seven days, or nights, a week for six months without stopping to reach an out output of 300 engines a week. 'After the six months, TB was rampant, obviously because your resistance was its its lowest, so it was decided we should get Saturday night off, or Saturday during the day.'

Absenteeism was common and it occurred on average twice as much among women as among men for an obvious reason. Elaine Burton put it scathingly:

It didn't seem to dawn on the government that any woman in war work really had two jobs, because she had a home to run. It took ages for anyone to realise she had to do her shopping and the shops were closed when you'd finished work, so of course women had to stay away to do the shopping. By December 1941, the Ministry of Labour was trying to persuade employers that shorter shifts must be worked and women were given time off for shopping. The discovery was also made that shorter shifts increased output.

Celia Fremlin left her job as an air-raid warden after the Blitz was over and took a job in a wartime radar equipment factory. She produced a report for Mass Observation in which she conjured up vividly the feelings of a young woman towards the end of a twelve-hour shift:

At about three o'clock one gets the feeling that the time will never pass. You think to yourself after a whole hour it will still be only four o'clock and there will be two more hours to go after that. A bewildering sense of helplessness comes over you. You make idiotic bargains with yourself – if I drill 100 of these holes without looking up then by the time I do look, five minutes will have passed. Between three and five in the afternoon more slacking and idling goes on than one would have thought possible. Not more than one girl in four is actually working. One will be sitting with her hand on the handle as if just about to pull it down, another will be patting her hair, another staring out of the window, another settling down after a visit to the cloakroom. People stay half an hour in the cloakroom, eating sandwiches, talking, reading, doing nothing at all, in spite of the fact there are no chairs to sit on.

Although firms were discouraged from working more than a sixty-hour week by Bevin and his Ministry, local officials would still urge them on, in an attempt to reach higher output. Research showed that overlong hours did not pay, however. They resulted in factory friction and low morale, as well as absenteeism. As Celia Fremlin pointed out acutely, the state was trying to get the best out of workers who had had years of economic insecurity and fear of the sack and who therefore had no goodwill towards the management. 'No amount of pep talks or regulations are going to make everyone go flat out until the pattern of responsibility between management and workers is seen in a fresh way. It is a question of starting with the emphasis on the human being operating the machine, not the machine operating the human being.'

Meanwhile, one useful palliative that was discovered were the daily

53 Women in dungarees assemble the fin of a barrage balloon. Women not only manufactured them but took over the crewing of the balloon sites

broadcasts of 'Music While You Work' which the BBC began in June 1940. There were two half-hour sessions of continuous music daily, in mid-morning and mid-afternoon, and in 1942 a night session was added for night workers. 'For an hour or an hour and a half after a programme production is increased by $12\frac{1}{2}$ to 15 per cent,' reported one managing director. In that case, one might wonder why there were not more frequent music sessions. No doubt the rest of the BBC's listeners might have objected to hearing more of the seamless flow of what now would be a perfectly normal background of taped music. The BBC reported that experiment had shown that extremes of loudness or rhythm or tempo distracted attention and disrupted production. So did vocal items, organs and 'hot' music; it was best if the music had something of the monotony of the task the listeners were performing at the factory bench, preferably with tunes they could hum. 'Music helps us to forget the cold, so we can do more work,' reported a factory worker, 'Please may we have more?' But they didn't get more. 'A musical tonic diminishes in effect if applied in overdoses,' ran the BBC pamphlet. 'It is better to give too little than too much.' The voice of Aunty, this time, anxious that there should be no spoiling with too many treats.

One of the treats that women brought into common practice was the tea-break, to which they (but not men) were entitled under the factory acts. Jack Jones remembers fighting for the right of men to have one too.

I remember our shop stewards going in to the manager at one firm asking for a ten-minute break and the managing director saying, not on your Nellie, you come to this place to work, not to sup tea. And just as he was making this point, in came a girl with a tray of tea and put it on the desk for him. Of course the shop steward said, 'If it's good enough for you, then it's good enough for us,' and he had to concede the principle.

Among the wide-ranging powers enjoyed by the Ministry of Labour was the right to make regulations affecting every area of industry. One of these was Regulation 1305, which made strikes illegal. However, it would be a great mistake to assume that there weren't any, although they often went unreported. In October 1943, a Mass Observation survey found that unauthorised strikes were almost a daily occurrence on Clydeside shipyards. There was a dock strike at Liverpool and innumerable disputes in the coal fields. The aircraft production industry, usually held up as an example of smooth productivity, was often disrupted by local wild-cat strikes affecting a single factory, some of them over wages or piece rates, others about supervisors, inspectors, or canteen facilities or alleged victimisation – even over one management's refusal to allow collections during working hours for the Red Army. The Rolls Royce strike at Hillington in November 1943, described by Agnes McLean, cost 730,000 man-hours.

But it was not only strikes that held up aircraft production; it was often management inefficiency and bad planning. Vickers-Armstrong aircraft division was reported on in 1943 by a Ministry of Aircraft Production team who found, for instance, that shifts completed their quotas by 3.30 p.m. and skilled men then stood around with nothing to do until the shift ended at 7 p.m. Sometimes workers went slow deliberately. When PAYE was introduced at her factory, said Mona Marshall, 'once the men had made so many shells at the beginning of the week, they'd slow down because if they didn't, they'd be working the last day of the week for nothing.' But often it was the workers who complained of being left with nothing to do by inefficient management. A Mass Observation survey of opinion about industrial output in 1941 came up with a series of outspoken criticisms: 'We only seem to be working at half capacity. The workers are willing to do more but nobody seems to want them to.' . . . 'Men are idle through lack of materials, lounging about all day and warned to pretend to be busy if anyone makes a tour of inspection.' . . . 'A man engaged by the firm means a profit for the firm, whether he is working or not.' . . . 'The large number of people employed is to keep the company's overheads at a high level to present the image of a wonderful war effort.' . . . 'Forty per cent of the factory's hands are nothing but rotten slackers who are honestly quite pleased that they can do the government.' . . . 'Several people consider that the war is looked upon as a heaven-sent opportunity for the workers to get rich.'

Most of these faults were blamed on the system of payment instituted by the government for firms producing war materials. There was no competition between suppliers, which would have been impractical. So the manufacturers were paid on the basis of 'cost plus' – their costs plus a margin of profit, usually 10 per cent. Hence they were assured of making profits – not huge ones, as some people did in the First World War, but solid profits which they could count on without any danger of being undercut by a competitor. Waste of men, or time, or machinery, did not pay the penalty that it would have done under competition.

In 1942 the shop stewards of the Coventry arms firms held a conference, together with employers, works managers and the war production board for the region, at which the managements were severely criticised for inefficiency in obtaining the maximum output. Jack Jones, as district secretary of the Confederation of Engineering Unions, was in the chair.

We called people to the rostrum to say what was happening in their plant. There was a factory employing 4000 on the day shift and only 150 on the night shift – imagine all that machinery unused. There was one plant on highly secret work held up by a shortage of draughtsmen but which was keeping a drawing office working full pelt on designing post-war buses – in 1942! In another factory they had fifty aero engines lying on the floor waiting for carburettors. We made out a very strong case that management was not organising for maximum production.

The shop stewards demanded the setting-up of joint committees of managements and unions to enquire into production hold-ups. The result was the Joint Production Committees, which spread to many industries, with variable results. They were highly praised by Sir Stafford Cripps, who was Minister for Aircraft Production from 1942 onwards. Cripps toured the aircraft factories with crusading zeal – he had come back from a mission to Soviet Russia – calling for the breaking-down of traditional suspicions between management and the workforce. In the year war broke out, 1939, aircraft production was still a moderate-sized industry, employing 350,000 workers and producing 8000 planes. By 1942 it was the biggest industry in the country. There were 1.7 million workers turning out the myriad components for 26,000 or more war planes a year. Many of these were heavy bombers, like the Lancaster, which required 2 million parts made in a wide variety of factories spread over a large area (factories had been widely dispersed to avoid presenting a single target to German bombers). Motor-car factories had turned over to aero engines; carpet factories, a hangar, a bus garage, even a disused quarry, were being used for making components. Dozens of 'shadow factories' were built by the government to increase capability. On the face of it, aircraft production was a great success story of adaptation to the demands of a new, very sophisticated industry requiring enormous organisation.

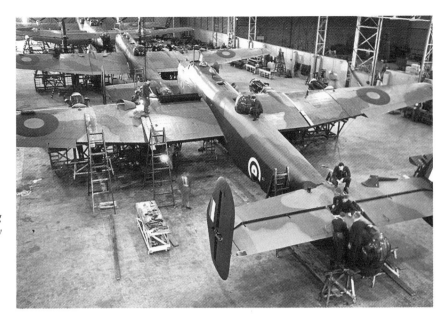

54 Aircraft production expanded hugely to become the country's biggest industry, employing 1.7 million workers. Heavy bombers, like the four-engined Halifax, required some 2 million components, assembled from dozens of factories

Arthur Varney, the manager of nine Alvis motor-car factories near Coventry, turned over to aircraft engines, remembered watching Lancasters coming off the production line at the A. V. Roe factory.

The hangar doors were never closed and you could see the long line of aeroplanes being built and the one in front practically finished. A little man, not very well dressed, trilby hat on, no collar and tie, stood at the doorway looking down the line. His job was to see that the aeroplanes came off the line at the planned rate, about one an hour. That strikes me as fantastic because they were big aeroplanes.

In the course of the drive to increase production the industry became a legend for high wages, and Coventry, as a boom town, was viewed as a sort of El Dorado. Arthur Varney remembers his workers getting about £10 a week before overtime but, with bonuses, some skilled engineering workers were earning £20 and more a week by 1944 – about £300 in today's terms – in comparison with national average earnings for manual workers of £6 10s.

'Earnings were high, but the effort was correspondingly high,' said Jack Jones. 'The high piece-work rates ensured that at least the nation got effort.' Yet when the Production Efficiency Board visited Coventry in 1943, it reported that the high prices paid for piece-work allowed workers to get 'high earnings without a corresponding high effort. In each factory there is evidence of slackness and lack of discipline.' Is there an explanation of these contradictions?

Sir Alec Cairncross, the economist, who worked as a planner in the Ministry of Aircraft Production, the sole boss and customer for the whole tangled skein of aircraft firms and sub-contractors, cast some light on it:

What holds up aircraft production is the failure to make the right decisions at the right time. It's management. It will show itself as a shortage of the things you didn't provide. When I joined the Ministry in 1941, I was told there were 300 Wellington bombers lying on the beach at Blackpool for lack of propellers and I thought, that's a frightful muddle. But I thought that no doubt the rest of the organisation was very much better. I came to see in time that it was really one great muddle modified by a certain amount of organisation. At the time it seemed impossible that you could put a gang of people together and they could be so muddled. But I was a bit harsh. Other organisations that I joined afterwards showed me that almost any large organisation is by definition a bit of a muddle.

If the lavishly financed aircraft industry was not the paragon of efficiency that it has been made out to be, how much worse was the story of old-established, traditional industries, such as coal, steel and shipbuilding, which were run down in the Depression years, hidebound in outlook and working practices and dogged by the bitter legacy of hostility between men and management? The answer is, very much worse. Shipbuilding had lost a third of its workforce in the Depression, when output at times almost ceased. The war and the sinking of merchant shipping by U-boats at the rate of 4 million

55 Giant barrels for naval guns in production. The view through the gun barrel's breech reveals the scale: the workman framed by the aperture is working on the muzzle at the other end

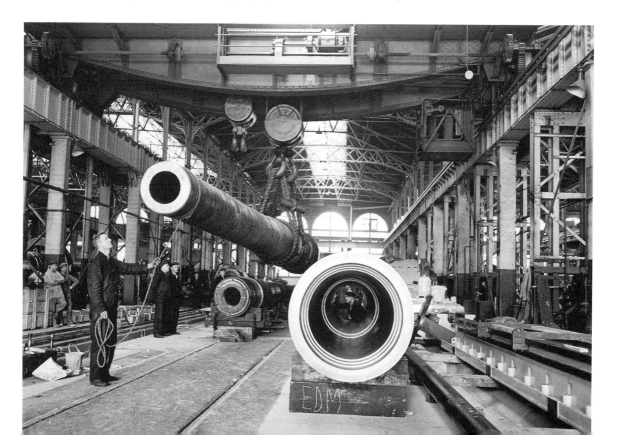

tons a year in the Battle of the Atlantic placed a huge new demand upon it for replacements, which it was ill-placed to meet, and by the time the shipyards had been re-equipped at an investment of £6 million, the worst of the U-Boat war was over. Little over 1.5 million tons of new merchant and naval shipping was produced each year, well below the target figure.

Strikes and demarcation disputes continued and the 'dilution' of jobs, by introducing extra, unskilled labour to do parts of them, was strongly resisted. When power-riveting came in, requiring only one man instead of two, the union insisted that a second man, with nothing to do, should still be employed beside each riveter. And strikes were frequent, especially on Clydeside. In the summer of 1941, at the peak of the Battle of the Atlantic when German U-Boats were sinking 700,000 tons of shipping a month, there were 33 labour disputes in Clyde shipyards, and during the whole of that year 110,000 working days were lost in 147 wage disputes. The biggest strike occurred over the dismissal of a yard convener 'who dedicated his enormous energies to embarrassing the management', ran a Mass Observation report.

> Irritations and tensions are simmering under the surface. . . . The Essential Work Order has brought complete security for the worker. The peacetime discipline of the sack for slacking is no longer operating. Some men exploit this, remembering with natural bitterness the long periods of unemployment and ill-use that they received from the shipyard employers before the war. Underlying all is the men's feeling that after the war they'll be back on the scrap-heap, where they were before.

In the coal industry, feelings of bitterness and suspicion towards the mine-owners were, if anything, more violent. 'Hatred – perhaps blind hatred', was how Monmouthshire miner, Ernie Way, described his feelings towards management. 'I was aware there was a war going on, but my enemy was within my workplace. Miners felt very indifferent to the war effort. The enemy was management.' 'I suppose that as a body of employers, coal-owners were in the top class of tyrants,' agreed Ben Morris, who started work at the pit at fourteen. 'After the 1926 dispute they took savage revenge by victimisation. Thousands of men were driven from the pits by the tactics of the coal owners. Their word was law and if you didn't obey, they sacked you. Now, in wartime, they couldn't sack workmen and, frankly, they didn't know what else to do.'

Miners' strikes were responsible for almost half the working days lost in nearly every year of the war. Wages were already very low, 80th in the wages table of 100 industries, when war began. Then came the drive to recruit women to war factories and this caused renewed bitterness. 'Housewives went to work in the war factories and were earning more money than I did as a piece-work collier,' said Ben Morris, and Ernie Way remembered thinking, 'God, why should I go down that pit for such a pittance when women are

56 *While the aircraft industry paid record wages for piece work, miners were left far behind in the wage tables and realised that housewives in munitions factories were earning more than they did. The result was a wave of strikes*

getting three times as much as us?' The Miners' Federation was asking for £6 a week minimum underground. A tribunal offered £5 but when the government refused to pick up the bill the mine-owners withdrew their agreement. A spontaneous 'unofficial' strike began and was joined by colliery after colliery: 100,000 men came out in South Wales, 120,000 in Yorkshire. The miners held out and were eventually offered the second highest minimum wage in the country after the munitions workers.

Coal output dropped steadily in every single year of the war, for a number of reasons. There was no new recruitment, leaving only the older miners to work underground; absenteeism, through sickness or simple exhaustion, grew higher year by year, and productivity per worker declined as pit machinery wore out. Basically the problem was lack of manpower. Many young miners had seen the war as a heaven-sent chance to get away from the pits – and volunteered for the forces. Bevin's appeal for ex-miners to return voluntarily fell on deaf ears, so 30,000 men who were registered as having had mining experience were given no choice in the matter and were directed back to the pits. Production remained too low, however.

The Miners' Federation was constantly demanding nationalisation of the industry, but the coal-owners were still being led intransigently by the man who had been their spokesman in the General Strike. Instead of pressing for nationalisation, which he knew would divide the coalition government, Bevin in 1943 agreed to an awkward system of dual control: the mines remained the property of the coal-owners but they were operated by the newly set-up Ministry of Fuel and Power, under Gwilym Lloyd-George. This was only agreed after much dissension in the Labour party, which favoured nationalisation whatever the consequences.

At the end of 1943, supplies to industry had to be cut by 10 per cent and, in a hasty and desperate attempt to raise manpower and production in the pits, the 'Bevin Boy' scheme was introduced. One out of every ten young men coming of age for calling up to the forces was chosen by ballot to go into the mines. It was an extremely unpopular measure – with the Bevin Boys as well as the miners. 'I'd grown up looking forward one day to putting on a uniform and being admired and then suddenly I get sent into the coal mines and I'm not entitled to wear a uniform at all. That really hurt,' remembered David Day, who was the only Bevin Boy in Evesham. There was no possible glamour in being sent into the mines – it was considered a fate worse than the forces.

Bevin Boys felt both cheated and apprehensive, almost as if they were being sent to prison. They found that they were also resented as misfits at the pit, where the miners took them down a peg or two, especially those from middle-class and educated backgrounds. But not only those resented it. Apprentices in the Tyneside shipyards came out on strike in protest that, at the end of their apprenticeships, they might be directed into mines and ditch their prospects of an engineering career. In the event, four of them went to prison but were released on appeal after a campaign by Aneurin Bevan, MP. On the other hand the Bevin Boys who worked at the coal face – and only about 7000 did – learned to appreciate what a physical strain it was for a miner to cut his stint of fifteen tons a day. Ben Morris recalled, 'I was the first miner in South Wales to have a Bevin Boy – by trade he was a dental mechanic. On his first day he shovelled about a ton of coal on to the conveyor and said, "Well, that's that, I've earned my keep for today." And I remember telling him how much that coal he'd shovelled was worth to me – sevenpence halfpenny.'

Very few Bevin Boys stayed on in the coal industry – or were of much use to it, though a few went on to be mining engineers and one even became an area manager. But the experience did have a useful legacy in opening young men's eyes to the way the miners had to live. Brian Rix, then a very young actor, who volunteered for the mines when sinus trouble prevented him from training as an RAF pilot, remembered this well:

It was a culture shock of tremendous proportions as far as I was concerned. I think it was a marvellous thing because it taught me a great deal. But I had an idea of it as a character performance. I went down the mine on the first day wearing pig-skin gloves. I explained to this guy as we stepped out at the bottom of the shaft, 'I'm an actor, you see, I've got to look after my hands,' and he said, 'If you wear them gloves, you'll look like me.' And he held up a hand with the first three fingers missing. So I took my gloves off.

It was not only the physical hardships and the social injustices of the Depression years that he learned about. A political education resulted from this mixing of the classes. 'I don't think we ever became integrated. We were the sort of rogue elephants of mining and the miners were, I think, amused by us in a sort of avuncular way. But as a class it levelled us off. It was the first

time I'd really met a socialist. A lot of well-to-do young men become rabid socialists theoretically, but I was faced with socialism and deprivation practically and it had a great effect on me.'

Coal-mining was the industry that came closest to defeating Bevin, according to his biographer, Alan (later Lord) Bullock. But it was an exception to a remarkably successful tenure of power. In spite of his dictatorial powers, Bevin was never a dictator. 'I have an inherent faith in our people which they understand,' he said in 1941. 'In spite of the criticism showered on me, I have stuck to leadership as long as I can, rather than resort to drastic compulsion.' That came soon afterwards. By 1943 there had been 400,000 people directed to war work – but the great majority went willingly. Legal proceedings were taken against only 1 in 10,000 workers, and only 1 in 50,000 was sent to prison for refusing to comply. It was a testimony to Bevin's success in winning the confidence of the nation. 'His performance as Minister of Labour was outstanding,' was Jack Jones's verdict. 'He made a contribution to the war effort second only to Churchill's . . . I think equal in many ways.'

Bevin's legacy, which far outlasted the war, was the concept of union–government cooperation. This was only possible given fair negotiations, the arbitration of disputes and welfare provisions – factory inspections, canteens, good working conditions and holidays, even factory entertainment. Under his influence a remarkable change came over the embittered industrial relations that he inherited from the Thirties – and it far outlasted the war.

57 From the end of 1943 one in ten young men called up was chosen by ballot to go down the mines as a 'Bevin Boy'. It was considered a fate worse than the forces. This group of raw recruits is being taken underground by the experienced miner in the centre

CHAPTER SIX

WOMEN AT WAR

IN SOME WAYS women could be said to have achieved more for their cause in the First World War than in the Second. In 1915 they had to campaign for their 'Right to Serve'; in 1941 they were begged to volunteer. The beginning of male conscription in 1916 and the urgent need to replace conscripted men, especially in munitions factories, only gradually overcame the prejudice against employing women. From 1942 onwards women were conscripted willy-nilly and directed into women's services or into war work. In both wars they were speedily disbanded or dismissed once victory was won, yet in the first case they won a great advance – the women's vote, which passed through Parliament in 1917 with great ease. Mr Asquith, who, like most leading politicians, had been unmoved by the campaign of the suffragettes up to the eve of the war, now called the case for votes for women 'unanswerable'. 'How could we have carried on the war without them?' he asked the House of Commons. 'Short of bearing arms there is hardly a service in which women have not been at least as active and as efficient as men.' After the Second World War, however, in which twice as many women were mobilised and half a million were part of the fighting forces, they were granted nothing comparable, least of all equal pay. A Royal Commission on Equal Pay had been appointed in May 1944, in the wake of many wrangles on the subject. By the time it reported, inconclusively, in October 1946, the war and women's war work were long past and the 'problem' could be shelved again. Women remained far from equal.

Women bore the brunt of the upheaval of war. Apart from the fact that 7.5 million of them were mobilised, either in the factories or the auxiliary services, it was women who had to face up to losing their husbands or men friends to the forces, losing their children to evacuation – or to receiving other people's children as evacuees. Others put up relatives seeking refuge from bombed areas, and troops or war-workers who were billeted on them. In a population of 35 million in wartime Britain, 60 million changes of address were registered – almost two moves per person. Every one of these concerned women who, amid such a fantastic degree of disruption, were trying to keep homes and families functioning. Fear for those in danger and loneliness due to prolonged separation were their usual lot, as well as the endurance needed for the trials of rationing, queueing, disrupted transport and the blackout. Yet the voluntary services, coping with the casualties and upheavals of bombing, were provided to a great extent by these same hard-pressed women. A people's war meant to a large extent a women's war.

In 1939 there was a lot to be liberated from, if you were a woman. Of the 6 million women who worked, 2 million were in domestic service, receiving wages as low as 5 shillings (25 pence) a week. The remainder were mostly confined to low-paid industries such as textiles, boots and shoes, food and drink manufacturing or light engineering, or they had lowly jobs in shops and offices. Few entered the professions and nearly all – doctors, teachers, civil servants (as well as factory workers) – were required to leave work on getting married. This was partly because men expected it and partly because during the Depression it had not been thought right for a household to have two incomes when many had none, but it was also because marriage and motherhood was the best career available. Home was considered to be a woman's proper place. When war broke out there was a rush to volunteer for war work – and, paradoxically, many women were told in the first eighteen months that they were not wanted. Elaine Burton was one.

> I had applied for so many jobs and got nothing that I wrote an article about it. It was accepted by the *News Chronicle* and out of that I got a job writing a weekly article on women and that's how I found out what other women felt. They were so anxious – everybody wanted to help – and they just didn't seem to be accepted. What we all felt was that we weren't being used, we weren't wanted. The unemployment figures among women at the beginning of the war actually went up by some 300,000 and we said to ourselves, 'How can this happen?'

To general disappointment, the Ministry of Information announced that women should stick to their jobs and their homes unless particularly well qualified. 'Every time they ask for women, I go along and they won't take me, they say I'm too old,' a 41-year-old woman said angrily to Mass Observation. 'There's a lot I could do if they'd let me. They don't want women and that's that.'

Even those women who could claim to be extremely well qualified – as pilots – received a churlish welcome when the women's section of the Air Transport Auxiliary was set up to ferry new planes from the factories to the RAF stations that were to use them. Letters poured into the press, hostile to the very idea of women being used as pilots. 'Women are not seeking this job for the sake of doing something for their country but for the sake of publicity,' said one. 'Women anxious to serve their country should take on work more befitting their sex instead of encroaching on a man's occupation.' This was a common attitude, a mixture of scorn and fear of competition, and it might have lasted far longer had not the war situation become desperate.

After 43,000 volunteers had been admitted to the women's services in the first three months of war, recruiting fell off badly. One reason was the disapproval of men. Almost all husbands were against their wives volunteering, and fathers were far from keen about their daughters joining up. A 1941 survey by Mass Observation came up with these typical reactions: 'I wouldn't let my wife join. She's been talking quite seriously of joining the ATS as a cook. I told her I wouldn't hear of it.' . . . 'It's bad enough when your wife has to go out to work, but I don't like to think of them in uniform.' . . . 'I wouldn't want to see my daughter in it, although I wouldn't stop her if she wanted to go.' When soldiers were asked whether they would like their wives to join the ATS (the Auxiliary Territorial Service, now the Women's Royal Army Corps), 85 per cent said they would not. Half of them explained their attitude by saying it was immoral and dirty. Clearly the ATS had a bad name.

'All the forces seemed to have a bad name, particularly the Army,' recalled Terese Roberts, who volunteered for all three at seventeen, and was accepted by the ATS. 'My parents were furious. They said, oh, they're going to be officers' playthings and stupid things like that. My friend's mother signed her form because she said she'd run away otherwise. I finally persuaded my father to let me join. When eventually the papers did come through we sent them back saying we'd changed our minds, but unfortunately the army had already enlisted us. We were hooked. They'd got us whether we wanted it or not.' It was not only fathers who feared the worst. Micky Hutton Storie wanted to join at the age of seventeen and twice cut out the form in the newspaper recruiting advertisement, requesting joining-up papers to be sent to her. 'Twice my mother burnt them on the fire because she didn't want me to go. So the third time I went to the Labour Exchange and volunteered in person and my mother could do nothing about it.'

'Those ATS girls are a disgrace. They come in this pub at night and line up against that wall. Soldiers give them drinks and then when they're blind drunk they carry them out into the street. And we're paying public money for them too.' (A remark overheard by a Mass Observer in Chester.) What was the opinion of the soldiers whom they had to work with? 'I think that while the majority of soldiers appear to look down on and sneer at the ATS, they are glad that they are there, although they do not like to admit it,' wrote one officer about his men. 'There are some very good friendships; some bad and rather unhealthy ones, of course, but several marriages have taken place.' An anti-aircraft gunner felt that: 'The clerks and cooks are usually efficient and keen, mostly secretaries and typists in civil life, but the scrubbing ATS are very poor on the whole, unintelligent and inefficient, and they usually get into trouble. One girl complained of being given a black eye by a gunner. Another girl told the battery captain to get out of her bloody kitchen.'

'I know the Wrens were considered the élite corps and possibly the WAAFs came next because of the glamour of the pilots, and somehow the

Russian women fight and die side by side with men on the most wicked battlefield of all time.

German women (...two of them...to one of you) work doggedly to strengthen the hideous war machine of our common foe.

Your place is in the A.T.S. Volunteer to-day. Time is very short.

CUT THIS OUT AND POST IT TO-DAY

Address it to The Auxiliary Territorial Service, AG18/IIV, Hobart House, Grosvenor Gardens, London, S.W.1

Please send me full story of life in the A.T.S. and details of the opportunities it offers. This does not commit me in any way.

Mrs./Miss ....

Address ....

Age .... (in confidence)

ATS

Adventure through Service

Unsealed envelope, penny stamp.

You can still be adventurous or domesticated. You can still drive...or cook...or cater...go into army offices...or go into the Signal Corps ...or into army stores...or hangars...do

Radiolocation...work on anti-aircraft. You can make a vocation of this war work...now and in the future. But volunteer you must! For the A.T.S. And at once!

Please call and have a talk at any Employment Exchange or A.T.S. or Army Recruiting Centre.

58 The ATS relied on volunteers in the first two years of war but many girls were put off joining by the disapproval of parents or husbands because the women's services had 'a bad name', in particular the ATS

ATS at the beginning were looked down upon. But I'm sure when the public found out we weren't in there for a good time, that we were in to do a job of work, that made a great deal of difference,' said Micky Hutton Storie.

In the early days, the women's services naturally attracted the girls with wanderlust, who may well have imagined a romantic, carefree life in uniform with plenty of men for company – a break from a restricted humdrum life. This was encouraged by the most effective recruiting poster of the day – the 'blonde bombshell' in uniform seen in glamorous profile, looking like a Hollywood film star. There were protests in the House of Commons that it was encouraging girls to volunteer by false, romantic promises, and it was withdrawn in favour of a far more regimented, less glamorous girl, marching past a line of soldiers with the unexciting message, 'You are wanted too.' This poster embodied the very uniformity that put most girls off joining – along with the dislike of leaving home. When conscription was introduced for girls in their twenties, only a quarter of them chose the services rather than factories or civil defence. At one stage in 1942 all girls of twenty-one to twenty-two were directed into uniform to make up the numbers. 'I know two girls who've said they hope they would die before they were called up. They are frankly terrified at the prospect' . . . 'I have not yet met a woman in her twenties who is not in an awful state about conscription, nine times out of ten because she does not want to leave home' – two unenthusiastic reactions, to put it mildly, collected by Mass Observation.

It was felt that conditions in the women's services left much to be desired, so the government announced a Committee of Enquiry – consisting of four men. Elaine Burton regarded that as typical government thinking, though

59 Anti-aircraft batteries began to have mixed crews from 1941. The ATS members took over range-finding and aiming mechanisms but were not allowed actually to fire the guns. Some battery commanders said women were better on the instruments than men

later, after ridicule, the Committee was given a top dressing of women. 'There were two very obvious problems, physical training and lavatories. It was ridiculous to expect the women to do physical training with the men under a male instructor and there's no use having a long line of lavatories for women without doors, because women won't buy that – and they didn't. No woman would have allowed that.'

The initial shock of joining up was much the same for women as for men. Terese Roberts conjured it up vividly:

> We seemed far from home; we were very miserable, everything was so rough, the food wasn't all that nice and the whole atmosphere seemed so cold and unwelcoming. We didn't like the sergeants shouting and yelling at us. We found it very hard at first to accept being ordered about so constantly and also the fact that we couldn't go out when we liked, we had to go only when we were told.

She managed to avoid the cookhouse by volunteering for ack-ack (anti-aircraft) mixed batteries which began training in 1941.

> We were guarding the ICI works. When planes came in we were meant to shoot under them and in front of them. It meant they had to go higher and they were off their target. When we thought we'd got one, we were all elated – until we were given a thorough telling off and told that wasn't the idea. When you stopped to think, had we got that plane full of bombs it could have come down right on top of the ICI works.

Women gradually replaced men as 'technical control officers', vital for the correct aiming of the guns. They were debarred from actually firing them but Churchill, whose daughter Mary served with an anti-aircraft battery, decreed that they should be known as 'Gunners', like the men. 'There wasn't very much glamour, particularly on an ack-ack site,' said Terese Roberts.

> In one camp we had no water on, we used to break the ice on the fire buckets in the morning to get a wash. We had quite a bit of comradeship but at times we were very unhappy. I don't think there was anyone who didn't have a weep and want to go home at some time or other. But I would never say I regretted it. There were times when I hated it but I'm glad I had the experience.

The commander of the first battery to bring down a German plane paid the women under his command an unexpected compliment: 'If I were offered the choice of a mixed battery or a male battery, I would take the mixed battery. The girls cannot be beaten in action. In my opinion they are definitely better than the men on the instruments they are operating. Beyond a little natural excitement, which shows itself in humorous and quaint remarks, they are quite as steady, if not steadier, than the men.' What the 'quaint' remarks were, and how they differed from men's, we can only guess.

Although cooking and scrubbing and clerking were the commonest jobs in the ATS – the largest of the three women's services (198,000 strong) – a great many of them became drivers and mechanics, including Princess Elizabeth, who, wrote her mother, was so caught up in her training that 'we had sparking plugs all through dinner last night'. The ATS had the highest casualties of the three services – 335 killed, 94 missing, 22 taken prisoner. There was also an élite all-women corps, the 93rd Searchlight Regiment, the only women's searchlight regiment in the world. It was equipped with radar, which the men's searchlight regiment had not got, because women's finer touch made them better operators of this sensitive equipment.

General Sir Frederick Pile, anti-aircraft Commander-in-Chief, wrote of the unit which guarded London, 'The girls lived like men and alas some of them died like men. Unarmed, they often showed great personal bravery. Like all good things they were in short supply.'

Micky Hutton Storie, one of the pioneer trainees, who became a sergeant major in charge of a searchlight site, found the work thrilling. Radar would locate the enemy bomber in darkness, then she would order the switch to be thrown. 'Three beams would converge with the German plane sitting on top, very brightly illuminated. We worked with the planes from Northolt and they'd shoot them out of the sky. It's terrible to say it, but we were so thrilled because this was our job, this was what we'd been trained to do. In fact, we almost became machines.' The searchlight units also guided home severely damaged English planes coming across from the Channel – a crippled bomber would fly along their beam to an airfield and land.

> We would get three minutes to take post – not a long time to get up. You couldn't dress, you went out in your blue striped issue pyjamas with just your steel helmet clamped on top of curlers. It was a very specialised job and we were very proud to belong to it. I cannot stress enough how well these girls behaved in action, even though sometimes German bombers would dive down the beams with machine guns blazing away, trying to put the light out. They still went on duty, even when the telegrams arrived that their husbands had been killed or injured at Arnhem. It was a marvellous feeling of just working together. It was utterly marvellous.

The WAAF (Women's Auxiliary Air Force, now the WRAF), offered girls jobs as radio-operators, bomb-plotters, photographers and mechanics, but the heaviest physical work was crewing the barrage balloons. At first it was thought that women were not strong enough to handle them, but from 1941 they started taking over the sites until half the balloon barrages in the country

60 *Members of the all-women Searchlight Regiment – the only one in the world – pose for an off-duty photograph in Trafalgar Square. Their sergeant major, Micky Hutton Storie, is at bottom left*

were operated by women. It took sixteen women to replace a crew of ten airmen.

The only women allowed to fly aircraft were the women ferry pilots of the Air Transport Auxiliary, which delivered new planes to their RAF or Fleet Air Arm squadrons. To begin with, a pool of eight women pilots at Hatfield were employed to fly training planes, such as Tiger Moths, but as aircraft output soared sheer necessity meant that every woman pilot available to deliver them was needed. From 1941, women were cleared to fly operational aircraft such as Spitfires and Hurricanes, and within two years they were flying four-engined Lancaster bombers to their airfields. Joan Hughes, one of the original eight ferry pilots, remembered that at first they would only take women who had 600 hours' flying experience, whereas the qualification for men was 300 hours. 'The men didn't mind us flying the Tiger Moths because it was terribly cold – there was no heating and an open top. No matter what you did to avoid it, your face froze. We were so thrilled to be doing it that the idea of the freezing cold didn't bother us.'

The strength of prejudice against women pilots is hard to believe now.

61 A woman ferry pilot of the Air Transport Auxiliary climbs into a new Spitfire to deliver it to an RAF fighter station. There was strong resistance to using women ferry pilots at first, but before long they were flying four-engined bombers as well

The editor of *The Aeroplane* wrote: 'What do these social butterflies think they're doing?' 'There were masses of letters from other women saying how dare we fly? We should be at home cooking our husband's dinner,' said Joan Hughes. 'In the end they didn't care if you were a monkey, just as long as you didn't smash the aeroplane up. That was the best time of all, really. The fact that you were a woman didn't mean a thing.' 'We flew all over the country without radio – almost impossible to believe now,' said Diana Bernato-Walker, who joined ATA for training when she had only a few hours' flying to her credit. 'We used maps to guide us, but eventually we knew the country so well we hardly needed them. I was never frightened at the time. It was only when I thought about it afterwards that my knees would shake. The women's accident record was better than the men's. I put that down to the fact that the women were determined to prove themselves.' In the course of the war 120 women ferry pilots served, compared with 700 men. From 1943, once they were flying every type of aircraft, they were paid at the same rate.

For women there was an added bonus in the fact that they were piloting types of planes that they would normally get no chance to handle. 'To be actually allowed to fly brand-new planes before even the RAF got their hands on them was beyond one's wildest dreams,' said Joan Hughes. 'It was five years of absolute bliss.' Which was more than most people could say of their war.

By 1943, 375,000 women were in civil defence, a quarter of the total, and women air-raid wardens, discouraged at first, constituted a sixth of the force. Others staffed control centres, first-aid posts and shelters. Most air-raid ambulance drivers were women – 36,000 of them – and there were also 2600 women firemen (some drove fire engines) and another 47,000 part-time auxiliaries. Pay for women in full-time civil defence was £2 15s a week, but most of the women were unpaid volunteers – until 1943, when civil defence work was made compulsory. This made it all the more disgraceful that compensation for injury in air raids was not the same for women CD workers as for men. Elaine Burton, who campaigned for equal compensation, said: 'A woman was assessed at two-thirds the value of a man, if you were bomb-damaged. I saw one woman who had lost both legs below the knee in hospital alongside a man who had lost one arm below the elbow. The woman got less compensation than the man.' Only after four petitions had been presented to Parliament was the compensation made equal.

The job of the ambulance volunteers was harrowing psychologically as well as physically. Hetty Fowler, a married woman in business with her husband running a fish and chip shop when war broke out, joined the ambulance service while he was in the National Fire Service – each on duty for twenty-four hours at a time but on opposite shifts. 'I reported at 9 a.m. just as he would be leaving. He would walk past and say, "Good morning, Mrs Fowler" and I would say, "Good morning, Mr Fowler" and that was all we saw of each other.' Driving in the black-out was the worst part of the job.

> You drove by guesswork really. I was the oldest on the station, the others were young wives with husbands at the war. The younger ones never seemed to show fear, so of course I wasn't going to, although I really was frightened. We made a joke of everything. Once there were three of us in the driving seat, one doing the steering, one the accelerator, one the gear lever – hair-raising. One girl pulled the gear lever right out of its socket and waved it, with the vehicle still moving. 'Look what I've got,' she said. You made a joke of everything – you had to. You'd be called out to an incident and you didn't know what you'd find.

The social miseries of the war, especially the aftermath of the air raids, were the province of the Women's Voluntary Services – the 'women in green and maroon' – who provided an immediate welfare service for the homeless while they were too shocked and disorientated to cope for themselves.

Founded in 1938 by a Viceroy's widow, Lady Reading, they had no pay, no system of ranks and no politics and they organised a million volunteers from the ages of seventeen up to sixty-five – the majority being of matronly years. (A total of 241 WVS members were killed – the highest casualty figure after the ATS.) No one was turned away for being too busy to offer much time or for being less than physically fit. Famous for providing cups of tea in a crisis, the WVS tackled an extraordinarily wide range of services as a second

62 *The WVS operated no age discrimination. Most of their million volunteers doing all kinds of welfare work were of matronly years. Their clothing depots distributed donated clothing to the bombed-out and needy*

line of defence in air raids. They provided food, shelter and information, and a sympathetic mother substitute – often badly needed. Over 180,000 of them were deputed to run rest centres for the bombed-out on behalf of the local authority, and their Incident Inquiry Points reunited families with each other, their pets and their valuables. Pets were of great importance, as WVS worker Alice Myers discovered in a rest centre in Hull.

They kept coming in, their bare feet cut and bleeding because they'd walked over glass, the men carrying the children, and only pyjamas on. They were in a state of shock because they couldn't believe they'd lost everything and the children brought pets with them. They wouldn't go to sleep unless they had their kitten, or their dog or rabbit. We had a budgie in a battered cage with no feathers, just one on its head, and a lot of stray dogs, following the crowd, which the RSPCA took. The children would settle to sleep with their animals; they seemed to bother more about the animals than they did about themselves.

The WVS were great improvisers of field kitchens out of the rubble and bricks of air-raid damage – they were always cooking in 'dustbin ovens'. They also staffed the Queen's Messenger Convoys, British Restaurants and mobile canteens for troops, for the bombed, for people in shelters, for dockers and building-workers repairing bomb damage. They took pies to farm-workers in the fields. They ran hostels for women in the services, nurseries for working women's children, clothing depots and mobile laundries, knitting parties and parties to make camouflage netting or jam or toys. They collected salvage and distributed books. Their motto was 'If it should be done, the WVS will do it.' Clemency Greatorex, a WVS organiser in Lymington, remembered organising one section of the town to offer hot baths to soldiers, and billeting bombed-out evacuees from Portsmouth on retired admirals. 'One captain's widow took six and had them all doing PT on the lawn before school. There was no Lady Bountiful swanning in and giving away glorious gifts. For one thing we had nothing to give away, except work.'

But this was not always how they appeared to others. Yvonne Gilbert, a thirteen-year-old schoolgirl who waited to help welcome the evacuees to her small Cambridgeshire village, saw them not as Lady Bountiful but as Lady Bossy.

> Four WVS ladies arrived. They seemed to come in two sizes, very large, with hair scraped back in a bun, or very small and weedy-looking. The large lady came complete with clip-board and talked about 'them' rather than the children. One of the mums lit a cigarette and was pounced on. Another wanted to breast-feed her baby but that was frowned on too. I remember one WVS lady saying to a mother who would not be parted from her children, 'Come, come now, this is war! We can't all do what we like.' Since that day I've never been able to think well of those do-gooders with their leather handbags, who didn't take in evacuees themselves.

In all these fields women tackled work that was new to them, but no organisation staffed and run by women broke new ground more visibly than the Women's Land Army. Milkmaids were traditional but women driving tractors and operating threshing machines, ploughing, tree-felling, hedging and ditching, sheepshearing or shepherding in winter were a novel sight, though it soon became usual and accepted in many parts of the countryside. The WLA expanded from 20,000 in 1941 to 80,000 in 1944, a third of them girls with a town upbringing. They wore a not unattractive uniform (when it fitted) of corduroy breeches, leggings, boots, green jumper, brown jacket and khaki broad-rimmed hat. After four weeks' training they were paid only £1 8s (increased to £2 8s in 1944) for an arduous fifty-hour minimum working week – in practice much longer at harvest time. Out of their wages they often paid 25 shillings for lodgings. There were WLA hostels, though their rules were strict, with fines for untidiness and early lights-out – but then the day might start with milking at 5 a.m. Like every town girl, Joan Shakesheff, who joined at eighteen, discovered how hard country life could be.

> The first week I thought I'd drop dead from tiredness. It was hay-making

time. I had two or three blisters on each finger from using a pitch-fork and when we came in at five-thirty the first day, I could hardly stagger up the stairs to bed, I was so tired. And we never seemed to get enough to eat. I always seemed to be hungry. We were given an extra amount of cheese but it wasn't really enough. There wasn't an ounce of flesh on any of us, thin as pins. I can remember being hungry most of the time.

Kitty Murphy, who suffered skin complaints from the effects of cordite at Woolwich Arsenal, volunteered for the sake of fresh air and a healthy outdoor life. She got it in a farm foreman's tied cottage with no running water, gas or electricity in a small Essex village. But at least food was plentiful. 'I remember the first time I walked in there they had two hares hanging up in the kitchen. They frightened me at first, I'd never seen anything like it. Oh, I was well fed there, I looked a picture of health, living off the fat of the land, jugged hare, pheasant, chicken.' Without any formal training, except by watching others, she learned to milk, hoe, hedge and ditch, dig drainage trenches, and pick everything from strawberries to sugar beet. 'That was the worst job, pulling sugar beet, you couldn't wear gloves because of the ice on the leaves, your fingers used to be numbed.' In Joan Shakesheff's opinion hedging and ditching was the worst – 'up to your knees in water most of the time. But muck-spreading, which sounds a terrible job, was a lovely job in the winter because you really got warm.'

The girls were usually sent from one farm to the next for the potato harvest, the hoeing or whatever was the task of the season. 'I don't think the farmers thought we'd be very much good – girls coming on to the farm, disrupting everything and giggling,' said Joan, 'but I think they were quite surprised. They were very glad to have us in the end when they were short of men. There wasn't anything we didn't tackle. We were very proud of it, proud to think we were really doing something worthwhile.' This opinion was confirmed by Sir Emrys Jones, speaking for Gloucestershire, as its wartime Cultivation Officer.

They were the most trainable human beings I have ever had. I could teach a land girl to drive a tractor in half a day because they wanted to learn. Where they were brilliant was at looking after stock. I remember three girls from Bootle we put in charge of calves and they were marvellous, far better than any man. I suppose this was mother instinct. They became the most efficient tractor drivers. I was amazed. I didn't really believe a woman could drive a tractor – she wasn't built for it. But they got used to the knack of handling heavy work, humping potato bags, that sort of thing. Instead of two-hundredweight sacks we used one-hundredweight for girls. I can't think of anything else that they couldn't do. We had farmers screaming for land girls on the telephone every morning and the demand was far greater than the supply.

63 and 64 Appeals to join the Women's Land Army raised 80,000 recruits, many of them town girls who discovered the tough side of country life. The image on the posters was translated into the reality of snow and mud and frozen fingers, but the Land Girls were much sought after as good workers

It is interesting to contrast the wartime behaviour of women in Britain and in Nazi Germany. Hitler's concern with the purity of the race and vision of women as the 'mothers of the nation' prejudiced him against any occupation that might sully them as child-bearers. Conscription of German women was held up until 1943 by this doctrine and even after that Germany, though short of labour, failed to mobilise women for war work in large numbers. Women refused to volunteer and there were many loopholes to enable them to avoid conscription.

In Britain, on the other hand, women took up unfamiliar and unsung civilian occupations – 100,000 of them worked on the railways, for example, not only as carriage cleaners, porters and ticket-collectors but as plate-layers and mechanics in railway workshops. There were over 100,000 more in the Post Office, some of them as drivers, motorcycle messengers and cable repairers. There were women working in shipyards and as dock labourers. There were women plumbers, electricians, gas-fitters, house-repair workers and chimney sweeps. They drove all manner of vehicles – ambulances, corpse wagons, heavy lorries and buses – and even crewed barges on the Manchester Ship Canal. They proved endlessly adaptable to work which had been hitherto withheld from them simply because it was considered too tough or too technical for the 'weaker' sex. Psychologically, this was a breakthrough that took time to sink in.

Ellen McCulloch, women's officer of the TGWU, found this: 'Even in 1942 you'd talk to a girl and ask did she like the job and she'd say, "Oh yes, I never thought I'd be able to do it. After all, it's not women's work, is it, Ellen?" They had clearly in their minds that there was women's work and it was done by inferior people. But they began to realise that they weren't second-class citizens.'

Again and again women echoed this surprise and satisfaction at their newly discovered abilities. 'I think it surprised men that we slips of girls could make such a good job of it,' said Micky Hutton Storie of her radar-controlled searchlight battery, 'and I'm very surprised we got that opportunity when I remember how technical it all was.' 'You had these beautiful aeroplanes to fly. Fancy being allowed to fly them,' said Diana Bernato-Walker, the ferry pilot. 'After all, women weren't expected to fly, they weren't expected to do anything much.' 'The war did women a good turn. They found out there were a lot of jobs they could do just as well as a man and women had never thought like that before,' said Hetty Fowler.

In 1942, Clement Attlee voiced the amazement of a Labour politician at what women munitions workers were capable of doing. 'Precision engineering, which only a few years ago would have made a skilled turner's hair stand on end, is now being performed with dead accuracy by girls who had no industrial experience!'

No category of women found the change more liberating than those who had been brought up to expect domestic service as their lot in life. Mona

65 *Women took up all kinds of unusual occupations to release men for the forces. There were 100,000 women on the railways, as porters, ticket collectors, cleaners, plate-layers – and signal-persons*

Marshall, nursemaid turned steelworker, had no doubts of the benefits that war brought her:

> To be quite honest, the war was the best thing that ever happened to us. I was as green as grass and terrified if anyone spoke to me. I had been brought up not to argue. My generation had been taught to do as we were told. At work you did exactly as your boss told you and you went home to do exactly what your husband told you. The war changed all that. The war made me stand on my own two feet.

It would be difficult to find anybody who regretted being plucked from a life as a servant, however much life 'below stairs' has since been sentimentalised as a cosy, dependable world. Here is a real parlourmaid speaking, Margery Bailey: 'When I was in service, I wouldn't dare answer anybody back, I would be walked over. The head parlourmaid, she used to frighten me to death. It was the best thing I ever did, to go into a factory.' Phyllis Elms escaped from being a lowly kitchen-maid in a big house to making radar equipment in the Ekco factory set up at Malmesbury in rural Wiltshire. 'I worked very long hours, sometimes if they had dinner parties it was one o'clock in the morning. I loathed the work, I really hated it. I think I had a lot of pride and having to bow and scrape to people just wasn't on with me. So when the Ekco factory started up, it was like a gift from the gods.'

The initial prejudices, on both sides, against women joining trade unions were worn away fairly swiftly. In 1942 there were over a million and a half women in trade unions. The big catch-all unions – the Transport and General Workers and the General and Municipal Workers – had both recruited over a quarter of a million each. The craft union most doggedly opposed to women, the Amalgamated Engineering Union, which opened its membership to women only in 1943, had 143,000 women members, nearly a sixth of the total, by the following year. By then the men had realised that it was better that women should be organised and better paid, as employers would be less likely to take on women instead of men if they were just as expensive to employ. Nevertheless, equal pay was only achieved by a minority of women in engineering, and Jack Jones looked back on the disbelief it caused.

> In many cases we were getting the man's rate for women where they were doing highly skilled work such as aero-engine fitting. I had to come down to London and meet the Select Committee on National Expenditure to justify the fact that some women workers were getting as much as £25 a week. They were doing the same work as men, working piece-work day and night, so I was able to justify it easily, but it wasn't the case everywhere. In the Coventry area we developed trade unionism to a high pitch and the union stuck up for them.

In other industries or parts of the country it was more usual for women to earn half or, rarely, two-thirds of the men's rate. London bus conductresses, who were 100 per cent union members, got equality, but when the House of Commons amended the 1944 Education Bill to give women teachers equal pay, Churchill denounced the vote as 'an impertinence' and insisted the amendment was revoked on a vote of confidence. However, he bowed to public pressure to the extent of appointing a Royal Commission 'to consider the social, economic and financial implications of the claim of equal pay for equal work'. Mass Observation reported that 95 per cent of women were in favour of equal pay as a matter of simple justice and most of them were surprised that it was thought necessary to have a Royal Commission to discuss it. The Commission reached no conclusions but it illuminated the reasons given to justify *unequal* pay: women were considered to be less strong physically, more often absentees, and to look on full-time work as a temporary expedient until marriage. A dissenting minority of three women members questioned this. They pointed out that even if it was true it did not justify sex-differentiation in pay for equal work. But by the time it reported, in late 1946, some 2 million women workers had already melted away from the factories.

Mass Observation had already discovered in a March 1944 survey that there was a widespread longing to be done with the grind, boredom and weariness of war work: 'The two jobs of home and work are getting me

66 *Milkmaids are traditional, but the milkwoman on her round was another wartime innovation*

down. I'm tired. When the war is over I'll want a good long rest' . . . 'I only came as a wartime thing. It's a change from housework but I hope I'll go back and lead a peaceful life when the war's over' . . . 'Of course, when we get married I shan't want to work, I shall want to have children' . . . 'If he can get a regular job I won't go to work, I'll stay at home and have children' . . . 'What's going to happen to the men who come home, will there be jobs for *them*?'

These were understandable reactions and they were very widespread. Home and motherhood, with all their limitations, appealed strongly to women who had spent four years getting up and going to work in the dark and had spent their spare time queueing and trying to catch up with the rudiments of housekeeping between long, tiring shifts.

But there was also a general acceptance that jobs for ex-servicemen came first (with memories of the unemployment that awaited the 'heroes' of 1918). When it came to it, most women were given no choice in the matter. According to aircraft worker Barbara Davies,

> I went in one night and was told that my services were no longer needed. This displeased me very much, so straight round to the union representative we went. There was nothing he could do. I think we were really quite an embarrassment to him – if he could have rubbed our names off the list, he would gladly have done so. He said the jobs were needed for the men coming out of the forces. I understood that perfectly but I didn't approve. A lot of people I knew would have liked to have stayed on but we were given no option whatsoever.

Not everyone minded as much. 'The women knew that when they came back the men had to have their jobs,' said Kitty Murphy. 'They were earning good money but I don't think they minded very much.' 'A lot of women did fight for a long time to keep their jobs,' said Hetty Fowler, 'but we couldn't not give a man who'd been fighting for his country a job.'

The trek back to the home can be exaggerated. Although the nurseries which had at last been opened in reasonable numbers were mostly closed again, there was a net increase in women working compared with pre-war figures, especially in the new fields of engineering, vehicle manufacturing and transport, all of which retained double the proportion of women workers that they had in 1939. So did local government and the civil service. By 1948 the number of insured women workers had increased by 350,000 over pre-war, and the increase was largely in the ranks of older, married women. This was a small but permanent legacy of the war, which was to increase again in the full employment of the 1950s, when married teachers and nurses were begged to return to work as soon as their children were old enough.

Just as the coming of the war had set off a boom in marriages, so did the end of it. The pre-war marriage rate was about 325,000 a year; by 1947, it peaked at 400,000. Three out of ten brides were under twenty-one, and some 70,000 of them crossed the Atlantic as GI brides. There had been a phenomenal rise in illegitimate births during the war, reaching a total of almost one baby in three, but then in the year before the war, one baby in three was conceived out of wedlock. What had diminished was the number of shotgun marriages that legitimised 70 per cent of these children – because fathers were now serving overseas. American troops made their generous contribution; a figure of 70,000 illegitimate offspring supposedly fathered by them in Britain was quoted in Congress. So the general picture was one of a large number of couples, who had had little time to get to know one another, settling down to live together for the first time, often accompanied by young children. Of course it often proved a strain, as Mickey Lewis found: 'It was really difficult – suddenly he turned up and I didn't feel "how marvellous", I felt a bit resentful at first. I thought, oh, he's come home to spoil it all. I hadn't made any relationships with other men. I was just living a broader kind of life and it was very difficult to change.'

Sometimes the dream was very far from the way the reality turned out, as it was for Doris White:

> I think we were spurred on by romantic movies to be little home-makers. I knew my boyfriend would come home and we'd get married and I worked like mad and got the house nice, whitewashed the ceilings, colourwashed the walls and after I'd done all that he used to go out every night because he missed the comradeship. The men missed the war. It felt a bit of a let-down to be home with the missus and the garden. They just couldn't settle.

Inevitably the war had disorganised everybody's sex life and threw them into proximity with strangers when many were feeling alone, anxious and aware that tomorrow it might be too late to enjoy life. Ellen McCulloch, as a union women's officer, saw what troubles factory girls away from home and mother got themselves into, in the days when knowledge of contraception was minimal.

> It was really too easy for them to drift into a relationship simply because they were lonely. It was all very sad. They'd be put into homes to have the baby and it would be adopted within a few days of birth, when the girls were in no condition to consider adoption. There was no social security, no question really of being able to keep the child.

Even when both partners to a marriage were living at home and working in civil defence, like Hetty Fowler in the Ambulance Service and her husband in the Fire Service, the fact that their duties kept them apart caused complications.

> I made friends and I know he made friends. We all used to get invited to the camp to dance with the soldiers, in our thick soles on a concrete floor, but it was very enjoyable. We were thrown together in war and we all thought we hadn't much longer to live, so why not get what we could get out of life? You're dancing with a man, he thinks you're rather nice and you think, well, nobody's told me that for years and you rather like it. When you're back with your husband, you can't say to him, I know a man who thinks I'm nice, can you?

Women enjoyed their freedom but were often racked by anxiety, or remorse, as the agony columns in magazines betrayed. Constance Holt, wartime editor of *Woman's Own*, remembered that the magazine's advice to those who were tempted was quite uncompromising.

'You can't do this to your husband, or even your fiancé, while he is away fighting for his country. You must break it up or wait until after the war and resolve it. You must not see this man'. We'd go as far as that – that was the advice we gave them. Occasionally we'd hear from men who had read the magazine abroad and were worried what it would be like for their wives if they got involved with a service girl, just now and then. And we'd write on the same lines – she's alone, without you. Behaviour may not always have been perfect but there was a strong feeling that it ought to be.

'Drifting' was the euphemism for gradually succumbing to temptation. Mrs F., whose husband was out East in the Army, wrote to *Everywoman* about the man she met at a dance and confessed: 'I'm not excusing myself, but I drifted until I became unfaithful to my husband. Now I'm horrified. I've given the man up – but what shall I say to my husband? I'm not really an unfaithful type of woman at all!'

The answer, now that it was too late to be uncompromising, showed sympathy and commonsense: 'Do get that guilty feeling out of your mind or you will destroy every chance of future happiness for yourself and your husband. What happened is a direct result of the war. . . . Don't say a word to your husband. Silence is the bravest thing.'

But, bravely though they kept silent about it afterwards, such experiences placed an intolerable strain on many marriages. By 1945 the number of divorce petitions reached 25,000 – two and a half times the figure for 1938; 70 per cent of them were for adultery and over half of them were brought by husbands.

When one asks what good – or bad – came of it all for women, it is not easy to draw up the balance sheet. Certainly, women achieved liberation of many kinds during the war – occupational, geographical, psychological, economic and sexual liberation, not forgetting the liberation of wearing trousers as a matter of course. That the great majority went back home again afterwards to be housewives is not surprising, for their freedoms had been geared to the extraordinary demands of wartime, which had disappeared. But some experiences are more liberating than others and one of these was the discovery of all-female camaraderie, of loyalty of woman to woman, which had had no chance to flourish when women only related to one another through men, as husbands and as bosses. 'In the old days men used to think that women couldn't work together,' reflected Clemency Greatorex of the WVS. 'It's quite untrue. Women *can* work together, as they can work with men. We had the confidence of finding we could do that. There were a lot of us at it.' 'I don't think I've ever made friends like I made when I was in the Women's Land Army,' said Joan Shakesheff. 'We had the same money, we

wore the same clothes and we did the same things. We were all in the same
boat.'

Probably the most important change that the war brought to women was
the change in their picture of themselves and of their potential. 'If there hadn't
been a war I would have stayed in the little valley where I was born, married a
local boy and that would have been that,' said Barbara Davies, whose pre-
war life was as an apprentice weaver. 'It took a year or two to realise that I
didn't have to accept that way of life. My aspirations grew. I became a mature
student. There would never have been any chance of an education like I've
had before the war. It changed women's self-esteem.' If women did return to a
social coma when the Second World War ended, as they did after the First, it
was only a light trance and it did not last many years more.

CHAPTER SEVEN

DRIED EGG AND BOILED NETTLES

'THANK YOU SO much for the three eggs. It is wonderful to see three eggs together, almost a miracle – *one* is remarkable.' So wrote Rose Macaulay to her sister in September 1940 as she anticipated the pleasure of cooking one of them when the air raid was over. It was the sort of treat that made a day memorable in the years of shortages and austerity that began in late 1940. As merchant ships went down in the Atlantic, so did rations at home. By December 1940, a Mass Observer was reporting what a prized possession an onion was. 'The greengrocer had let her [a neighbour] have a large one for threepence. She tied a piece of ribbon round it and put it on the mantelshelf. She's going to keep it for Christmas.' Another Observer reported from a village near Newcastle: 'They've got some oranges in the village but they'll only sell them to children and they have to bring a note from the clinic to say they need them – such a business for one orange.'

By early 1941, when merchant ships were being sunk at a rate of three a day, shortages were at their worst. Even the small amount of meat allowed was often hard to find, the butter ration was down to two ounces, the ration of 'mousetrap' cheese looked like bait at only one ounce and, perhaps hardest of all, only two ounces of tea a week went nowhere. Egg and milk allowances varied with the season; at its worst, one egg a fortnight, at its best, two eggs a week. Milk sometimes went down to half a pint per adult per week; a large proportion of dairy cattle had been slaughtered for lack of feed for them. To supplement this, two of the most disliked wartime institutions, dried egg and dried milk, were brought in from the United States. 'Shell eggs are five-sixths water,' explained a Ministry of Food announcement. 'Why import water?' So from 1942, a packet of dried egg was doled out every two months 'equivalent' to twelve eggs – but somehow incapable of resembling them. When the water was restored, scrambled dried egg looked like badly made custard and tasted chalky. Omelettes and Yorkshire puddings of a rubbery sort could be made with it; the puddings looked like linoleum tiles. 'National Dried Milk' was no treat either, best flavoured with chocolate – if you could get chocolate.

A close rival to dried egg in unpopularity was the 'National Wheatmeal Loaf' of 85 per cent extraction, brought in to save grain imports and shipping space. The British were a white-bread-eating race in 1942 and it was judged too much to ask of them to eat brown wholemeal bread, whose healthy qualities could have been hymned with perfect sincerity. Instead the nervous Ministry compromised, making the bread 'as white as possible'. It came out dirty beige. Everyone hated it and ascribed their minor ailments to it. 'Nasty, dirty, dark, coarse and indigestible' were five blistering adjectives that were applied to it. A patriotic 22 per cent said it was better than white bread on its initial appearance but by the next year Mass Observation found approval had sunk to 14 per cent on closer acquaintance. A. P. Herbert burst into song on behalf of the disapprovers:

As I now salute the Red,
So will I bow to dear brown bread,
Because, as my wise rulers say,
We shall save tonnage in this way.
But let this point be understood –
No man can tell me it is good.

68 Ration books and the coupons that had to be cut out weekly ruled everybody's household, even at the smartest of addresses

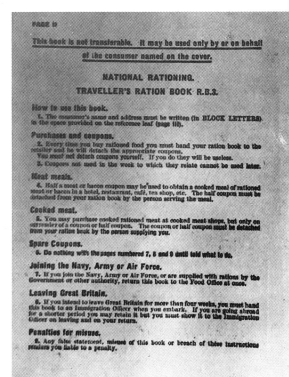

Whatever the privations, Britain was still in those days a bread-and-butter country. Bread meant white bread and butter did not mean 'marge'. Margarine, which made up most of the fats ration, was despised in spite of expensive advertising campaigns that claimed you could not tell it from butter. It was one piece of brainwashing that never worked. There was nothing most people could do to provide themselves with 'real' bread and butter but they swiftly turned into a nation of part-time chicken farmers. A popular song ran:

> I had a lot of chickens
> And a large chicken run,
> But owing to conditions,
> I'm now down to one –
> Hey, little hen,
> When, when, when,
> Will you lay me an egg
> For my tea?

Chickens were kept in back gardens, back yards, garden sheds, and on flat rooftops and balconies, even above the smartest London streets. They were fed on meal mixed with scraps, potato peelings, carrot tops, sprout leaves, crusts of National Wheatmeal bread, and their own ground-up egg shells. Feeding the fowls was an odiferous task.

By the end of the war a quarter of the eggs available were home produced. Sooner or later the hen that ceased to lay would need to be replaced by a young pullet and gratitude to a loyal servant was outweighed by need; owners would steel themselves against sentiment, wring its neck, pluck it and boil it. Others plucked up the necessary resolution to eat their pet rabbits. Some ambitious people kept a pig in the yard or garage and thousands joined a pig club. Pigs were admitted to the London Zoo in Regent's Park and sheep were grazed in Green Park.

'Food is a munition of war. DON'T WASTE IT.' So ran the tireless exhortations of the Ministry of Food, itself a wartime innovation, run rather like a university department at Colwyn Bay in Wales. Ministry nutritionists were eager to apply what was then a new science. Patty Fisher belonged to the scientific advice division headed by Sir Jack Drummond.

We knew what people needed for nutrients, we knew exactly how much of each nutrient and how many calories people needed for energy. We knew the calorie values of foods and so it only remained to do the calculation. Then we had to calculate which foods to choose, which we could grow and which to import on the basis of their nutritional value.

This was vital to the war effort, this evaluation which was the basis of rations. The Ministry of Food was far ahead of its time.

Another Ministry food scientist, Dorothy Hollingsworth, pointed out the social gains behind the policy.

I think Jack Drummond particularly was quite determined from the outset that the war situation would be used to improve the nutritional condition of the people. Special arrangements were made for young children and expectant and nursing mothers. There were special milk supplies, cod liver oil and orange juice; special rations for children in schools. Adults really got what was left over, equally divided. The great slogan really was fair shares for all.

Admirable as this was, it was possible for scientific measurements of calories and nutrients to get too divorced from human likes and dislikes. Something called 'the Basal Diet' was worked out, promising that if the worst came to the worst the normal adult could be adequately fed on a minimum quantity of bread, potatoes, oatmeal, vegetables and three-fifths of a pint of milk. When this was put before Churchill, he was horrified. 'Almost all the food faddists I ever knew, nut-eaters and the like, have died young after a long period of senile decay,' he snorted in a letter to Lord Woolton, the Minister of Food. 'The way to lose the war is to try to force the British public into a diet of milk, oatmeal, potatoes, washed down on gala occasions with a little lime juice.' No more was heard of the Basal Diet. But the scientists were correct in their calculations and the British people emerged from the war healthier than they went into it.

Pre-war surveys of the nation's diet showed that a quarter of the population was undernourished. Half the women of the working class were in poor health, infant mortality was at a high rate of 62 infant deaths per 1000 births and rickets was common – 80 per cent of under-fives showed some bone abnormality, 90 per cent had badly formed or decayed teeth. It was a disgraceful picture. Now everybody bought their rations – and could afford them thanks to controlled prices. 'The result was that all the measurable statistics improved – infant mortality, growth rate of children, and the condition of children's teeth, almost certainly due to the shortage of sugar and sweets,' said Dorothy Hollingsworth. It was a source of satisfaction to a nutritionist but less so to children who had to wait four weeks for their next sweet coupons to become valid and then make the agonising decision whether to spend them all on one half-pound bar of chocolate or on boiled sweets, toffees or liquorice allsorts. Then came the character-building discipline of trying to make these last.

The Ministry of Food prided itself on its publicity, which told people what was good for them and how to cook it, in Food Fact advertisements in the newspapers, 'Food Flashes' at the cinema and most of all the 'Kitchen Front' broadcasts after the 8 a.m. news. For these Lord Woolton recruited Elsie and Doris Waters, in their music hall characters 'Gert and Daisy'.

GERT: Did you know, Daisy, there's as much nourishment in a pint of milk as there is in a cut off the joint and two veg?
DAISY: Good gracious me! Is there really?
GERT: It's good for your teeth too.
DDISY: You don't say! I'd better put me teeth in a glass of milk tonight.

And so on, with improving tips and recipes from knowledgeable Gert to help dim Daisy make her scrambled egg go further with oatmeal. The Kitchen Front also included health tips from the Radio Doctor, Charles (later Lord) Hill, whose favourite cry was 'Lovely grub' and who liked nothing better than a heart-to-heart – or bowel-to-bowel – talk on constipation.

The shortage of sugar led to a desperate search for sweetness. 'Raw carrots added to steamed puddings and cakes will sweeten them,' promised the Ministry, which also encouraged women to jam-making orgies, for which extra sugar was made available. Carrot jam was well to the fore, along with parsnip, beetroot, marrow and green tomato jam. 'Dr Carrot', with a doctor's bag marked 'Vitamin A' (alleged to enable you to see in the black-out), was one of the many cartoon characters who were unleashed in their advertisements. Another was Potato Pete, who would sing the praises of spuds ('Every day serve 1 lb. per head . . . use potatoes in pastry . . . serve mashed potatoes as sandwich fillings'). Other omnipresent members of this unattractive menagerie were the Squander Bug, who tempted housewives to spend more than they needed, and the Fuel Demon.

One of the Ministry's jingles ran:

> Those who have the will to win
> Cook potatoes in their skin
> Knowing that the sight of peelings
> Deeply hurts Lord Woolton's feelings.

After the potato, the vegetable that roused the Ministry propagandists to unwonted frenzies of enthusiasm was the swede – 'Don't forget swedes!' was their constant cry. Potatoes, swedes and carrots were the chief ingredients of the Ministry's *chef d'oeuvre* among its recipes – Woolton Pie, named after the popular, avuncular Minister (it was made with potato pastry, naturally). Fatless pastry, eggless cakes, sugarless puddings and meatless soup ('by adding one or two Oxo cubes to your vegetable water a delicious soup is quickly made') were the reward of the virtuous – along with such recondite suggestions as mock haggis or mock oysters (sardines on oyster shells hidden

by breadcrumbs), date-and-nut loaf and boiled nettles ('once thoroughly wet they lose the power of stinging'). *Country Life* carried 'A note on nettle tea': 'Nettles can be used satisfactorily as a vegetable, for nettle tea and soup, even when in flower but the flowers can always be discarded and the young leaves used, just as one treats perpetual spinach. The young shoots are much more tender. It is advisable *not* to use the coarse large leaves.'

Country-lovers may have been reduced to boiling and drinking nettles but they drew the line at acorns. Acorn coffee was famous as something the Germans had to drink. 'Camp Coffee' essence, with a strong taste of chicory, may or may not have tasted better but at least it was British, as the label demonstrated with its Empire-builder sitting at his camp fire with a steaming cup.

69 *'Gert and Daisy' – music hall artists Elsie and Doris Waters – were recruited by Lord Woolton, Minister of Food, to add light relief to the recipes and food tips that were broadcast every morning*

In the matter of drinking, the war left much to be desired. Churchill opposed rationing tea as 'the only luxury of the working woman, whose morale should not be jeopardised' (he could probably not conceive of the idea that men drank tea; when offered a cup at an RAF station he replied 'Good God, no, my wife drinks that. I'll have a brandy.'). But he lost that battle and people were admonished by a jingle which ran:

> One spoon each and none for the pot,
> When you make tea you mustn't use a lot,
> Just one spoon each and none for the pot.

Pubs were crowded and glasses were in short supply – often you had to wait to pounce on an empty one and hand it back at the bar – but the beer, though unrationed, was always running out. When you got it, it was watery, to say the least. 'Don't think much of this wartime beer,' said a cloth-capped character in a cartoon. 'Nor me,' his drinking companion agreed. 'I'll be glad when I've had enough.' Spirits were harder to get unless you 'knew someone' and didn't mind the expense. Ernie Preedy, a Romford market trader, recalled deciding to have a party and looking for something to have it with. 'Somebody comes along and says, "We've got Scotch to sell." It was expensive, 25s for a bottle of Scotch then. But when we actually drank it, it was hooch, definitely methylated spirits, doctored. But people drank it, you put a bit of orange with it, and it didn't seem a bad drink.'

70 'Potato Pete' and 'Dr Carrot' were just two of the menagerie of cartoon creatures who were ever vocal with advice. These were 'goodies'; among the 'baddies' was the Squander Bug who urged housewives to spend more than they needed

[160]

Naturally, people who were in many cases earning more money than they had ever seen in their lives, were prepared to pay extra to improve the diet of their families. Some things, like fish and game, fruit and vegetables were never rationed. One result was the eternal fish queue, which did not disperse even when an air raid began, and there were always those who would pay high prices for luxury foods, salmon or trout, grouse and pheasant. Grapes, when they could be found, cost £1 or more a bunch and a melon might be £2. But by the end of the war, very few children knew what a banana was.

It was notorious that butchers' social standing in the community soared to great heights. They did very well for Christmas presents and were well supplied with drink and cigars. Some customers, it was said, asked them to their cocktail parties. Isobel Murphy recalled her childhood in Liverpool:

Everyone had to be nice to my father and more or less nice to us, even if they didn't like us, because my father was their butcher. A customer would bring a parcel in and another would be brought out from under the counter. I'd nudge my brother. We both knew there was a leg of lamb in that parcel and probably we had got sugar or butter in exchange. But we never thought what he was doing was anything to do with the real black market. It was a question of survival. My dad would always have a little bit of something put by, in case a neighbour's son came home on leave unexpectedly.

Besides barter there was simple favouritism. Irene Brewster remembered when she was an assistant in a Hull grocer's shop: 'You'd get a dozen tins of salmon in. Well, you had two or three hundred customers, they couldn't all have a tin of salmon, so the manager used to say, save that for Mrs So-and-So, save that for this one. We used to put one aside for ourselves, if we could. Why should they have it when we were working for it?'

'Under the counter' was the generic description of all such deals and few people were puritanical enough to be above temptation when they had families to feed. They would be disapproving only if someone else had been luckier. 'They'd say, "I know you've got some because Mrs So-and-So's had some. You've got it under the so-and-so counter, I know",' said Irene Brewster. 'Currants and raisins were wanted for Christmas cakes. We'd say, "We haven't any today" and we'd save them for the special customers. They didn't like you for it, the customers. Some who were getting the stuff did but the others used to grumble.'

Lord Woolton wrote after the war:

Because the public grew to realise the essential fairness of rationing, there were constant demands that more and more commodities should be rationed. People who found that their neighbours had occasionally been able to get tinned salmon or sardines, tinned meat or dried fruit, demanded that the Ministry should ration all these things. They did not realise the impossibility of the task. It is only possible to ration if there are sufficient supplies for everybody to have some. In the end we borrowed from the Germans a system of rationing by points. The articles that were in shortest supply cost the largest number of points.

Under the lend-lease agreement with the United States in 1941, Britain, which had run out of dollars, could postpone payment until after the war for munitions and food. This brought corned beef and Spam across the Atlantic to eke out the meat ration; spam was one of the tinned foods rationed on points. It was left to the customer to choose what his or her 'points' should be spent on each month. Corned beef hash became quite a favourite and so did Spam in the form of Spam fritters (the mysterious name actually stood for 'Supply Pressed American Meat'). Dried eggs were also US imports, which were forced on Lord Woolton by the uncertainties of shipping. One consignment of millions of shell eggs had been kept hanging about on the New York dockside and by the time it arrived, Liverpool dockers had to be paid extra to unload the hatches. The eggs were finally disposed of by being dropped down a disused mine at Skelmersdale by the truckload.

Restaurants, including the extremely cheap, one-shilling-a-head 'British Restaurants' provided by local authorities, enjoyed a boom during the war; eating out saved rations at home. From 1942, restaurants, however smart, were not allowed to charge more than 5 shillings per meal, only one main course could be served and most choices on the menu were swiftly 'off'. Horsemeat was certainly served but never mentioned – although the Commons dining-room menu included 'Canapé Cheval' on occasion.

Later, almost at the end of the war in January 1945, the oily delights of whalemeat steaks were offered as a fish course, and the notorious tinned snoek (actually barracuda) made its appearance, to be the subject of innumerable jokes.

There were 1.5 million allotments by 1943 and half the manual workers in the country were digging for victory in their spare time in gardens or allotments, advised by 'Mr Middleton' in his weekly gardening talk on the radio. Windowboxes grew tomato plants, rubbish dumps and bomb sites grew marrows, railway sidings and the edges of football pitches were planted with potatoes – even the moat of the Tower of London was full of pea- and bean-poles. But this could only dent the problems of an island that imported 60 per cent of its food in peacetime. The answer had to be intensive farming: mechanisation, chemical fertilisation and ploughing-up of spare grassland or wasteland on a huge scale. There was certainly room for improvement because agriculture had been grossly neglected during the Twenties and thirties when the price of corn fell to its lowest for 300 years. Sir Emrys Jones, wartime cultivation officer for Gloucestershire, was born on a farm in mid-Wales and remembered the changeover from the scythe to horse-drawn mowing machines and binders. Tractors only began to arrive in any number in the late 1930s. 'As far as the countryside was concerned, I can only describe it as a wilderness in modern terms. The hedges were overgrown, the whole place ridden with millions of rabbits. It looked hardly possible to grow any sort of corn crop; if the rabbits didn't have it, the mildew caught it.'

Tractors and fertilisers were rationed and allocated by the War Agricultural Executive Committees, which set production targets for each county. Farms were graded for efficiency: A, the top-class 10 per cent; B, moderately good; and C, bad farmers who were told to pull their socks up and who, if they failed to do so, could have their land taken away from them. Despite the reluctance of fellow farmers, who made up the district committees, to do this, quite a few were evicted, whereupon the 'War Ag', as it was called, had to take over and farm the land instead. Ten million acres of grassland were ploughed up (a subsidy of £2 an acre was paid for this) and much of the additional 17 million acres of derelict moorland and marshland were brought into cultivation, some of it for the first time since Saxon days. It meant revolutionary changes in the conservative countryside, as John Wheeler, a farm worker, realised when he worked for the Mendip district War Ag:

> We started up with a few tractors and a few men and, as the farmers requested us, we moved out into the surrounding countryside ploughing up land which had been requisitioned to be ploughed. It made a tremendous impact because, instead of the old horse-drawn vehicles, they'd begin to see the first agricultural machinery. The local farmers didn't really appreciate us coming and ploughing up their best bit of pasture. Many of them were a bit canny and gave us the roughest ground to plough, land that was lying derelict. Through doing that they increased their production.

Farmers, being individualist, did not appreciate being told what to do with their land, even by other farmers. 'The bigger farmer resists and says he can't get the seed to plant it; when is the government going to send it?' wrote Victoria Sackville-West from Kent. 'They resent being dictated to.' Sir Emrys Jones remembers farmers threatening him and his local agricultural committee district chairman with guns, but they appreciated the subsidies that war brought for drainage, ploughing, fertilising – virtually all branches of farming. 'There was no trouble at all in getting subsidies through government. They would bring the money down in a barrel for an extra bit of food.'

The shortage of 100,000 farm workers who had left the land before 1940 was wiped out partly by the 80,000-strong Women's Land Army, partly by 40,000 Italian and German prisoners of war and by some conscientious objectors who were given farm labouring as an alternative form of war work. There were also campaigns to persuade troops on leave, factory workers and school children on holiday to 'lend a hand on the land' at a farming holiday

PLOUGH NOW! by day and night

GROW FOOD FOR THE NATION
FEEDING STUFFS FOR YOUR FARMS
KEEP OUR SHIPS AND MONEY FREE
FOR BUYING VITAL ARMS

71 *The landscape of Britain was altered as 10 million acres of grassland and 17 million acres of wasteland were ploughed to grow crops to save imports. Farmers were encouraged to plough by night as well as by day – ignoring the black-out – by a subsidy of £2 for every acre brought into cultivation*

camp. Wartime farming proved a remarkable success story. Crop acreage more than doubled, the number of tractors quadrupled and between them they produced record harvests.

As farm machinery made more and more impact, agriculture took off. Food imports were halved, then reduced to a third of their pre-war level. All in all, the 1940s saw the change from neglect and near-wilderness to the beginnings of scientific farming – 'more changes probably than in the whole of the history of agriculture', according to Sir Emrys Jones. And, unlike in previous wars, farming did not return to depression once the war was over. 'The war made British agriculture what it is, one of the most efficient in the world.'

Food was the main, ever-present, preoccupation of most civilians. The drabness of daily diet was relieved by small treats and tiny victories – an extra orange, a present of a chicken or a rabbit (even a Christmas turkey) from the country, the hens starting to lay, watching eagerly the first tomatoes ripening, the discovery that it was a good year for blackberries – or crab apples or quinces – for making jam or jelly. One legacy that marked those who lived through it for years afterwards, possibly for life, was a feeling of uneasiness at the sight of food left on a plate. However unappetising, wartime meals were finished to the last morsel, the plates scraped or wiped almost as clean as if they had not been used.

But it was not only food that was short. Sooner or later there was a shortage of almost everything and the oddest thing acquired rarity value. Paper, for example. It was a matter of course to write on the back of letters, to readdress envelopes several times, to plaster one economy label over another, to save all paper bags and wrappings and to smooth out the brown paper from parcels to use again – and again. The genteelest lavatories were provided with home-cut squares of newsprint on a spike or string and there was much discussion of which newspapers were best for the purpose. Books carried the legend 'produced in conformity with the authorised economy standards', while their pages were spotted with impurities from the re-pulping and were so thin that the type on the reverse side showed through.

Cleanliness was another problem, owing to the short supply of both fuel and soap. Fuel rationing was narrowly voted down by Tory MPs in 1942, when coal stocks were at their lowest, but instead the public were persuaded that it was their patriotic duty to take fewer baths and to run no more than five inches of bath water. Many baths were shared – excusing another inch or two. In some perverse way this seemed an honourable and British depriva-tion. The response saved even more coal than had been requested. Plimsoll lines to indicate the five-inch level appeared round baths in hotels and public baths and it was widely believed, on what authority nobody quite knew, that the King had had such lines painted round all the baths in Buckingham Palace. Soap was rationed in 1942, one tablet (or three ounces in various forms) being allowed every four weeks. Shaving soap was unrationed but hard to find; razor blades were even harder and often were made to last longer by running them round the inside of a glass tumbler – that was, provided you had not broken your last tumbler.

Glasses were seldom to be had. Neither were cups. There was a crockery and bottle famine, and you could only buy a bottle of beer if you presented an empty. At one time the only cups made were without handles, and cutlery, especially kitchen implements, was also in short supply. The manufacture of soup spoons was totally prohibited and sugar spoons were chained to café counters. You could spend weeks on the look-out for a bicycle, a bottle, a thermos flask, a ballcock, an alarm clock, a lighter, a comb, a pram, or even matches, pens, pencils, packets of rubber teats, needles, kirby grips, or safety pins – so widespread were the scarcities. Many household goods could only be bought secondhand. A children's birthday party would be a nightmare to

72 This Anton cartoon from Punch was a comment on the plaster tiered wedding cakes that still decorated confectioners' shop windows. Icing cakes was a forbidden activity under the austerity regulations

"Are you ready to cut the cake, Madam?"

organise for there were no toys, no crackers, no balloons, no paper hats and a regulation which stated: 'No person shall put or cause to be put any sugar on the exterior of a cake after the same has been baked.' Tiered wedding cakes in confectioners' windows (and at weddings) were usually made of cardboard or plaster of Paris, and could be hired for decoration.

Two of the most annoying shortages were of tobacco and cosmetics. Cigarette queues wasted much time and patience and the favoured brands often disappeared under the counter to regular customers, leaving Turkish or Rhodesian or nothing at all for casual callers. After a twelve-hour night shift at a Sheffield shell factory, Mona Marshall remembered, one girl would start queueing for cigarettes on a Monday and by Wednesday would still be queueing all day, not having had any sleep. Cosmetics production was down to a quarter of the pre-war level and, as luck would have it, the fashion was for a heavily made-up look, with red, red lips and face powder plastered on thickly. Women melted down the ends of lipsticks, cooked beetroot juice was suggested as replacement, and even more drastic home-made substitutes were tried. 'We put our fingers up the chimney to get a little bit of soot to put on our eyes and we looked for long red liquorice sweets – that would be our lipstick,' said Elsie Thompson, recalling her eighteen-year-old days when she worked

73 *Queuing for almost
every necessity took up
much of women's lives.
Fish queues (fish being
unrationed) were some of
the longest. Even an air
raid would not disperse
them*

in the NAAFI and lived for dancing. It was easier to make up her legs, to resemble the stockings she had not got: 'We used to put this gravy browning all over our legs and your friend would stand at the back with a black pen or eyebrow pencil and she'd mark a seam down the back. Mind you, if it rained, you were in a right mess. The dogs used to come round, sniffing your legs.'

Alongside the shortages ran the constant appeals for salvage. The earlier of these was the notorious aluminium appeal launched by Lord Beaverbrook ('We will turn your pots and pans into Spitfires and Hurricanes') and organised through the WVS, whose chief, Lady Reading, broadcast in July 1940: 'We can all have the tiny thrill of thinking, as we hear the news of an epic battle in the air, perhaps it was my saucepan that made part of that Hurricane!' The stuff poured in, the sacrifices were made with enormous enthusiasm. Lord Harrowby donated the aluminium body of his Rolls Royce. Irene Brewster, newly married with a brand new set of saucepans and a three-tiered steamer she was particularly proud of, heard her husband pronounce their doom. 'He said, all these can go and I'll buy you some more. He stamped on every one of them to flatten them so that nobody could take them out of the bin. And that was the end of my poor pans. But I never did get any more. I never got a steamer like that again.'

Families with a conscience about salvage had to keep several dustbins, one for pigswill, one for paper, one for tins, one for rags, one for bones, one

74 Saucepan mountains appeared in 1940 when Lord Beaverbrook appealed for aluminium utensils to be turned into Spitfires and Hurricanes. A thousand tons were quickly contributed. Sadly, many of these sacrifices were hardly necessary, as there was plenty of scrap aluminium without them

for jamjars and bottles. Dauntless WVS workers collected rabbit fluff and dog combings to spin for wool, laddered stockings were made up into rugs and old sweaters were unravelled to be reknitted. Some 50 million books were pulped and iron railings were removed from houses, parks, churchyards and London square gardens, the weight of scrap iron salvaged reaching over a million tons. It would have been more satisfying if many of the scrap piles had not remained where they were, rusting, for years. Everywhere there were posters and advertisements condemning waste. 'Take all empty tubes – shaving cream, toothpaste, ointment, paint, etc, to your chemist: do not put with other metal salvage or the vital tin and lead will be lost in the smelting. They are wanted for munitions,' ran one of them. Salvage was a complex business.

The policy of austerity, which was carried out under Dr Hugh Dalton as President of the Board of Trade, was mitigated by the introduction of 'Utility', which applied to clothes, furniture and household utensils as well as clothing. Its principle was standardisation, the greatest possible economy of materials, and it had the virtue of good plain design, often by leading designers. But there was very little choice. From 1942, with an acute timber shortage, all furniture manufacture was reduced to twenty-two articles, each in three standard designs at fixed maximum prices and each bearing the 'Utility mark', CC41, which was to become a guarantee of quality at a

75 Railings from houses, parks, churchyards and the gardens of London squares all joined the salvage drive. Some people thought cities looked friendlier without them. A million tons of scrap iron was salvaged

reasonable price. A 4ft. 6in. double bed in the first Utility range cost £3 10s 9d in oak and £4 11s in mahogany, and you could furnish a new home with twelve items for £54 in oak, or £73 in mahogany. Sir Gordon Russell, chairman of the Utility design panel, felt that the scheme did much for British taste and raised the whole standard of furniture for the mass of people. 'Good Lord, it wasn't the best work I've ever done but it was the most important. At least furniture never went back to what it was before the war – thank God.'

The Utility mark, CC41, stood for 'Civilian Clothing' and the date 1941, which was the year that clothes rationing began. At first, 66 coupons a year were allocated, intended to cover one complete outfit (a man's overcoat took 16 coupons, a woman's 14) but by the next year they were reduced to 48, which meant that a family might have to pool its coupons in order to send a father or working mother respectably to the office or, while uniform was still insisted on, a child to a new school. Utility clothes, which accounted for 80 per cent of output, were standard designs made from a restricted range of materials at controlled prices, sometimes little more than half the uncontrolled price for non-utility garments. Since the women's range were designed by such top names as Hartnell, Molyneux and Hardy Amies, among others, they were greatly sought after. The regulations did not permit more than so much cloth per garment and strictly regulated the number of pleats, pockets or buttons, or the maximum length of skirt allowed. Fashion settled on a standard, square-shouldered, boxy look, with a straight skirt to just below the knee and an absence of trimmings. Some liked its simplicity, others found it too severe – 'civilian battledress'. Constance Holt, wartime editor of *Woman's Own* was one who approved:

They were plainer than the sort of dresses people had been buying before but they were good trim lines. Before the war there had been a lot of bits and bobs and what you might call 'in bad taste' clothing. I remember one of my directors saying, 'Don't the girls look good walking about the streets, don't they look good!' They were wearing well cut, well shaped clothes. I didn't hear any grumbles about them at the time.

Fashion historian Doris Langley Moore was not so impressed:

They were dreary and drab. I never wanted anything that was utility – the quality was shoddy. I think people felt quite happy with the food rationing, quite patriotic about it, but I don't think they were ever wildly happy about their clothes. Of course, the French fashion industry just carried on with many of the same couturiers making clothes just as lavishly as before for the German conquerors and continuing in a main stream of fashion. That's why in 1947, very soon after the end of the war, Dior brought out his feminine sloping shoulders, nipped-in waists and very full skirts, the 'New Look'. The government resented it very much

76 and 77 'Utility' became a new trademark from 1941 onwards. Furniture-making was simplified to twenty-two articles in standard designs, some of them grouped together here. Utility clothing accounted for 80 per cent of what was on offer: the amount of material and trimmings used was severely controlled

and urged women not to buy these new vulgar fashions. But we wanted that kind of thing and as soon as we could, we got it.

One innovation that caught on everywhere was the head scarf, or turban, which began as a safety measure to keep hair out of factory machines, recommended by the Ministry of Labour. It was adopted everywhere by women seeking a quick cover-up for hair which they had neither the time nor the shampoo to do properly. Until then headscarves were part of peasant costume. 'Headscarves were not well looked upon when they first appeared, made of rayon not silk,' said Doris Langley Moore, 'but they were widely adopted because they were easy to put on, although hairstyles were sort of birds' nests on top of the head, and the head scarf over that was not a very good design for surrounding the face.' One very useful fashion innovation was the siren suit, which zipped up as you dashed for the shelter, and was popularised by Churchill. And women wore trousers, known as 'slacks', for all kinds of work from ambulance- and lorry-driving to air-raid warden or land-girl duties. Women's trousers were never made with turn-ups but, it now seems strange to reflect, the prohibition of men's turn-ups to save cloth was looked on with great hostility and dismay. No one would then have predicted that the turn-up's peacetime days were also numbered; at the time men felt naked without their reassuring weight at the bottom of their narrowed trousers. For women, trousers had the added convenience of making stockings, which required two scarce coupons a pair, unnecessary – far too much time had to be spent hunting down stockings as it was. Hats, however, were never rationed and were the chief way of 'dressing up' the standard two-piece suit or plain black dress for an occasion.

Most people for most of the time had to put up with the clothes they had, which men on the whole were quite happy to do, since shabbiness and the old, leather-patched sports jackets they tended to prefer were sanctioned now by austerity. Women exercised ingenuity in making clothes from all sorts of unlikely material. Curtain material, even black-out material, was used to make swirling skirts; parachute silk was cut up for underclothes or used to make wedding dresses; children's clothes were made out of their parents' discards ('Never mind when father's grey flannels get too worn for him to wear. They'll make a most attractive skirt for your daughter'). The WVS ran clothing exchanges for growing children and 'Make Do and Mend' was the slogan for renovations and alterations to the millions of garments sent over from the United States and the Dominions as gifts.

Even grey army blankets could be turned into something unrecognisable, as Irene Brewster discovered when the WVS gave her some after she was bombed out. 'They gave me two great big army blankets and somebody said, "Do you want to have a coat made with that? Mrs Carter will make you one." So I went to Mrs Carter and she made me a beautiful swagger coat and I had it dyed maroon. It lasted for years.' 'Make Do and Mend' was encouraged by another sickly puppet character offering advice in the advertisements – Mrs Sew and Sew, the creation of the Board of Trade, whose publicity never caught the public's enthusiasm like the Ministry of Food's did. 'To discard clothes that are not completely worn out is as unpatriotic as to waste good food,' ran one of their advertisements, recommending 'Patriotic Patches' as something to be proud of.

Stockings were one of the mainstays of the black market, where they sold for upwards of 5 shillings a pair. The 'Spiv', with his camel-hair coat, wide lapels, wide tie but thin moustache, beneath a gangster-like trilby worn at a jaunty angle, was to be found in every market and could be relied on to supply stockings – or clothing coupons themselves. On the whole, Spivs were tolerated as amusing figures who might have stepped out of Ben Jonson's *Bartholomew Fair*, and comedians like Sid Field were loved for their imitations of them. People were too fed up with shortages and regulations to take a holier-than-thou attitude to defeating austerity in small ways. Blind eyes were turned to market traders who didn't ask for clothes coupons but adjusted the price.

But there were organised criminals who planned to defeat rationing on a big commercial scale, and this was the sort of black market that the police were concerned about. Jock Joiner, a CID officer in the Leicester police force, dealt with break-ins at warehouses, factories or garages where sugar, butter, cloth, or petrol coupons were stolen.

> We had a well known hosiery factory broken into one weekend. Thousands of pounds worth of stockings were stolen and they found their way on to the London black market. They forced the lock on a Friday night, got a van inside and then put a fresh lock on, so the offence wasn't discovered till Monday morning. By that time the stuff was all down in London, on the market. Very valuable commodity, ladies' stockings.

The docks and railways were, of course, prime opportunities for rationed goods to go astray. The classic set-up required a corrupt checker, a lorry-driver accomplice and a dealer to receive the unaccounted-for goods. Peter Gannon, who worked for the Port of London Authority police, explained: 'The lorry would arrive in the docks for, say, 100 sides of beef and the checker would ask him if he wanted some extras. If he was that way inclined, he'd take 110, sign for 100 and then, on the way to Smithfield, drop the extra off at a butcher's shop. Or, if it was fruit, at a greengrocer's shop.'

Statistics of railway thefts were pretty staggering. The LMS lost more than half a million pounds' worth of merchandise in 1941 and the other railway companies – the Great Western, LNER and Southern – lost another half a million between them. The railway police, men brought back from retirement in many cases, were not very energetic and were past running after thieves, claimed Cliff Harrison, an LNER train-driver. Drivers, too, had their perks. 'When the fish trains came in, the fish was transferred to horse-drawn wagons. Then one of the boxes would come off the back of the wagon and we'd have a couple of haddock, or four kippers on a shovel, cooked up in the engine.'

The largest black market theft of its kind occurred when the new clothing ration books for the district of Romford were awaiting distribution at the local food office. They were in the charge of Fred Barnes, the district food officer:

> It was an old house with a huge cellar and I thought, this is the place for the ration books to be stored. I fixed two huge padlocks on the cellar door, an electric alarm bell, and had two night watchmen sitting in the office, in touch with the police, with strict instructions not to open the door to anyone. One morning the police rang – 'You've been done, your ration books have gone' – and I just couldn't believe it. The cellar had an outside lavatory over its far end and the thieves had pulled up the floorboards of the lavatory, hopped through on to the ration books and loaded them into sacks. Meanwhile the watchmen upstairs were ringing through and saying 'Everything under control'.

With a street value of £5 per book of coupons, there were about £500,000 worth, about £7 million at today's prices. 'In other words, it compared with the Great Train Robbery,' said Fred Barnes. 'It wasn't the sort of thing you mentioned – you would destroy confidence in the rationing system. It got no publicity, thank God.'

The 'basic' petrol ration, enough for about 120 miles of motoring a month at first, was reduced and then withdrawn altogether in 1942. As a result the number of cars on the road fell to 700,000, compared with 2 million pre-war, and any driver could be stopped and asked if his journey was really necessary. People could still get petrol coupons for 'essential' travel, however, and it was possible to obtain black-market coupons or petrol, usually 'commercial' petrol, which was dyed red. An ingenious use was found for the disregarded gas mask: by pouring petrol through its filter, the red dye was removed. Joy-riding was a risky business, though. If you used your petrol allowance for purposes other than that for which it was granted, you could be prosecuted and jailed, as Ivor Novello was – for four weeks.

Many people were prosecuted for black-market offences, but most of them were small fry. Obviously, from some of the above examples, there were bigger fry organising break-ins and thefts. 'The black-out was a thieves' paradise,' said Jock Joiner. 'I went to back-street warehouses that were stacked from top to bottom with sugar, butter, flour and tinned stuff. People made a lot of money.' And yet, since the essence of a successful black-market coup is that nobody hears about it, it is hard to estimate how serious the black market was. The Ministry of Food employed 900 inspectors on the look-out

"The price of petrol has been increased by one penny."—Official.

78 This Daily Mirror *cartoon was a powerful reminder of the true cost of petrol in the lives of seamen braving the U-boats. But Churchill took it as a slur on the profits of capitalism and the* Daily Mirror *was reprimanded, even threatened with suppression*

for major offences. The penalties in fines (£500) and imprisonment (two years) were very heavy, and black-marketeers could in addition forfeit three times the capital involved in the illegal transactions – quite enough to ruin them. 'The fact that, in spite of all the scarcity of supplies and the rigidity of rationing, there was little or no black market in Britain was a tribute to the British people,' wrote Lord Woolton. He may have been looking on the rosy side a little, but it is hard to disagree with him.

All the privations of austerity bore most heavily of all on one type of person, the housewife – unglamorous, unappreciated and unsung. She was the one whom all the exhortations were aimed at – to shop and cook and clean and salvage, to save fuel and food and clothing, to make do and mend, to raise livestock and vegetables, to sacrifice her own rations of food or clothes if necessary for the sake of her family – and on top of this do a wartime job, full-time or part-time, as well. Mary Bloomfield was a policeman's wife, who also worked in the council offices in Coventry.

I was just an ordinary housewife. I worked nine to five-thirty and until twelve-thirty on Saturday, so you did everything else – washing, ironing, washing your hair, whatever cooking you could do in advance, everything like that, on a Sunday. I would never have dreamt of doing the washing on a Sunday before the war. I was cleaning my floor one Sunday afternoon and I suddenly thought, I don't know how long it is since I was in town. So I went. It was deserted. Everyone was doing what I was doing, straightening up their homes so that they could go to work on Monday morning.

I was brave during the war. I never complained to my husband. I never whimpered. I did what had to be done – spent hours on my own in the shelter and lived by routine, just like other women. That's what kept us going – routine. But it was misery for 99 women out of 100. We lost our husbands or sons or parents. We suffered from grief. But everything that happened to us we accepted. We were very different people. Our peaceful life was shattered and we were never the same again.

CHAPTER EIGHT

TIME OFF FROM WAR

WORLD WAR TWO was the first war of the radio era and with the war, the medium came of age as an organ of national consciousness. The pre-war BBC, which its director-general Sir John Reith handed to the nation as his legacy on resigning in 1938, spoke to only half the people, at most, although there were 9 million 'wireless' licences in 1939. On Sundays the BBC remembered the Sabbath day and kept it unbearably holy: church services, organ music, appeals for good causes and talks about cathedrals were the staple output, unsullied by anything that could cause levity, even light music. The news was read by announcers who used to put on dinner jackets to do it, although they were invisible, and they all had indistinguishable 'BBC' accents behind which they maintained anonymity. Suddenly there was a huge audience confined to their homes by the black-out, with nothing else to do but listen in. They did not enjoy what they heard on the Home Service (as the National Programme was now named), consisting as it did of news bulletins (when there was virtually no news), religious services and a surfeit of the BBC 'theatre organ' – hours of it, played by one Sandy McPherson – varied by pep talks on such themes as 'Making the Most of Dried Fruit'. There were loud complaints and a massive switchover by the troops in France to Radio Fécamp, a French commercial station, or to German stations.

This was a challenge that the BBC could hardly ignore. Reith's BBC had given the listeners what Reith thought good for them; now the Corporation had to ask the troops what they actually wanted to hear. The result was the new Forces Programme, instituted in February 1940, which concentrated on sport, variety and dance music, besides news bulletins. Soon its audience, at home as well as among the troops, was one and a half times the audience for the traditional Home Service. The BBC had taken the first step towards identifying with the majority of its audience, instead of remaining stuffily aloof from them. The war was to bring it right out of its ivory tower.

The news was easily the most avidly listened to of the BBC's programmes once France had fallen. The nine o'clock news bulletin regularly attracted an audience of half (sometimes two-thirds) of the adult population. The newsreaders – Alvar Lidell, Frank Phillips, Bruce Belfrage, Joseph MacLeod and others – began to announce their names ('Here is the news and this is X reading it'), so that listeners came to recognise and to trust these voices. They were pictured in the *Radio Times*, giving details of their backgrounds and hobbies (most of them had been singers in earlier life). Halfway through the war, to show that the BBC recognised that not all regions of the country spoke in a standard accent, they were joined by the Yorkshire tones of Wilfred Pickles.

Trust was all-important. Was the BBC to become a tool of the government, the poodle of the new Ministry of Information, just as German radio was the tool of Dr Goebbels and his Ministry of Propaganda? The listener needed to believe that it was not. The Ministry's job was to 'guide' the BBC, which had to submit the names of its broadcasters and their scripts for approval; this gave the Ministry powers of censorship on the grounds of national security which it would be hard to refuse in times of war. Somewhere in Broadcasting House there was a 'switch censor' who could press a button and cut off a programme in mid-air if it deviated from its approved script, but this was not the same as telling the BBC what it had to say, although there were plenty of public busybodies who would like to have done so. The service ministries, for example, thought of news as a nuisance and were very reluctant to divulge details of their operations. The BBC benefited, if no one else did, from the acknowledged incompetence of the Ministry of Information in its early days under a series of unhappy ministers, including Reith himself, but eventually Brendan Bracken, a personal friend of Churchill's, was appointed Minister in 1941 and deliberately sought the BBC's co-operation. He refused to interfere in BBC policy, saying in 1943, 'The governors and staff often consult us and sometimes they condescend to ask us for advice. But no attempt has been made to influence the news-giving or any other programme.'

This was not precisely true of the earlier, jumpier phase of the war in 1940–1, as the case of J. B. Priestley demonstrated. His 9.15 Sunday evening *Postscripts* after the news on the Home Service were designed to stop the audience switching over promptly to Hamburg radio and Lord Haw-Haw to see if they could learn more. When Priestley began to give them in June 1940, immediately after Dunkirk, listeners recognised that here was a broadcaster of rare compulsiveness who was saying what many of them wanted to hear, and not in a 'BBC' voice. Priestley soon averaged an audience of 30 per cent or more of the adult population, a percentage only exceeded, on occasions, by Churchill. Critic Peter Black in his unofficial history of the BBC, *The Biggest Aspidistra in the World*, wrote:

> He was instinctively in touch with what his hearers felt. Spoken in a voice as rich and unpretentious as a good Christmas pudding, the effect was overwhelming. As his popularity grew he developed the vein of social

79 'Here is the news and this is Alvar Lidell reading it . . .' War brought the BBC newsreaders out of their anonymity and made them national celebrities. A regular audience of at least half the adult population listened devoutly to the nine o'clock news. Lidell, like many of the newsreaders a former singer, was photographed in an underground studio in Broadcasting House beside his bunk

comment and criticism that ran through all his best work – a refusal to forget that things were wrong with Britain that ought to be put right. I, and virtually everybody I knew, felt enormously uplifted by this powerful voice. He said what most of us knew was right and just.

One of the things he said was wrong was that a house he knew, left empty by an absentee owner who had gone to America for the war, was being left empty instead of being requisitioned for the homeless and its ground used for allotments. This was the sort of comment that made property-owners nervous. Letters began to be written accusing him of getting political, and mutterings of complaint and alarm were heard on the Conservative back benches. Priestley took himself off the air for the winter, but when he returned in January 1941 he sounded even more like the voice of Us against Them in condemning the old, bad, social system which obtained before the war and arguing for change after it. His broadcasts were as popular as ever, and at times he reached an audience of 20 million. A deputation from the Tory back-bench 1922 Committee protested to the Minister of Information at his reappearance on the air and Churchill himself complained that a *Postscript* had expressed war aims that he did not subscribe to; it was inevitable that they would be stopped. A minute duly appeared of a BBC board meeting in March: 'Priestley series stopping on instructions of Minister'. If it was on the 'instructions' of the Minister (of Information, presumably), the BBC had failed to stand by the most popular and influential broadcaster it had yet discovered in war. No subsequent *Postscript*-giver ever matched his power of uplifting the audience.

Graham Greene wrote after his departure, 'We shall never know how much this country owed to Mr Priestley last summer. For those dangerous months when the Gestapo arrived in Paris, he was unmistakably a great man.'

Perhaps that was the trouble. Priestley himself claimed he was never given the real reason for being gagged; the BBC blamed the Ministry and the Ministry blamed the BBC. To the end of his life he believed that the initiative for taking him off the air came from the man who could be described as his only broadcasting rival – Churchill himself. His muzzling was by no means unwelcome to some of the nervous BBC mandarins. As Priestley wrote of the episode, 'To its senior administrators, men who wanted a quiet life and an hour or two in the garden, I looked like trouble . . . when I left, the sigh of relief followed me down the street.'

If the BBC was not brave enough to champion Priestley against the powers that be, it also appeared shifty and lacking in courage over its next great popular hit, *The Brains Trust*. *The Brains Trust* (originally *Any Questions?*) seems an obvious enough idea in retrospect, but at the time it seemed original and daring. BBC talks and discussions in Reithian times were a form of enlightenment, handed down from the summit by experts who could not be questioned to the grateful populace waiting in ignorance at their receivers. The prime attraction of *The Brains Trust* was hearing the 'Brains' disagree and argue with one another. They were often asked to discourse on

80 *The Brains Trust was listened to by 11 million people who delighted in the arguments of the regular panellists, Dr Cyril Joad, Julian Huxley and Commander Campbell – seen here (left to right) with question master Donald McCullough (centre) and behind him the programme's producer, Howard Thomas*

quirky and less serious questions – 'How does a fly land on the ceiling?' 'Why do women always have cold knees?', 'Why nod your head for Yes and shake it for No?' (they didn't know the answers) – as well as on subjects on which anyone could have views, such as 'What is civilisation?' The resident team of Brains, assembled by the producer Howard Thomas, was astutely balanced to provide a charismatic, unpredictable mixture of human characteristics. Julian Huxley, secretary of the London Zoological Society, had scientific prestige. Dr C. E. M. Joad, teacher and populariser of philosophy, offered lucid expositions of ideas and could be snappish ('Astrology is bunk' was one of his best-known short answers). The third 'regular', Commander A. B. Campbell (RN, retd.) was the endearing and irrepressible non-expert on everything, with a stock of amazing sailor's yarns, exotic experiences (often beginning 'When I was in Patagonia') and eccentric acquaintances. He sorely tried the patience of the two intellectuals but that was part of the entertainment. He would assure them and us, perfectly seriously, that he knew a man whose head 'steamed' whenever he ate marmalade. This was not allowed to become the general level of discussion. The panel took the listeners' questions seriously and debated them with no thought of scoring a cheap point or getting an easy laugh (there was no studio audience, the bane of so many 'discussion' programmes since).

The questions poured in: 3000 postcards a week arrived from servicemen and civilians, while the audience climbed to 10 or 11 million a week. The trio became celebrated national figures – perhaps the first non-professional entertainers to be so elevated through radio alone. They were joined by many eminent panelists – Bertrand Russell, William Beveridge, Ellen Wilkinson, Jennie Lee, Barbara Ward, but it was the original three who were the favourites.

Why did this simple idea take off to such an extent that local 'Brains Trusts' sprang up all over the country and abroad, in Army or Air Force units, schools and institutions, towns and villages? It was partly that the programme satisfied a widespread hunger for (fairly) serious argument and discussion. It was partly because it came so unexpectedly from the paternalistic BBC to allow, indeed positively encourage, a questioning, slightly sceptical outlook. Huxley, for example, expounded the case for Humanism and Joad, in his dry, high-pitched cackle, argued without academic stuffiness for truth, beauty, and tolerance in moral questions (later he proved tolerant to a fault over the matter of not paying for his tickets on the railways).

People found it liberating to be encouraged to think for themselves instead of being told what to think by superior persons – at which point superior persons (politicians, the Archbishop of Canterbury, academics, the BBC board of governors among them) began to feel very uneasy. So much popular influence for non-conformists was not what the ruling class expected and it was jealous. Sniping at the programme became standard practice in educated circles and the heavier weeklies. The BBC's controller of programmes, Basil Nicolls, who already vetted the questions personally, directed that discussion of religion should be excluded. The Archbishop complained that no one on the panel represented the orthodox Christian viewpoint; he was assuaged by the founding of an all-churchmen's 'Brains Trust' programme, which failed to excite anyone. By 1943 the governors, who had been itching to interfere, took matters into their own hands, banning religious and political questions altogether and 'questions that might embarrass the government over foreign policy or the war effort'. An example of a question which they deemed too hot to handle politically was 'Should there be equal pay?'

It was a tribute to the power of radio that three such non-political speakers – a philosopher, a biologist and a raconteur – should be so feared by the authorities that a governors' edict went out that they must no longer appear all together. 'The governors considered them too powerful,' said Howard Thomas. 'They insisted they were rationed to one appearance every three weeks. I was told no religion, no more politics. This programme was more than a programme, it had become something of a power and the BBC governors were trying to dilute it.' Soon after that Thomas resigned, but the show continued, without much loss of popularity, until 1949. Its tendency to start people thinking had caused the BBC to be regarded as 'dangerously subversive' in some quarters.

The BBC was never accused of subversion through its variety programmes, however. The war was a boom time for comedians. It could be said that anyone with the slightest degree of comic talent could get an ENSA booking for *Workers' Playtime*, a twice-weekly factory canteen entertainment dreamed up by Ernest Bevin in 1941. It was played to easily pleased audiences longing for relief from the relentless war production-line. If they were lucky, they got Elsie and Doris Waters, George Formby or Flanagan and Allen. They might, on a red-letter day, have got Robb Wilton, a bucolic monologist with beautiful timing and the sort of ruminative style which might have been given by Shakespeare to one of the yokels in Dogberry's Watch. Wilton always began: 'The day war broke out, my missus said to me . . . What are *you* going to do about it?' When he did do something about it, by putting on his Home Guard uniform, she was sceptical as usual.

> The missus looked at me and said, 'What are you supposed to be?' I said, 'Supposed to be? I'm one of the Home Guards.' She said, 'One of the Home Guards, what are the others like?' She said, 'What are you supposed to do?' I said, 'I'm supposed to stop Hitler's army landing.' She said, 'What *you*?' I said, 'No, not me, there's Bob Edwards, Charlie Evans, Billy Brightside – there's seven or eight of us, we're on guard in a little hut behind the Dog and Pullet.'

Whole books have been devoted to the phenomenal success of *ITMA*, a

81 *The mystery of* ITMA's *stranglehold on the nation's attention is not made much clearer by this picture in which Tommy Handley is telephoned simultaneously by two of his regular callers, Funf the spy (Jack Train, left) and Signor So-So (Dino Galvani, right)*

programme which began on the eve of the war, when the *Daily Express* repeated a running headline to denote Hitler's latest doings – 'It's That Man Again' (it was also assuring its readers that 'there will be no war this year'). When the prophecy was proved wrong and there was a wartime outburst of institutions known by their initials, It's That Man Again was shortened to ITMA for the programme. That Man was Tommy Handley, a fast-talking Liverpool comedian, who was already a familiar star of radio but who had never had a show built round him such as Arthur Askey had with *Band-Wagon*. A weekly comedy show with a fixed cast was a new development. Instead of a partner or straight man, such as Askey had in Richard Murdoch, Handley was given a cast – a whole world – of lunatics with absurd names, caricatured voices, and memorable catch-phrases or tricks of speech. As everybody knows, the entire national audience, which increased to 16 million on both Home and Forces programmes when the show became a regular fixture in 1941, were soon repeating them to one another. The first to catch on was the telephone voice of the spy, Funf, spoken sideways into a tumbler by Jack Train, which came out something like 'Dis iss Funf spikkig'. It was almost impossible to get through a day without somebody saying it to you, especially on the telephone. It always put the speaker into a state of euphoria – why, it is hard to explain.

Nobody who did not experience *ITMA* at the time can hope to under-stand what all the fuss was about. To listen to it now would be merely mystifying. In the scripts, Handley's lines look like a high-pitched burble of embarrassingly bad puns better forgotten. But it worked then as no radio show had worked before and few have since. This was partly because Handley had a warm cheekiness that cut through the microphone and he spoke like an express train – indeed the show induced the mesmeric effect of travelling on an express train constantly on the verge of derailment. It also freed comedy from static situations. The most important sound effect was the *ITMA* door, which opened and closed continually to admit or eject, for no reason whatever, the host of characters – or wilder improbabilities:

HANDLEY: Let's see what's in this cupboard . . .
(Door opens)
(Sound effect: horse neighing)
(Door closes)
HANDLEY: Funny place to keep a horse and cart.

Radio had not exploited the freedom of sound to play with the absurd before and it was exhilarating to hear it let itself go. As for the catch-phrases, which depended on their utter predictability, they embodied the sort of stereotypes at which the British have always loved to laugh, at least as far back as Dickens. Many of them were comic foreigners, like Funf, the incompetent German spy; Signor So-So, an Italian in an endearing muddle with the English language; or Ali-Oop, the slippery oriental postcard-pedlar who, though sent about his business, warned ingratiatingly 'I go – I come back', as they invariably do. The native characters were drawn from the national repertory of character types: Colonel Chinstrap, in eternal search of liquid refreshment, saying thickly, 'Brandy, sir? I don't mind if I do'; Mrs Mopp, the classic Cockney char, with her quavery greeting 'Can I do you now, sir?' and her farewell 'Ta-ta for now', shortened to TTFN; the pair of handy-men of exaggerated deference – 'After you, Claude', 'No, after *you*, Cecil'; Miss Hotchkiss, Handley's overbearing secretary, whose withering tones, like those of Lady Bracknell, demanded, 'Mr Handlay! Do you expect anyone to listen to this rubbish?' Many of the verbal mannerisms were founded on real people whom Handley or his scriptwriter Ted Kavanagh had come across – like the diver who solicited pennies on the pier from seaside crowds ('Don't forget the diver, sir. Every penny makes the water warmer') but never actually seemed to dive for them ('I'm going down now, sir,' was the nearest he got). In war, where people were sharing so many experiences of danger, hardship or sheer dreariness, there was a great need for conversation-looseners, and *ITMA* provided a perfect recipe for helping conversation with strangers, a fund of common frivolity to draw on. Many of the catch-phrases adapted themselves to war situations – pilots waiting to dive into the attack would say over the intercom, 'After you, Claude'; no lift descended without a voice saying, 'I'm going down now, sir'; and other catch-phrases such as 'I'll have to ask me Dad' or 'It's being so cheerful as keeps me going' (spoken in a lugubrious voice) had endless possible applications. They continued to delight huge audiences for over 300 programmes into the post-war period, until Handley's sudden death in 1949. He received the unique distinction for a radio comedian of a memorial service at St Paul's and the programme died with him.

ITMA was one of the most popular shows with the forces, but their special favourite was *Sincerely Yours*, a vehicle for the 'Forces Sweetheart' Vera Lynn, who had as personal a following as Priestley or Handley did. The format of the programme was her weekly letter from home to the listening servicemen, giving messages from England along with news of such events as babies born to their wives. A thousand letters of request came in each week, often asking her on behalf of a couple to sing 'our song'. The songs requested, such as 'We'll Meet Again', 'You'll Never Know', 'Only Forever' or 'The White Cliffs of Dover', were songs with a strong emphasis on sentiment, optimism and happy reunions. This did not commend itself to the busybodies or to certain high-ups of the BBC, who thought sentimental ballads might undermine the aggressive spirit of fighting men. The board of governors 'deplored' the programme. The controller of programmes suggested 'more virile lyrics' and the 'elimination of crooning, sentimental numbers, drivelling words, slush, innuendoes and so on'. He favoured waltzes, marches and cheerful music. So did the War Office, as Howard Thomas, who produced the programme, remembered:

82 *The 'Forces' Sweetheart' herself received a thousand requests a week to sing 'our song' for faraway servicemen and those they had left at home. Amazingly, the BBC controllers and the War Office brasshats thought Vera Lynn's songs would sap the men's fighting spirit*

> The War Office thought that this sentimentality was sapping the will to win and was a little dangerous. The Air Force had a different view. They thought it was inspiring and sent men off on their missions with a good heart. The Navy was also pleased with the sentiment of it. But the generals of the War Office muttered in their beards about what it was doing to the Army's morale.

There was an element of the age gap and the class gap in these objections, as dance music and especially 'crooning' was then thought to appeal only to the rank-and-file and to the young. This was not true, according to Howard Thomas – plenty of requests came in from naval officers and the like. Dame Vera Lynn remembered the controversies that surrounded her name in those days but which are seldom recalled now:

> The BBC thought the programmes were too sentimental and could be lowering morale, which was ludicrous because all my letters from the men said how much the programme encouraged them. They could think of home and actually it built up their courage. It was a simple programme and the songs were simple, a bit on the corny side perhaps, but they were home-bred songs. I didn't use Americanisms and my accent stayed English. I stopped listening to American singers' records so that I wouldn't sub-consciously copy them. You couldn't help but visualise

boys sitting somewhere listening round a truck, or in a barrack room beside a bed, and I would direct my song to a person rather than to the empty air. I suppose it must have come through because they used to tell me that they felt I was singing just to them.

Ever since she became a girl singer with pre-war bands such as Ambrose, Vera Lynn insisted on choosing her own songs after visiting the music publishers to listen to what was new. 'I had to feel they were sincere. It had to feel natural to me to say these words. I wouldn't sing sexy songs or suggestive songs. I came from an ordinary working-class family and I didn't try to get sophisticated. Maybe that's why people liked me and stayed loyal.' What neither Vera Lynn nor her critics realised at the time was that she also had an audience in enemy-occupied Europe. People listening in secret to the BBC news broadcasts in Holland, Denmark or Norway would stay on in their cellar or haystack hideaways afterwards to hear her programme on Sunday evenings. Even Germans used to listen to her in secret, running a considerable risk, not only of discovery but of undermining their morale – if the War Office view was to be believed. (The Japanese actually announced her death in an air raid to demoralise their prisoners.)

By this time the pre-war BBC rule of no dance music on Sundays had long been swept away. The big bands of pre-war fame – Jack Hylton, Jack Payne, Roy Fox, Joe Loss, Ambrose – gradually lost their best musicians to the services. But there, it was soon realised, they could do better service with saxophone and trumpet than with rifle and Bren gun by forming top-class services dance bands, such as the RAF's Squadronaires, or their rivals the Skyrockets. The Army countered with the Blue Rockets and the Navy with the Blue Mariners, but the RAF always had the edge in reputation.

The Second World War produced very few popular songs of quality, nothing like as many as did the First. As a result many wartime sing-songs turned back the clock to include 'Pack Up Your Troubles' or 'Keep the Home Fires Burning', an Ivor Novello hit which he rivalled just before the second war ended with the saccharine ballad 'We'll Gather Lilacs'. The fall of France produced 'The Last Time I Saw Paris'. But the irony of the London Blitz was that a sophisticated cabaret number turned itself into the siren song of the bombing: 'A Nightingale Sang in Berkeley Square'. All kinds of people in shelters very far from the West End night-spots, in pubs and dance halls and variety theatres, sang the lyric about 'such a romantic affair' to the muffled accompaniment of the raids.

> I may be right,
> I may be wrong,
> But I'm perfectly willing to swear,
> There were angels dining at the Ritz,
> And a nightingale sang in Berkeley Square.

The glass in Berkeley Square had been shattered and a minuscule proportion of those who sang the song had any plans to dine at the Ritz at any time, with or without angels, but the song served as a token of the days when extravagant escapism would be possible again. People liked the idea of it, however unlikely they were to want it once the bombing was over.

For the most part, English World War II songs were relentlessly and martially cheerful – 'Roll Out the Barrel', 'Bless 'em All', 'Kiss Me Goodnight, Sergeant Major', 'I'm Going to Get Lit Up When the Lights Go on in London' – or they were sentimental in the Vera Lynn manner – 'That Lovely Weekend', 'Moonlight Becomes You', 'You'll Never Know'. There were few attempts at wit. The most notable was Noel Coward's 'Don't Let's Be Beastly to the Germans'; this was too subtle for the Ministry of Information, which did not realise that it was meant to be ironic.

> Don't let's be beastly to the Germans
> When our victory is ultimately won.
> It was just those nasty Nazis
> Who persuaded them to fight,
> And their Beethoven and Bach
> Are really far worse than their bite –
> Let's be meek to them,
> And turn the other cheek to them,
> And try to bring out their latent sense of fun,
> Let's give them full air parity
> And treat the rats with charity,
> But don't let's be beastly to the Hun.

Coward was invited to Chequers by Churchill in 1943 (they sang Cockney songs together) and was asked for a rendering. Churchill enjoyed it but the Minister, Brendan Bracken, continued to ban it from being broadcast or recorded because there were lines Dr Goebbels might twist. 'I am sick of the bureaucratic idiots,' fumed Coward in his diary.

But the outstanding popular song of the war was the (pre-war) German number *Lilli Marlene*, sung in the desert with as much enthusiasm by the Eighth Army as by their enemy, the Afrika Korps, who relayed it through loudspeakers to the British lines. An English version was recorded later in the war by Anne Shelton and by Marlene Dietrich, who subsequently made the song her own. Why 'Lilli of the Lamplight' exercised such fascination across national frontiers is hard to fathom, for the melody, though haunting, was uninspired and the lyrics were trite. It was simply that the competition was not up to much.

During the war people went dancing mad. The great outlet for frayed nerves, boredom or exhaustion was dancing – there were dances in the lunchbreak in factory canteens, in big *palais de danse*, at service camps and village halls, and in West End nightclubs, at the Lyceum Theatre and the Royal Opera House. Dancing in the early part of the war still meant the quickstep, the slow foxtrot and the 'last waltz', accompanied by discreet, unobtrusive bands and sedate singers. The arrival of the American troops from 1942 onwards, bringing their own bands with them, changed all this completely. Billy Amstell, a musician with the pre-war bands of Ambrose and Roy Fox, remembered the effect they had:

> We always tried to copy the American musicians because they were so much better – I don't know why, it seemed to be in the air over there. But English band leaders were very reserved; they had never wanted to offend the public. At the pre-war Embassy Club we played very softly not to drown the conversation. If Ambrose couldn't hear the dancers shuffling, the band was playing too loud. But the Americans didn't worry about playing big arrangements, some of them very loud, and the public liked it. Jive and jitterbug caught on like mad. Everything was jitterbug.

Nobody, of course, could have imagined jitterbugging to the Henry Hall or Debroy Somers bands or Victor Sylvester's Ballroom Orchestra. But there was jitterbugging by a minority to numbers like 'In the Mood' or 'Woodchoppers' Ball' before the Americans arrived. The sheer professional polish of the Glenn Miller (Army Air Force) or the Artie Shaw (US Navy) Orchestras was, however, an eye-opener even to the musicians who knew them from their records. Glenn Miller spent six months in Britain giving concerts and making broadcasts in 1944 before he took off on his fatal flight to Paris; by then the GIs had made jitterbugging more than just an exhibitionist display for a few

83 Dancing was the great outlet for frustration, boredom or the nervous strain of war – the quickstep, slow foxtrot and waltz until the GIs arrived bringing their bands, their music and jitterbugging. There wasn't much room for it here at Rainbow Corner, the American forces' club off Leicester Square

acrobatic specialists surrounded by a gaping throng. English girls had not only been converted but infused with a dynamism they did not know they had. 'They wouldn't do any of our waltzes and foxtrots, they were just jitterbugging, so naturally we learnt it quickly,' said Jessie Robins, whose small Devon village was transformed by the arrival of the GIs. 'The first night they arrived they set up a dance and we could hear the trumpets blowing and the rhythm of the music, and it was lovely. We'd hardly heard it before except in films. To hear it live was quite something. They were full of life, exciting compared to us, they were like dreams come true. That's how I felt, anyway.'

'I thought, I'll never be able to do that. I liked ballroom dancing,' said Kitty Murphy, a regular patron of the Lyceum and Covent Garden, 'But it's funny what music can do. Seeing other people do it, you easily pick it up. Thrown over shoulders and under legs. . . . Oh, dear, it was great, it was really nice.' Elsie Thompson, a Liverpool girl who used to go to Burtonwood US Air Force base, was equally enthused at the memory. 'Once you'd learned to do the jitterbug there was just nothing else for it. It was marvellous. They'd throw you over their shoulder and throw you under their knees and it was absolutely fabulous, really lovely. You'd dance your heart out and forget everything for a few hours.'

It was not only popular music that was in demand during the war. Classical music also experienced its greatest boom to date. In 1940, for example, Jack Hylton, an astute showman, sent the London Philharmonic Orchestra on a tour of provincial variety theatres, playing twice nightly under its conductor Malcolm Sargent. In ten cities – Glasgow, Manchester, Liverpool, Birmingham, Coventry, Newcastle, Leeds, Bradford, Sheffield, and Edinburgh – the regular patrons of their local Empire or Palace found the stage occupied by seventy musicians in white tie and tails under the suave, carnation-in-buttonhole Dr Sargent. To many people's surprise, including their own, they liked it, and the takings broke records. Besides the twice-daily concerts, a third, at lunchtime, sometimes had to be fitted in to cope with the demand at the box office. The programmes were popular classics, leaning rather heavily on Tchaikovsky, Wagner and Grieg, with leavenings of Johann Strauss waltzes, Pomp and Circumstance marches and the 'Londonderry Air'. But, said Sargent, 'hundreds of galleryites, normally entertained by conjurers, contortionists and red-nosed comedians, listened for an hour to heaven-sent music'. In one theatre, at Edinburgh, an old lady in a shawl who had just listened to the plaintive cor anglais solo in the 'New World' Symphony, called down from the gallery, 'Play something cheery!' Sargent called back that the next movement *was* cheery. In another theatre a stage-hand said, 'You're going over big, Doc. Your only rival on the halls is George Formby.' The tours were repeated and several of the concerts took place immediately before a night-time Blitz, such as the one that burnt out the Free Trade Hall in Manchester.

On 10 May 1941, Sargent was the last conductor to give a concert in the

Queen's Hall in London, then the site of the Proms, which was utterly destroyed that night. The Proms moved to the Royal Albert Hall, with twice the capacity, and promptly attracted twice the audience. It was not all for popular classics, however. In 1942 Shostakovich sent the score of his 'Leningrad' Symphony, written in the besieged Soviet city, for performance at the Proms; the score and orchestral parts arrived on microfilm via the diplomatic bag from Moscow. There were wartime oddities such as performances by the Czech or Polish army choirs or the spectacle of a contemporary composer, Edmund Rubbra, conducting his new symphony's first performance in battledress (he was a private in the artillery). In 1943 Sir Henry Wood, the founder of the Proms, had a stroke while conducting in full view of the audience, but he survived to put in an appearance at the Jubilee Season in 1944, before flying bombs caused the concerts to be suspended. The remaining programmes were broadcast by the BBC Symphony Orchestra under Sir Adrian Boult from its wartime home in Bedford. A week after the Jubilee Concert Wood died, having seen his ambition of taking classical music to a mass audience fulfilled in wartime as never before. Destruction put a new value on creation. To pick one's way through the rubble of the bombing to a theatre for an afternoon symphony concert made the *Enigma Variations*, for example, sound unbearably poignant. A Bach Suite played by Myra Hess beneath the damaged roof of the pictureless National Gallery, at the famous series of shilling lunchtime concerts, seemed all the more perfect a German achievement by contrast with what they had done to the surroundings. As Malcolm Sargent said during a noisy raid on a northern city, as he picked up his baton to conduct Beethoven's 7th Symphony: 'There are certain things that will last forever. This is one of them.'

ENSA (Entertainments National Service Association) was also said, cruelly but with justification, to stand for 'Every Night Something Awful'. But as well as running concert parties by the hundred to entertain troops or munitions workers in their lunch-hour, it instituted 'Symphony Concerts for War Workers'. The opening concert in East London, at the People's Palace, Mile End, was attended by Ernest Bevin. All the leading orchestras were employed, as well as artists like Pablo Casals, who played for fees of only two or three guineas to audiences that had never heard them before.

The more 'highbrow' counterpart to ENSA was CEMA (Council for the Encouragement of Music and the Arts), which after the war became the Arts Council. CEMA's encouragement took the form of employment for war artists such as Paul Nash, who painted a memorable 'Battle of Britain'; John Piper and Graham Sutherland, who painted the still smoking ruins of the Blitz; and Henry Moore, chronicler of the tube-station shelterers. It also sponsored theatre and ballet tours by the Old Vic and Sadler's Wells companies in drama-starved industrial areas.

The new drama that emerged in the war was mostly escapist comedy, such as Noel Coward's *Blithe Spirit*. There were exceptions – Terence Rattigan's

84 *Popular music in the war wasn't all American or modern. After the Proms were bombed out of the Queen's Hall, they found a new home and a much larger audience at the Royal Albert Hall, the kind of mass mixed audience their founder, Sir Henry Wood, had always aimed for*

85 *ENSA took entertainment, good and bad, to service camps, factories and, here, even to the people sheltering in the (closed) Aldwych tube station in October 1940. While the accordion ensemble took the platform the audience passed right down on to the track*

Flare Path (about RAF wives waiting for their men to return from a raid) and Emlyn Williams's *The Morning Star* (about London under German bombing) – but the main demand on the serious stage was for classics revived with the lustre shed by a generation of remarkable actors then in their prime – Gielgud, Olivier, Ralph Richardson and Donald Wolfit, Edith Evans, Sybil Thorndike and Peggy Ashcroft. Gielgud's fourth *Hamlet* in 1944 was adjudged 'the best Hamlet of our time' by the leading critic, James Agate, and Wolfit's *King Lear* in the same year was, he said, 'the greatest piece of Shakespearean acting I have seen'. But for many the performances which eclipsed all else were those of Olivier and Richardson in their spell-binding resurrection of the Old Vic Company in 1944 and 1945. Richardson's fantastic Peer Gynt and definitive Falstaff were matched by the malignity incarnate of Olivier's Richard III – soon hackneyed by other people's imitations, but blinding when it was first revealed. Then came his virtuoso coupling in *Henry IV* of the strapping, stammering bully Hotspur in Part I, followed in Part II by the senile Mr Justice Shallow, in which he shrank into a quavering scarecrow. He went on to astonish audiences anew by combining in a single programme the roles of Sophocles' awe-striking Oedipus and Sheridan's absurd theatre critic, Mr Puff, as light as pastry. Those who saw the 1944 performances, which at once annihilated all consciousness of the London of the doodlebugs that lay outside the New Theatre in St Martin's Lane, knew that they were watching theatrical history. A new era of acting magic was being created. Its performers have never yet been matched, let alone surpassed.

The cinema also experienced some of its great days, if only because blackout, bombing and boredom saved the British cinema from near-extinction and transformed it into an industry attracting 25–30 million paying customers a week. Many people went more than once. The films they went to see fell into two main categories: escapism provided by Hollywood and realism about the war provided by British film-makers. Of the two, escapism was easily the favourite. *Gone With the Wind* opened in early 1940 and was still running in the West End shortly before D-Day. The queues in Leicester Square used to circle the cinema from early morning throughout the Blitz, whatever the state of chaos produced all around by the night's bombing. The war years produced such vintage Hollywood titles as *Casablanca*, *Citizen Kane*, *The Little Foxes*, *Maltese Falcon*, *Going My Way* and *Meet Me in St Louis*, as well as a profusion of Preston Sturges comedies and Busby Berkeley musicals.

By comparison, the British cinema was dour and dutiful but at least it had a quality of truthfulness that had been lacking in the pre-war days of quick, cheap 'B' pictures, which were made to fill the quota of British films required to be shown by law. Hollywood's early war film about Britain, *Mrs Miniver*, was embarrassing in its sentimental 'wrongness'. In Britain, documentary film-makers, formerly working for the Post Office or in commerce, now

86 Great days at the wartime Old Vic company led by Ralph Richardson and Laurence Olivier, here duelling stagily as Richmond and Richard III at Bosworth

brought their skills to the Crown Film Unit. Humphrey Jennings, in particular, was responsible for two films about the Blitz – *Fires Were Started* and *London Can Take It* – and Harry Watt for *Target For Tonight*, the account of a Wellington bomber's flight over Germany, in which the pilot was played by an actual RAF bomber pilot. The most ambitious documentary was the story of the battle of El Alamein, *Desert Victory*, edited by Roy Boulting from 1.5 million feet of film shot over the ten days of actual battle by over twenty Army Film Unit cameramen – three of whom were killed and two badly injured while shooting it.

> They are the men who deserve the credit for the film. No one knew *Desert Victory* was being made. I had been given the go-ahead by my boss to keep me out of harm's way. But once the battle was won, the War Office, urged on by Churchill, said they must have a film about Alamein and my commanding officer told them we had nearly finished it. We were given a completion date and we finished it in three days and nights without sleep, with several bottles of whisky to keep us going. I carried the film myself down to the Odeon, Leicester Square, for the press view. I sat in the foyer, absolutely exhausted and I heard a roar from inside and they were cheering.

> After the long, long silence building up to the dawn artillery barrage that begins the battle, audiences generally responded by cheering. 'The only other

[193]

time I remember this was in *Henry V*, when the English archers fired their arrows at the charging French knights,' said John Huntley, who worked as a wartime projectionist. *Henry V*, too, was a war film, dedicated to those who led the attack on Europe on D-Day. It was shot in 1943 in Ireland at a cost (£500,000) that would have been unthinkable in the British film industry until war made its reputation. It was epoch-making not only for its artistic standards but for the control allowed to one man, Laurence Olivier, as producer–director, with the final say in sets, music, lighting and camerawork. With a long life ahead of it, it paid for itself.

Documentary realism had its effect on contemporary feature films, helping to create the understated, stiff-upper-lip style of acting that looks in retrospect like a parody of Britishness. It was partly a response to the wartime newsreels, where cheer-up-at-the-back-there commentaries were delivered in an unvaried high-pitched bark: 'Is Dover down-hearted? No! Dover can take it!' It was always the officer-class that affected this gritty carry-on-sergeant-whatever-happens style. Other ranks were allowed an occasional human reaction. In Carol Reed's Army film, *The Way Ahead*, the officer class, represented by a somewhat unsympathetic David Niven, bawls out the other ranks in a way likely to inspire sympathy for the common soldier. And the common girl soldier certainly emerged as the heroine of *The Gentle Sex*, which might have been designed as a recruiting film for the ATS. Women are shown working efficiently alongside men, driving in convoy all night without complaint, operating anti-aircraft rangefinders on gun-sites under attack and drilling as well as a company of Guardsmen. In spite of this, the dialogue cannot help underlining its message with incredulity: 'Cor, stone me – women working all night!' or 'Where have those women got to? I suppose they're having their hair done.' The film's voice-over commentary, spoken by Leslie Howard, the producer, gives its heroines a final, paternalistic pat on the back as though they were a different species: 'There they are, the women. Let's admit at least we're really proud of you, you strange, incalculable creatures. The world is going to be a better place because you are helping to shape it.'

The world is always going to be a better place in war films, once Jerry has been dealt with. 'What are we fighting for?' – there is nearly always a reflective moment when somebody asks the question, in this case the ATS heroine enjoying the moonlight with a handsome pilot. His answer, as was usual, tends towards vague, rhetorical, manly reassurance: 'Mainly, I think, to create a world fit to live in. For the first time in history we have something to live for, not just to die for. You have to fight to win peace just as hard as you have to fight to win a war.' And in case this strange, incalculable creature hasn't appreciated the depth of these enigmatic words he adds, 'Were you listening?'

The high point of Britishness in word and deed was touched in Noel Coward's *In Which We Serve*, probably the most praised British war picture of any. It was written by Noel Coward in collaboration with his friend, Lord Louis Mountbatten, whose destroyer *HMS Kelly* had been sunk in May 1941. This authenticity was not enough to convince the Ministry of Information of the desirability of filming the story. The Ministry refused to be associated with it as bad propaganda. 'When I asked why it was considered bad propaganda,' wrote Coward of his interview with the head of the Ministry's films division, Jack Beddington, 'he said, "Because a ship was sunk in it."' Mountbatten intervened by taking a copy of the script to show King George VI, which may have helped get clearance for the film and its finance (the King brought his family to the studio to watch it being shot). The film mirrors the class structure both of the Navy and of the nation as a whole. The upper-class officer was represented by Noel Coward as Captain, in his most clipped consonant-snapping style ('I want this ship to be a happy and efficient ship. It won't be efficient unless it's happy and it certainly won't be happy unless it's efficient'). The lower class and lower deck were represented by John Mills, speaking Cockney, assisted by Richard Attenborough. And the middle-class middle ranks of petty officers were portrayed by Bernard (later Lord) Miles.

I'd made a five-minute propaganda film called *Home Guard*. Noel Coward saw it and said, 'You're the only person who can be my bo'sun. What we want is someone to represent Drake – Francis Drake's West Country seamen.' I was asked to do an audition, not to the producers but to the admirals in the Navy, and they said, 'He'll do, he'll do, jolly good, excellent, Chief Buffer (Chief Bo'sun's Mate), yes.' The film followed the

87 Noel Coward as the stiff-upper-lipped upper-class Captain of In Which We Serve, *the film he wrote and produced with the advice of Lord Louis Mountbatten, based on Mountbatten's ship, HMS Kelly*

pattern of society in the 1930s, namely that there were three decks that represented what English society was like then. The wives were the same – Kay Walsh was Johnny Mills' wife, lovely Joyce Carey was my wife and Celia Johnson, the Captain's. They couldn't be more perfectly chosen to fit the three-deck society.

Great pains were taken with authenticity – 120 naval ratings on leave were brought from Portsmouth to crew the fictional 'ship' in the studio. But the most unexpected touch of reality was when the battle began. Richard Attenborough's naval rating actually showed fear under fire and ran away – something that had never been permitted in a British war film before. 'I can remember the impact on audiences when they first saw it, the stunned silence and the waves of feeling,' said John Huntley, the projectionist.

In Which We Serve was directed by David Lean, one of the rich vein of new talent in the wartime British film industry, which included Carol Reed, the Boulting Brothers, Launder and Gillatt, Powell and Pressburger. Pre-war American domination ended when the Americans went back to the United States and allowed native talents to emerge – also new British stars, some of them of the calibre of James Mason, Celia Johnson and Rex Harrison. They made their quota of trashy melodramas too, of course – such films as *Dangerous Moonlight*, with its 'Warsaw Concerto' sounding like ersatz Rachmaninov. But taken all in all there were notable steps towards truth in a medium hitherto devoted to make-believe and fairylands. Discussing what you had seen at 'the pictures' – like what you had heard on the radio – became one of the common bonds between people who had little choice of entertainment. They not only provided emotional relief, they helped to draw the nation together and break down some of the class-oriented barriers of taste between people.

While indoor entertainment flourished in war, sport languished. Large crowds were forbidden as air-raid risks in the early days, players were some of the first to volunteer or be called up to the forces, and sports grounds were in many cases requisitioned for military or civil defence purposes. Epsom racecourse was seized by the military, Kempton Park became an internment camp, the Oval a prisoner-of-war camp, the Arsenal ground at Highbury a civil defence headquarters, Wimbledon's All England Tennis club a parade ground for the Home Guard, while Twickenham rugby football ground served for civil defence and as allotments. Although Lord's cricket ground and pavilion were used by the RAF, Sir 'Plum' Warner of the MCC defended the sacred turf against all comers on the ground that it would be a great propaganda coup for the Germans to be able to claim that they had stopped the English from playing cricket at Lord's.

Racing was banned in 1940 and all but suspended again as war wore on. It was branded almost as unpatriotic to back horses in the midst of austerity, and early in 1942 Sir Stafford Cripps announced the withdrawal of the 'basic'

petrol ration for pleasure motoring on which most racegoers relied to get them to the course. Only six courses still functioned, on a regional basis, and substitute Classics, like the Derby and the St Leger, were run at Newmarket. But people still wanted to go racing and to gamble, despite Sir Stafford's disapproval.

The Football League also had to reorganise itself by regions in order to save on travelling, and Saturday afternoon attendances were much reduced by the fact that many fans were working a shift in the war factories. Many clubs went under temporarily and those that played on frequently had to rely entirely on substitutes. Inter-services matches drew crowds to Wembley, however, often with sides composed almost entirely of international players. Football pools were 'nationalised' as Unity Pools and their coupons were printed in the newspapers to save postage and paper.

The county cricket championship was suspended for the duration, but most of the players of that golden age – Hutton, Compton, Edrich or Washbrook – could still be seen turning out for services or 'representative' elevens. Lord's still managed to attract some 250,000 spectators a year and among them you were liable to see familiar wartime faces – like Sir Charles Portal, the Chief of Air Staff, nursing his pipe, or Ernest Bevin himself – taking an hour or two off from the war.

88 There wasn't anyone for tennis at the All England Club at Wimbledon, but there were cups for something or other proudly displayed by the local Home Guard company

[197]

CHAPTER NINE

THE LONG, HARD SLOG

'I ALWAYS HESITATE TO SAY anything of an optimistic nature because our people do not mind being told the worst.' So Churchill, late in 1940, assured the House of Commons. But the time was coming soon afterwards when for a whole year he had nothing but the worst to tell them and they began to mind a good deal. There was general complaint of government incompetence, of loss of confidence in the direction of the war. Talk of replacing Churchill with another leader – if only one could be found – began to be heard.

Hitler's surprise attack on the Soviet Union at 4 a.m. on 22 June 1941 took much of the heat off Britain, however. The concentrated bombing of the Blitz ended just when it was becoming almost intolerable and the prospect of being invaded receded, at least until after German victory in Russia – though many people expected this to follow quite shortly. Three weeks, then six weeks, then three months was the longest that people expected the Russian forces (which had collapsed ignominiously in the First World War) to hold out. Meanwhile, the stimulus of imminent backs-to-the-wall confrontation had faded and the realisation sank in of a long, hard, miserable slog to come, lasting for years. In these uphill conditions morale was bound to sag. People were tired of hearing that Britain could take it; they wanted to see proof that it could dish it out. A large majority (never less than 75 per cent) still believed in ultimate victory, but they now realised that the war was not going to end by 1942, or even 1943. British confidence was very largely confidence in Churchill himself, and at worst approval of him as war leader never fell below 78 per cent of the people. By contrast, the number expressing satisfaction with the conduct of the war was no higher than 63 per cent during the bleak year of reverses up to November 1942. But, however gloomy the prospects, defeat was never seriously contemplated. The authorities had prepared for widespread psychological distress, breakdown and neurosis among civilians involved in war, but when it came to it the medical and psychiatric services were hardly needed. Civilians were less neurotic, not more, than they were in peacetime. Servicemen had more breakdowns under stress than they did.

Throughout the second half of 1941, the British held their breath waiting to see if the Russians could hold the Panzer assault at bay; it was obvious that if they did not, Britain was the next target. In October, with Leningrad surrounded, Kiev captured and the advance getting uncomfortably close to Moscow, Hitler prophesied, 'The campaign in the East is decided. The Soviet Union is finished as a military power.' It was a major propaganda blunder, which became obvious when the German armies settled down to endure their first Russian winter.

On the night after the Germans attacked, Churchill had declared Britain's out-and-out support for Russia. Asked by his secretary Sir John Colville how he, as so outspoken an anti-Communist, could change his tune like this, he replied: 'I have only one purpose, the destruction of Hitler, and my life is much simplified thereby. If Hitler invaded Hell, I would make at least a favourable reference to the Devil in the House of Commons.' In his broadcast that night he painted an idyllic picture of Russian villages, hardworking peasants, laughing maidens and playing children (not a word about commissars or purges) threatened by 'the dull, drilled, docile, brutish masses of the Hun soldiery plodding on like a swarm of crawling locusts'.

Once it was clear how ferociously the Russians were going to resist, the majority in Britain were enthusiastically pro-Soviet. But, wrote David Low, the greatest cartoonist of his time, 'A sizeable section of the community resented the company of the Soviet Union as a partner. Pleasure at the thought that Germany might now lose was balanced by mortification that

89 'Tanks for Russia' weeks in munitions factories meant that the whole week's output was dedicated to the Russian front, like these tanks bearing the V-for-Victory sign. Admiration for the Russians' ferocious resistance was universal

Russia might win. Even moderates felt that the new circumstances released Britain to become a spectator and watch Hitler and Stalin destroy one another.' This possibility, which was expressed by more than one Tory politician (including a minister, Colonel Moore Brabazon), was probably the reason behind the still unexplained flight to Britain of Rudolf Hess, the Deputy Führer. Hess left behind a letter to Hitler ending, 'You can always say I was crazy' – which is exactly what Hitler did announce. But there is evidence that he must have known of Hess's intention to fly to Britain and it is likely that Hess, for his part, knew the secret date of the imminent attack on Russia, originally set for 15 May, then postponed to June. Hess flew on 10 May. It was his third attempt at a flight which would have taxed the nerve of any pilot. Nothing suggests that he was crazy.

Whatever support there was for a separate peace with Hitler in the higher social circles, there was no hesitation among the workers in the munitions factories in supporting Russia. From August 1941, munitions convoys began to leave for the northerly Soviet ports of Archangel and Murmansk, carrying planes, vehicles, tanks, ammunition, boots, rubber and other supplies in their holds. Many never reached Russia but were sunk by German U-boats in the Arctic waters. In the munitions factories there were 'tanks for Russia' weeks, when the whole output was dedicated to the Russian front and the tanks were turned out named 'Stalin', 'Marx', 'Lenin' or simply 'Another for Joe'. Mickey Lewis, operating a centre lathe in a gun workshop, described the feeling:

This was a war in which working-class people knew what was going on. We had working groups and we used to meet to discuss politics. The feeling in the country was very pro-Soviet because of the heroic way they were fighting. People here felt tremendous admiration for the terrific heroism in the Leningrad siege. Everyone felt the same. There was absolutely no anti-Soviet feeling.

Margaret Cohen, a London teacher of twenty-two, went to join her husband in Coventry in August 1941 and threw herself into raising a public declaration of greetings and solidarity to send from the women of Coventry to the women of Stalingrad (not yet under siege).

In no time at all, 7000 women signed it. I don't remember any refusals – the Russians were fighting so heroically we got a tremendous response. Coventry people had suffered more than most. Everybody in the street seemed to be wearing little hammer and sickle badges. We constituted ourselves as a Women's Anglo-Soviet Committee and we took the signatures to London to present to the Soviet Ambassador's wife, Madame Maisky. Next year came the tremendous battle for Stalingrad, ending in the encirclement of the German army. Then, after it was over in

March 1943, came the response: 30,000 signatures from Stalingrad in an album addressed to the women of Coventry. By then many of those 30,000 women who had signed before the siege must have been dead.

There were Anglo-Soviet committees galore. One of the biggest was backed by the Foreign Office and presided over by the King's doctor, Lord Horder. In November 1942 the twenty-fifth anniversary of the Russian revolution was celebrated in London with an exhibition of Soviet Progress, and the twenty-fifth anniversary of the founding of the Red Army was celebrated with public meetings throughout the country and by a pageant, a play and a symphony orchestra in the Royal Albert Hall. The Aid to Russia fund was launched under the patronage of Mrs Churchill (the workers at Rolls Royce, Glasgow, gave a day's wages to it) and it raised the considerable sum of £8 million. Russian trade union delegations toured the war factories to great applause, and Russia was not only admirable but respectable in the highest circles. The august London club, the Athenaeum, elected the Soviet ambassador, the popular Ivan Maisky, as a member. Selfridges flew the Red Flag daily in Oxford Street. The BBC got into a tizzy about adding to its Sunday-night broadcast of Allied national anthems the Russian one, the Internationale. Churchill personally asked Stalin to send over the music of the new Russian anthem for broadcast by the BBC. Stalin complied, saying mis-

91 *The Soviet ambassador in London, Ivan Maisky, was liked in government circles, although it was his unpleasant task to convey to Churchill Stalin's incessant demands for an immediate Second Front to take pressure off the Russian one*

chievously that he hoped Churchill would learn the tune and whistle it to the Conservative party.

But was 'Russian fever' the same as an enthusiasm for Communism? Hardly. The Communist Party of Great Britain, which had been duly denouncing the 'imperialist' war until Moscow's orders changed, had sunk in membership to about 12,000 when the Nazi-Soviet pact was so abruptly terminated by Hitler's Panzers. It then rocketed to 65,000 members by September 1942, but this proved to be its zenith. Churchill had instructed Brendan Bracken, his Minister of Information, 'to consider what action was required to counter the present tendency of the British people to forget the dangers of Communism in their enthusiasm over the resistance of Russia'. But little action was required other than to found a few Anglo-Soviet Committees themselves; people were able to think well of Russia, while remaining hostile to Communism. There was such a relaxed attitude that Margaret Cohen, a Communist Party member from her student days, was recruited by the Ministry of Information to give talks in factory canteens about the women's war effort in the Soviet Union and to recruit more women munitions workers at street meetings.

The immediate response of Stalin to Churchill's offer of alliance was to demand a 'Second Front Now' to take the pressure off his own; this became a Communist Party slogan (and not only Communist) which began to appear on walls in 1941 when there was not the remotest chance of starting one. Churchill himself did not believe it was possible until 1943 (when in practice it turned out to be possible only in Italy).

'Russian resistance caused enormous admiration. Stalingrad made a tremendous impression,' recalled Tom Hopkinson, editor of *Picture Post*. 'We had a feeling not only that the Russians were defeating Hitler but that we ourselves had been saved. We'd been expecting an invasion and, as people said, "he's gone the other way". We were very grateful to the Russians.' But by 1942 people began to feel distinctly uneasy, even guilty, that the Russians were still bearing the brunt of the German attack in the field. It began to be said cynically that Britain was fighting to the last drop of Russian blood or that it offered the Russians 'all aid short of war'.

At this point, Britain's only role in the war seemed to be to suffer defeat after defeat. After losing much of what ground had been won in Libya, the outposts of the Empire in the Far East fell in unbelievably quick succession to the Japanese, who had attacked the American base of Pearl Harbor on Hawaii, on 7 December 1941. The Royal Navy's biggest and best warships, the *Prince of Wales* and *Repulse*, were sunk by air attack. On Christmas Day, Hong Kong fell. In February the Malayan peninsular was overrun and Singapore surrendered. In March and April Rangoon and Burma were lost. Privately, Churchill feared that Ceylon, Calcutta, Madras and part of Australia might follow. June brought the totally unexpected fall of Tobruk, which had been by-passed by Rommel's advance to the Egyptian frontier;

with a garrison of 33,000 men, it had been expected to withstand a long siege. Rommel was forty miles from Alexandria and Cairo lay beyond.

These were too many disasters to be borne with equanimity. It was the low point of war for Britain and for Churchill personally. He had faced one vote of confidence at the end of January and on that occasion was, for him, almost contrite before the House of Commons: 'In two and a half years of fighting we have only just managed to keep our heads above water,' he told them, 'If we have handled our resources wrongly, no one is so much to blame as me.' He added to his original list of offerings (blood, toil, tears and sweat) 'shortcomings, mistakes and disappointments.' Only the tiny Independent Labour Party of three voted against him.

The fall of Singapore, when it duly surrendered on 15 February with 85,000 troops, shook Churchill as few other defeats did. He called it 'the worst disaster and largest capitulation in British history'. He could not explain it. His broadcast to the nation that night lacked his usual defiant spirit, and those around him noted his irritability and lack of vigour. He even hinted to some of them that he might lay down his office. 'I am an old man,' he told the editor of *The Times*. 'No man has had to bear such disasters as I have.' The Singapore surrender had been preceded three days earlier by the escape of the battleships *Scharnhorst* and *Gneisenau*, which had been bottled up in Brest. They steamed up the Channel under escort, defying the Navy and the RAF, which were waiting for them, to stop their passage to the North Sea. It was a humiliation which caused public fury – it was called 'the blackest week since Dunkirk'. Was Churchill losing his grip? Was it time to look for a new leader?

It looked to some people as though there was an alternative leader in Sir Stafford Cripps, the ambassador in Moscow, who had returned in January 1942 in a blaze of (undeserved) glory as the man who more than anyone had got Russia in 'on our side'. Cripps was a devoutly Christian country gentleman who, paradoxically, had been expelled from the Labour Party for revolutionary extremism. He had the vegetarian's air of austerity, purity, near saintliness, combined with high intelligence and left-wing credentials. He had broadcast an impressive *Postscript* in which he compared the British war effort unfavourably with the Russian, and had refused the ministerial post Churchill at first offered him in the government. He was thus potentially a powerful critic of the government in the House of Commons and the press promoted him as a possible leader. 'Churchill's position is very shaky,' wrote George Orwell in May 1942. 'Up to the fall of Singapore people had liked Churchill while disliking his government but his popularity has slumped heavily. I wouldn't give Churchill many more months of power but whether he will be replaced by Cripps, Beaverbrook or somebody like Sir John Anderson is uncertain.' Under the pressure of criticism Churchill reshuffled his government and offered Cripps a seat in the War Cabinet and Leadership of the House of Commons. This time he accepted.

With demands for a Second Front, as British troops retreated before Rommel, Churchill's position grew shakier still. This was the period when only 78 per cent of people polled approved of him, and government candidates were defeated at four by-elections in a row. Sections of the press, led by the *Daily Mirror*, were violently critical of the way the war was being run and it was widely suggested that Churchill should be relieved of some of his burdens by ceasing to combine being Minister of Defence with the office of Prime Minister. Churchill would never have given up this post and with it his power to direct the war militarily in conjunction with the Chiefs of Staff.

Cripps seems to have nursed ambitions to take over as Prime Minister but, in the event, he never made a decisive bid to oust Churchill. Instead, he departed to India on an unsuccessful mission (at Churchill's invitation) to settle its post-war independent status, though his failure to talk Gandhi round did not harm his popularity. Then, on 21 June, Tobruk fell. The nation, like Churchill, was shocked. Was there no end to defeat?

A motion of censure was moved by Sir John Wardlaw-Milne, an influential Conservative, who astonished the House by suggesting not only that Churchill should give up the office of Defence but that the Duke of Gloucester, quite possibly the least dynamic member of the Royal Family, should be made Commander-in-Chief of the Army.

'I have sat in the House of Commons for many years but I have never heard such a furious noise emerge from all benches expressing dissent,' wrote R. A. Butler, then a junior minister. 'It was a mixture between a whistle and a howl. Wardlaw-Milne never recovered – and neither did the motion.' More effective attacks on the government followed from Aneurin Bevan, who declared: 'I know it is better debating tactics for the Prime Minister to wind up the Debate. In that way he will win the Debate. But the country is more concerned with the Prime Minister winning the war. . . . He wins Debate after Debate and loses battle after battle.' Hore-Belisha, a former Minister for War, pointed out how often Churchill's military judgment had been wrong. 'In a hundred days we lost our Empire in the Far East. What will happen in the next hundred days?' 'I am your servant and you have the right to dismiss me when you please,' said Churchill, winding up the Debate, 'What you have no right to do is to ask me to bear responsibilities without the power of effective action.' This time twenty-five votes were cast against him. Once more the House of Commons admitted there was no alternative leader.

The battle of El Alamein was fought from 23 October to 4 November 1942 and was followed immediately by the Anglo-American landings in North Africa. Churchill said that Alamein turned the 'hinge of fate' – it could almost be said that 'before Alamein we never had a victory. After Alamein we never had a defeat.' His instinct was sound in ordering the church bells to be rung for the victory for the first time in two years. There were never again to be any doubts worth considering about the leadership and morale at home recovered sharply. Cripps departed from the War Cabinet to the Ministry of

Aircraft Production – demotion for an overestimated rival.

The entry of America into the war after the disaster of Pearl Harbor was greeted by Churchill with almost excessive relief: 'Hitler's fate was sealed. Mussolini's fate was sealed. As for the Japanese they would be ground to powder. . . . There was no more doubt about the end.' The fact that he had tried so hard for so long to persuade his friend President Roosevelt to bring America in explains his euphoria, but it was not as intense among his countrymen. His meeting on board a battleship with Roosevelt which had produced 'the Atlantic Charter' – a declaration of vague democratic war aims such as that peace should bring 'freedom from fear and want' – had little impact at home. The arrival of American servicemen in 1942 and 1943 certainly did – but it was not one of overwhelming relief. Opinions on the GIs (the initials stood for 'General Issue'), who invaded Britain like an occupying army over a million strong, were sharply and almost equally divided, for and against. People liked or disliked them intensely, sometimes having both feelings at the same time. 'England is a small country, smaller than North Carolina,' ran a useful little pocket 'guide to Great Britain' issued to every American serviceman on arrival:

> The British dislike bragging and showing off. . . . If they need to be, they can be plenty tough. . . . You can rub a Britisher the wrong way by telling him 'we came over and won the last one'. . . . The British Tommy is apt to be specially touchy about the difference between his wages and yours. Keep this in mind. . . . Three actions on your part will slow up friendship – swiping his girl, not appreciating what his army has been up against and rubbing it in that you are better paid than he is. . . . Crossing the ocean doesn't automatically make you a hero. There are housewives in aprons and youngsters in knee pants in parts of Britain who have lived through more high explosives in air raids than many soldiers saw in barrages in the last war.

These warnings covered most of the points that were to cause friction – and plenty of it. There were two contrasting ways of seeing the American troops. One was to admire their obvious affluence, the high quality of their uniforms, their air of familiarity with the officers, their easy-going, gum-chewing ways. The other was to notice disapprovingly that many were poor physical specimens, lacking in soldierly bearing and discipline, and that they had no conception of the British idea of 'good manners'. They filled the pubs, drank all the beer, which they didn't like because it was 'warm', and tried to pick up any girl in sight.

George Orwell was 'struck by the mediocre physique and poor general appearance of the American soldiers' when they arrived early in 1942. In January 1943 he was writing, 'There is widespread anti-American feeling among the working class, thanks to the presence of the American soldiers

92 *The GIs arrived like beings from another planet. Their pay was far higher, their uniforms far smarter and their discipline far more relaxed. Nothing was more startling than the black American troops' habit of jumping high in the air and chanting while on the march*

and, I believe, very bitter anti-British feeling among the soldiers themselves. . . . If you ask people why they dislike Americans you get first of all the answer that they are "always boasting" and then come upon a more solid grievance. . . . An American private soldier gets ten shillings a day and all found, which means that the whole American Army is financially in the middle class and fairly high up in it.' By the end of 1943, after an encounter with two drunk GIs slurring out 'Down with Britain ... never trust a Britisher', he noted, 'The general opinion is that the only American soldiers with decent manners are negroes.'

They were the first black soldiers that many people in Britain had seen. In camp they were segregated and outside they were encouraged to patronise separate bars, clubs and cafés from white GIs. When fraternisation took place with British girls, white Americans were shocked. 'The girls here walk out with niggers,' said a disgusted American military policeman to a newly arrived GI. 'I can hear few good words for the Americans anywhere,' Orwell noted at the end of 1943. 'In two years since they arrived I rarely see US and British soldiers together. Obviously the major cause is the difference in pay. You can't have really close and friendly relations with somebody whose income is five times your own.' By May 1944 he was recording: 'The troops and the public, other than girls, are still very stand-offish.' One American soldier he met said a girl had come up to him on the pavement and seized hold of his penis with the words 'Hullo, Yank!' Another told him that 'Anti-British feeling is completely general in the American Army.'

Nevertheless there had already been 20,000 marriages between GIs and British girls, and a 'school for brides' was run by the American Red Cross. 'The trouble with Americans is that they're overpaid, oversexed and over here' – that comedian's taunt was repeated like a catchphrase and was founded on the Hogarthian scenes at places like Rainbow Corner off Leicester Square, where 'good-time girls' flocked round the 'Yanks' like birds of prey. Similar corners existed in most cities near American bases. But to balance this, the American Army or Air Force units showed their generosity and neighbourliness by giving parties for local children, orphans and, on Mother's Day (then a purely American custom) entertaining and making a fuss of local English mothers, as if they were their own.

A 1945 Mass Observation survey of attitudes to American troops put top of the list of likes their generosity, friendliness and the feeling that the two nations held ideals of freedom in common. Top of the longer list of dislikes was conceit; Americans were described over and over again as boastful, bumptious, bombastic, bragging, patronising, superior, talking and acting big. They were also thought by many to be naive, ill-educated and over-keen on money. People found them both courteous and discourteous to an extreme degree. It was a picture of thoroughly mixed-up feelings, tinged with ignorance of America's different social conventions – and envy. Naturally, in the Britain of 1942 and 1943, the Americans' PX stores glittered like Aladdin's Caves, while they themselves, to film-struck young girls, seemed to bring a little of the dazzle of Hollywood along with their accents. 'Every Yank was a film star – no matter how ugly he was,' said Elsie Thompson, who used to visit Burtonwood air base.

> They used to tell you these stories – they all had lovely places, plenty of money, some had ranches – and we used to believe it. It was their appearance, against our poor soldiers in their thick uniforms, and they talked with this American twang and you used to sit and look at them and say to yourself, I wonder if he'll marry me and take me back to America to live on a ranch?

Pamela Winfield, when still a seventeen-year-old schoolgirl, had her first encounter with the Americans at a dance at Wimbledon town hall.

> We were absolutely gaga looking at these gorgeous men walking in. They had beautiful uniforms that made them all look like officers, but the whole point was they seemed just like film stars. There was this great magic about America. It was to do with the films – we used to go to the pictures three times a week. We were so drab and it was another world, so glossy and clean, with picket fences and pretty white houses and Betty Grables and they all had lovely clothes. In fact we found out that the majority were

small-town boys, straight out of high school, and church-going. The vision that they were all wild and woolly was not fair.

She went back to school the next day wearing an American Air Force button on her gym-slip. 'My friends were horrified because nice girls did not go out with Americans.' Not every girl was GI-mad and some of those that were were interested in more material things than Hollywood dreams. 'They had cigarettes, they had lipstick, perfume, nylons,' said Hetty Fowler. 'We had one or two girls in the ambulance service who got, well, more than they wanted, so of course whoever could pay the highest price for them got their spare nylons, lipsticks and chocolates, even butter. I knew one girl who would always get a nice pat of butter from her American boyfriend. Some girls were quite brazen about what they got for their favours.' At Margery Bailey's radar equipment factory there were also girls who offered their surplus American goods for sale. 'There was a girl on our bench who used to say, "I can get you butter, I can get you sugar." Of course, I knew where she got it from – the Yanks. She would say, "I want so much for that." There used to be pieces of boiling bacon, tubs of margarine and stockings. I never had any. They were nearly a pound a pair, which was a lot for anybody to pay then.' 'We didn't like the Americans – only this certain type of girls did,' said Hetty. 'We were rather jealous that they had so much of everything and our boys had nothing.' 'To my eyes all they wanted was sex because the sights we used to see after a dance were unbelievable,' said Margery. 'Going to work one morning, three of us counted at least fifty contraceptives just dropped on the pavement, every so often. So they didn't care where they did it.'

The resentment on the part of some girls that the American troops had so much more to offer was, naturally, shared by British servicemen. Albert Levine, who served in Cairo in a services divorce office, heard a great deal about Army marriages broken by the temptations presented by the presence of allied troops to wives whose husbands were overseas.

> People almost expected that their wives had committed some kind of infidelity and there was a lot of bitterness about it, directed particularly against the Americans. They could give the girls a good time which the British servicemen were not physically there to do or, if they were, their pay was so lousy that you could not possibly entertain a wife or young woman in the fashion an American could. The Americans were very unpopular as a result.

Many parents of young girls were wary of their entanglements with Americans and the advice columns in magazines had their quota of worried letters from would-be brides. 'They would ask us what they should do if their parents disapproved of them getting engaged to a man who lived so far away,' recalled Constance Holt, wartime editor of *Woman's Own*. 'We used to advise caution – waiting – but if they were really in love, we urged them to get their parents on their side.' 'I couldn't take a Yank home,' said Elsie Thompson, an enthusiast who finally married not a Yank, but a British serviceman. 'My mother said, never get in a car if they offer you a lift, love, because you'll be taken away to the white slave traffic. She would never come to terms with the Yanks.' Pamela Winfield's parents objected to her GI because he was not Jewish and because America seemed such a long way away. They were married without her parents' blessing.

A great many GI romances came to an end with the embarkation for D-Day in June 1944. Jessie Robins, who was living in a Devon village when the Americans arrived, had been swept off her feet by a sergeant. By the time D-Day approached she was pregnant.

> We used to talk about our future together and what would happen after the war and it seemed quite natural to sleep with him. I thought I was going to America, he told me he wanted to take me, and I didn't think it was a dreadful thing to do. One Sunday morning, one of my friends in the village came running up and said, did I know they were all leaving? I left everything and ran all the way to the village. The convoy was getting ready. Jack, being a sergeant, was waving the men into the lorries and looking up the road for me. He said, 'We're going now' – the most terrible moment in my life, I think. He kept saying, 'Don't worry.' He wrote to me often and sent money for my daughter, but he never came back.

The Americans were blamed most for their attitude towards women. In June 1944, at the time of D-Day, the Ministry of Information Home Intelligence Unit reported people's dislike of their 'accosting, making love in

93 Rainbow Corner, off Leicester Square, run by the American Red Cross, attracted a swarm of American troops on leave and, in turn, 'good-time girls' on the lookout for Yanks and the rarities of their PX stores – cigarettes, lipstick, chocolates, nylon stockings or just bacon and butter

public telephone booths and their indiscriminate choice of women'. But it also reported, 'Blame of the girls is more widespread and sometimes stronger than that of the men. Their predatoriness is particularly censored. Some girls are said to be "dunning" as many as three or four US soldiers to provide for their coming child.' Mass Observation also found that though a majority of American soldiers liked England and the British, 'many strongly criticised the way in which children begged for sweets and the way Americans were being "done" by what some considered the low moral tone of British women'.

In order to improve relations between 'occupiers' and 'occupied' the Ministry of Information made a film called *Welcome To Britain*. Burgess Meredith was the visitors' guide to quaint British customs, such as rationing, shortages, British food in wartime restaurants, British pub behaviour and (comparative) British racial tolerance which made black Americans more welcome in Britain than they were at home. Although the film was highly praised by critics, it was never released to civilian audiences – unlike *The Way To The Stars*, which was set at an air base shared by British and American air forces, whose antagonisms were gradually reconciled through their common experience of the toll that bombing Germany took of them.

From 1942 to 1944, when the long-delayed Second Front was at last opened in Normandy, bombing was the only method available of keeping up the offensive against Germany (the invasion of Italy in 1943 engaged Hitler's armies but hardly threatened Germany itself). What was the attitude of the much-bombed British civilians towards their opposite numbers, the German people? There was surprisingly little enthusiasm for revenge raids among people who had seen 40,000 of their fellow-citizens killed in air raids by May 1941. Mass Observation investigators, constantly visiting towns in the aftermath of a blitz, found that people seldom talked of getting their own back on German civilians. Indeed, the desire for reprisals seemed to operate only at second-hand. One report ran: 'Before their own raid the people of A were very interested in the damage done at B, a neighbouring industrial town, and were very belligerent, demanding reprisals. But since their raid this has dropped entirely. No mention was heard of any demand for violent action.' People were more vindictive when they were asked what should be done with Germany after the war was won. About a third based their ideas on revenge and about the same number wanted Germany broken up into smaller units to prevent it ever making war again. 'Yet the distinction between the German people and the Nazis is still widely felt.'

This was also the attitude of Churchill – at least during the Blitz. Harold Nicolson described coming on him seated in the House of Commons smoking room on 17 October 1940, while a member was holding forth on the public demand for reprisals for the raids on London, then at their height. Churchill gazed at him, taking a long sip at a glass of port. 'My dear sir,' he said eventually. 'This is a military, not a civilian war. You and others may desire to kill women and children. We desire to destroy German military objectives. I quite appreciate your point but my motto is business before pleasure.' Of course it *was* a civilian war and women and children were being killed in large numbers all round them. The Germans could not claim that the raids on London were concentrated on railways, docks and military targets. But the traditional attitude that it was dishonourable to *aim* at killing civilians persisted long after the military had in fact abandoned it. In 1940 the moral issues were simple. Churchill's voice rallied the people in their ordeal by attributing the death and destruction to the personal evil of Hitler, 'this bloodthirsty guttersnipe', not to the German nation. 'This wicked man, the repository and embodiment of many forms of soul-destroying hate, this monstrous product of former wrongs and shame. . . .' That is what he told them they were up against and that was what lifted their spirits, for Hitler was palpably evil and Churchill's voice could make him sound as villainous as any foe could be. Dr Una Mulvany remembered the effect of hearing it during the hectic evenings of the Portsmouth raids: 'It would come over in the evenings, often when people were in their shelters or I was in the First Aid post. His voice was marvellous, absolutely. It's hard to understand how one man's voice could help you so much – but he did. He gave us the feeling that it was our war, that we were all in it and that we weren't going to be beaten.'

But this might not have been the effect if he had concentrated his fire on 'the Hun'. The First World War term was scarcely used in the Second World War and the Germans were not 'the Hun' but 'Jerry' or 'the Jerries', which sounded almost friendly. Similarly, Hitler reserved his venom mainly for 'the warmonger Churchill', while German radio talked about 'the Tommies'.

By April 1941, a poll found that just over 50 per cent approved of bombing German civilian targets but nearly 40 per cent still disapproved, with the rest undecided. It was a slender majority. Again, those who had experienced the most bombing – in inner London – were the least enthusiastic, whereas in the North of England three-quarters were in favour. All this was to be changed in February 1942, when Sir Arthur Harris took over as chief of Bomber Command and a new direction-finding aid, code-named 'Gee', became available for use with the new, big, four-engined Lancaster bombers. Until then Bomber Command had not been able to deliver the goods: its planes were too small and their accuracy too low to do significant damage to German military targets by night. There were plenty of critics and Harris was determined to prove that bombing could now destroy whole towns. An Air Ministry directive of 14 February gave the go-ahead for a full-scale attack on the morale of enemy 'industrial workers'.

Harris selected for his demonstration an easy target of no great military significance – the old Hanseatic port of Lübeck whose mediaeval centre, crammed with wooden houses, was still intact. It was, he wrote, 'built more like a fire-lighter than a human habitation'. On 28 March 1942, he sent 234 of his bombers to ignite it. The heart of the city disappeared in the fire and over 300 people were killed. There was much indignation among Germans, including the Führer, who promised them they would give blow for blow. 'As revenge, terror attacks should be carried out on towns outside London,' he directed the Luftwaffe; this was not easy, for the main strength of the Luftwaffe was now on the Eastern front. Before an attack could be mounted, however, the RAF in another demonstration burnt out the centre of the old town of Rostock. The German reprisals began on 23 April with three raids on Exeter. Bath followed on 25 and 26 April, Norwich on 27 and 28 April and York on 28 April. Both sides exaggerated the devastation they had caused. Goebbels wrote, 'There is virtually nothing left standing in Bath'. Harris wrote of 'the utter destruction of Lübeck and Rostock'. Goebbels wrote in his diary, 'Our task must now be to reply to terror with terror and to respond to the attempted destruction of German centres of culture by razing English cultural shrines to the ground.'

In fact they were not razed to the ground. The damage on such compact cities was considerable and over 900 people were killed, 400 of them in Bath where the bombers machine-gunned the streets, but although Exeter's ancient centre and York's fifteenth-century Guildhall were destroyed, there was less damage to historic buildings than might have been expected. The Georgian centre of Bath, for example, was largely untouched and all the cathedrals escaped major damage. Meanwhile, a German foreign office spokesman, Baron Gustav Braun von Sturm, turned the whole exercise into a propaganda blunder. He referred to the raids as 'Baedeker raids', and suggested that the Luftwaffe planned to attack every English city to which the well-known series of Baedeker tourist guide-books had awarded three stars

94 The 'Wings for Victory' campaign brought this four-engined Lancaster down – at the foot of the National Gallery, overlooking Trafalgar Square. The display was a tribute to the bombing offensive against Germany, which reached its height with the 'fire-storm' raids on Hamburg

for its cultural interest. The phrase went round the world: the Germans had categorised themselves as wilful barbarians – Huns after all. Goebbels was furious.

A lull followed in which he decided that the British were bluffing – rudely broken by the first 1000-bomber raid of the war, on Cologne. Nearly 1500 tons of bombs, two-thirds of them incendiaries, were dropped inside an hour and a half, devastating 600 acres of the city and causing nearly 500 deaths. The reply, next night, was the first of three raids on Canterbury. The Cathedral precincts were ringed with fire and several nearby houses were burnt to the ground, yet no one was killed or injured in its immediate vicinity. Firemen stood on the Cathedral roof hurling incendiaries on to the lawns below at a rate of dozens per minute, according to Dean Hewlett Johnson, who supervised in his gaiters and described the scene afterwards: 'The Cathedral shivered when the blasts and debris struck her, trembling like a ship buffeted by waves. Old iron frames, whose slender Norman wedges had held priceless Norman glass to stout Norman bars, were torn from the sockets where Norman builders had placed them seven centuries ago.'

As Canterbury was attacked, Churchill promised that as the year advanced, German cities 'will be subjected to an ordeal the like of which has never been experienced by any country in continuity, severity or magnitude.' The British dropped leaflets after the Cologne raid, which threatened, in the name of Air Marshal Harris:

We are bombing Germany, city by city, in order to make it impossible for you to go on with this war. . . . I will speak frankly about whether we bomb single military targets or whole cities. Obviously we prefer to hit

95 Exeter was the first historic city attacked in reprisal for the 1942 bombing offensive against the old Baltic ports like Lübeck. The cathedral survived, though badly damaged. The Germans described the series of attacks on towns of cultural interest as 'Baedeker raids', after the German tourist guidebook

factories, shipyards and railways. But the people who work in these plants live close to them. Therefore we hit your houses and you. We regret the necessity for this. . . . We are going to scourge the Third Reich from end to end.

The leaflet was the work of the propaganda department. Neither side was now aiming for factories or docks but for town centres and in any case were not accurate enough to discriminate between targets. But for a long time Bomber Command could not make good the threat of 'scourging' Germany in massive raids. To assemble the 1000-plane raid had taken every bomber, including obsolete aircraft, and crew, some of them still half trained, that could be mustered. It was not until 1943 that 'area bombing' with better direction-finding became possible and the US Army Air Force Flying Fortresses were thrown into the battle in daylight. It was believed that Germany could be crippled, indeed defeated, by bombing alone. In fact the damage inflicted failed to break the German will to resist or even seriously to disrupt German arms production, but the strain on German nerves 'approached the limit of endurance' according to a Cologne newspaper. 'The war has turned into something terrible which we did not expect,' said a Strasburg newspaper, and another complained, 'The British behave as though the sky above West Germany was their property.' In reality the RAF were paying a high price for it in bombers and crews lost.

As 1943 brought 'saturation bombing' to Nuremburg, Munich, Bremen, Essen and eventually Berlin, it also brought protests against the practice on moral grounds in Britain. George Bell, Bishop of Chichester, was the best known voice raised both in the House of Lords and in his pulpit. He called for the end of night bombing, provided the Germans would end it too. He was a friend of the German pastors Niemoller and Bonhoeffer, who had boldly opposed Hitler. On his side he was almost equally unpopular for opposing Churchill and the majority. He was not a pacifist – he did not object to bombing military targets – but he demanded 'How can the War Cabinet fail to see that this progressive devastation of cities is threatening the roots of civilisation?'

Vera Brittain, who was a pacifist owing to her experiences in the First World War, joined the Quaker-run Bombing Restriction Committee, publicising their views in her regular pacifist newsletter. She published an anti-bombing pamphlet called *Seed of Chaos*, which reproduced factual accounts of the destruction the raids were causing from neutral press sources. Descriptions of the Hamburg fire-storm in July 1943 rivalled the later horrors of Hiroshima. The surrounding air, sucked into the centre by the heat, stormed through the streets spreading fire and pulling trees out of the ground. No previous air raid compared with it. Charred adult corpses had shrunk to the size of children, reported a Swiss newspaper. People were wandering about crazed, throwing themselves at shelter doors which were locked against them, 'biting and clawing'. None of this was reported in Britain's press – rather there were headlines screaming 'No pity! No mercy!'

Those who protested, like Bishop Bell and Vera Brittain, were cold-shouldered by friends and acquaintances (some believe Bell would have become an Archbishop but for this). Worse, they were accused of pro-German sympathies, and a questioner in the House of Commons suggested internment for the Bombing Restriction Committee. Herbert Morrison, as Home Secretary (himself a conscientious objector in the First World War) replied: 'If people think obliteration bombing is wrong, I cannot see that it is terrible to say so. There is no danger that the bombing will leave off, anyway.'

Humanitarian protesters like these were exceptional but they were not entirely alone in their feelings. By the end of 1943, Mass Observation found that six people out of ten supported the mass raids ('It will shorten the war.' . . . 'They didn't think twice when they bombed us'); two out of ten thought they were necessary but had 'major qualms' about the civilian victims ('Nothing else to be done but I hate the idea of it all.' . . . 'It makes me feel sick.' . . . 'I feel terrible, when I think of what those poor bastard women and kids must be going through.' . . . 'I suppose they're necessary. Oh, I don't know. I don't see how they can *possibly* be necessary'). But one person in four definitely disapproved. The object of mass civilian bombing had never been frankly and unblinkingly admitted. Mass Observation added to its report: 'An interesting reflection of the depth of guilt felt about bombing people is afforded by the extent to which men and women still manage to believe that we are bombing military targets. Only one in ten said definitely that we were not aiming at military objectives.'

The acceptance of obliteration bombing, with the help of the fiction that it was 'really' aimed at military targets, was necessary to pave the way for the notorious obliteration of Dresden on 14 February 1945, which is believed to have killed more civilians than all the raids on Britain combined. At the time it was the logical conclusion of the decision to bomb civilians and beyond that, of course, lay the further extension of the policy to Hiroshima, Nagasaki and the nuclear age. By 1943 it was the Germans who were demanding reprisals. At first these came in what was called the 'Little Blitz' on London in early 1944, though not enough bombers could be spared from the East to repeat the scale of 1941. There were rumours, deliberately fostered in Germany, about new secret weapons being developed. By 1944 many Germans were expecting a near-miracle, a knock-out blow, their only hope, as they saw it now, of victory. On 12 June the 'miracle' arrived. Goebbels named it 'V1' to imply that a long series of V weapons were on the way – the 'V' stood for *Vergeltungswaffe*, 'reprisal weapon'. For a while Londoners were shaken by the eerie appearance of the pilotless flying bombs, 'buzz bombs' or 'doodle-bugs' as they were variously called, with their engines mounted on their tail-planes. The peculiar viciousness of the weapon resided in the last fifteen seconds of its flight, when the primitive rocket motor had cut out and all was silent as it nose-dived. Bert Sparling was taking a breather on a Croydon cinema roof with a fellow projectionist when this happened:

> Sid turned to me to say something and his face turned ashen, his jaw just dropped, his eyes went like saucers. Now Sid was a brave man, he'd been a senior warden all through the Blitz. I really didn't want to look over my shoulder to find out what it was but I did, of course, very slowly – and this thing had crept up on us from behind, very, very quietly and must have been gliding for some while. It seemed to be staggering through the air, falling slightly over to its right, which meant we would have been on the receiving end. There was nowhere to run. It was an agonising few seconds, it seemed to take hours. Then it settled on a level flight path again, went over to the left and dived straight down and we had a grandstand view. It hit some rising ground behind a row of shops. There was a flash, a half-circle of fire which spread outwards, then a lot of smoke and debris but no sound. I said to Sid, 'Where's the sound?' and as I spoke it hit us, with the blast, and blew us backwards.

At first these ponderous, noisy, grotesque flying robots caused considerable dismay. There was no longer any beginning or end to the raids. Life was one long alert, day and night. Bombers at least had gone home in the end, but V1s kept coming off the launching pads on the French coast, staggering to the end of their fuel supply in full view of everyone, and then falling silently and unpredictably out of the sky. Nobody who watched one approaching could avoid wishing, even praying, that its engine would stay alight at least until it had passed overhead – and then feeling a pang of guilt for wishing it on to

96 and 97 Hitler's secret weapon, the V1 or flying bomb, nicknamed the 'doodlebug', arrived in June 1944. Shaped like a pilotless plane with a primitive jet engine, it was launched from the Pas de Calais and aimed at London. When the fuel ran out, it stalled and fell. People below knew that they had fifteen seconds of utter helplessness in which to hope, or pray, that it would not drop on them

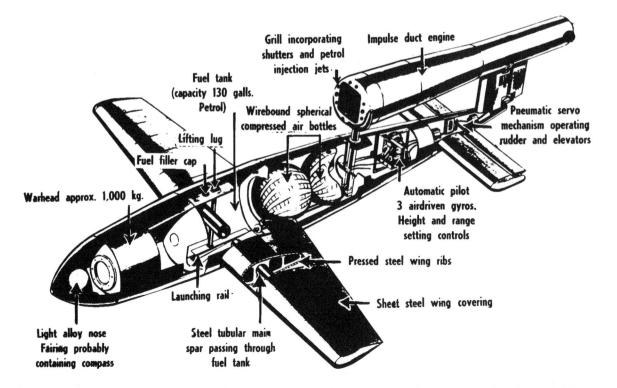

Grill incorporating shutters and petrol injection jets

Impulse duct engine

Fuel tank (capacity 130 galls. Petrol)

Wirebound spherical compressed air bottles

Pneumatic servo mechanism operating rudder and elevators

Lifting lug

Fuel filler cap

Automatic pilot 3 airdriven gyros. Height and range setting controls

Warhead approx. 1,000 kg.

Pressed steel wing ribs

Launching rail

Sheet steel wing covering

Light alloy nose Fairing probably containing compass

Steel tubular main spar passing through fuel tank

someone else. Watching one fall was an eerie experience. 'It seemed to take ages and it was the most helpless feeling I knew,' said Bert Sparling. 'At the bottom of the dive there were people waiting to die and you felt as if you wanted to reach out and catch it but there was just nothing anyone could do about it. It was a robot, it was totally inhuman and it fell wherever it was going to fall and nothing could stop it.' Overheard in a shelter was a remark from one woman to another that summed up the feeling: 'Oh, I'd rather have the piloted ones, they did have that human touch.' Another problem was the low altitude – the anti-aircraft guns were at first unable to aim at them, as Micky Hutton Storie found out bitterly at her AA gun-site:

> I shall never forget the night the first one came over, we hadn't a clue what was happening. There was this object flying very low with a huge exhaust, the flames spouting from its rear and we could do nothing about it. The guns were useless, their elevation was useless. To find all this expensive equipment was rendered useless by this thing made you feel all your training had been in vain at that particular moment.

At first the only defence against V1s were the RAF's fighters, which tried to shoot them down over the Channel or the Kent and Sussex Downs along what was called 'bomb alley', the route from the Pas de Calais launching sites towards London. Soon, anti-aircraft units were concentrated along the coast to explode them in the air over the sea – with increasing success, bringing down some 30 out of 100 daily. But for many weeks the bulk of them got through, carrying their pay-load of 1870 lbs (or four-fifths of a ton) of explosive – as big as all but the heaviest bombs – at a speed of 400 m.p.h.

The main attack lasted for eighty days, until the launching sites in the Pas de Calais were overrun by Montgomery's advancing army in September. During that time 10,500 V1s were launched, of which some 7000 of them reached Britain, but the guns and fighters destroyed nearly half of these. Only 2340 fell on their target – London – but they caused 24,000 casualties, including 5475 killed, a rate of 500 a week. There were more to come: over 750 were later launched in the air from planes and fell scattered over the country – some as far north as Manchester, Oldham and Yorkshire.

There was much discussion of whether the flying-bomb attack was as bad as the Blitz. It wasn't – but people were no longer in the mood that enabled them to rise to the Blitz so defiantly. They were tired and they were fed up with the war after five years of it. The long embattled stalemate after D-Day, the miserable summer and the impersonal nature of the flying bombs did not inspire the old resilience. People left the city in thousands, and a third evacuation took over a million, mainly children, out of the danger zone. This time the London evacuees on the whole were welcomed – some were invited back to their old billets by their country hosts of 1940. For those that stayed behind, three of the new deep shelters that had been built after the end of the Blitz were opened for the first time, as well as the tube shelters. 'Morrison shelters', which resembled a steel kitchen table with a wire cage around the legs, had also been supplied to many homes too late for the Blitz; now they were put to use, although many people did not shelter but took their chance.

Within a fortnight or so people adjusted to the new threat and treated it as a temporary nuisance rather than as the terror that had been anticipated from the 'secret weapon'. Life, work and entertainment carried on, although people became more adept at detecting the cutting-out of a spluttering rocket motor and at diving for cover. But on 8 September 1944 a new kind of explosion was heard, actually from Chiswick, but so shattering that people

98 Eros was protected by its pyramid-shaped air-raid shelter decorated with war slogans – here, one using the widespread V-for-Victory sign which appeared on buildings all over Britain and in occupied Europe. The flower-seller was a fragrant reminder of pre-war Piccadilly Circus

heard it all over West London and felt the shock of the blast for miles.

'We heard this huge explosion and we thought a gasometer had blown up,' said Micky Hutton Storie, the AA sergeant-major, 'It transpired that it was the first rocket dropped on London and it was utterly devastating. We hadn't got over the buzz bombs – they were still going strong – and now we had this to put up with. I'm awfully glad that we were just about winning the war at this point because there wouldn't have been very much of us left had it continued.' No official explanations were forthcoming of the thunderous explosions which followed on subsequent days. They were all supposed to be 'gasworks explosions'. If that was the case, there soon would not have been a gasworks left in London. It was not until 10 November that Churchill revealed that a new weapon, the V2, was in operation, launched from bases in Holland. V2s were eerier than V1s, besides being far more powerful; being supersonic, they gave no warning whatever of their arrival – until after the explosion, when the tearing sound of the approaching rocket followed it 'like an express train', according to Bert Sparling. In one way they were less menacing than their predecessors. No avoiding action was possible so it was pointless to worry whether one had your number on it – if it did, you would never know.

The V2s were huge steel canisters, forty-five feet long, carrying one-ton warheads. They were the most destructive weapons yet seen and the damage was heavy, although Londoners learned to live with them – uneasily. Over 1000 were launched and 518 fell on London over a period of six months, killing 2700 citizens and badly injuring 6000 more – only half as many as the V1s. But between them the two weapons damaged 1.5 million houses, at the rate of 20,000 a day at their worst. By the end of the raids, London had had 130,000 houses wiped out by bombs – more than the rest of the country put together. Only one house in ten in inner London had escaped damage completely.

The final grim arithmetic can be tabulated as follows for the whole of the war:

	Great Britain	*London*
Number of civilians killed	60,595	29,890
Seriously injured	86,182	50,507
Slightly injured	150,833	88,842
No. of houses destroyed	222,000	133,000
Weight of bombs dropped (metric tons)	71,000	12,222

The last V2 fell on 27 March and the last V1 on 29 March 1945. Allied troops were across the Rhine and the sirens fell silent for ever. The black-out had already given way to a 'dim-out' in the previous September, and in the same month the Home Guard had officially stood down. As the armies

inexorably ground on into Germany from the West and East during April, it was obviously all over bar the victory shouting. Then British feelings about their enemy, the Germans, altered with the overrunning of Buchenwald and Belsen. There had been White Papers on German concentration camps published in 1939 and in 1942, giving details of what was known of Jewish extermination from Polish sources, but the public were quite unprepared for the scale of the SS cruelty, for the discovery of Belsen's female warders, for the photographs of the state of the inmates, dead or only just living. The immediate reaction was to accuse the German people as a whole of responsibility. It was argued that the Nazi regime, which instituted these crimes, had been accepted by the vast majority of Germans without protest.

Until then, Mass Observation, which repeatedly questioned people on what should be done with Germany after the war, had consistently found that 'few people think that the crimes of war should be visited on the ordinary citizens of Germany. About one person in three will contemplate punishing the Nation, the abstract group.' But there was a very general desire to see the leaders punished as war criminals – with or without trial – and a noticeable anxiety that they would be allowed to get off unpunished. After the discovery of the concentration camps, there was no danger of that.

The fact was that throughout the first five years of war, the British people proved rather bad at hating another people. During the first three years, when everything was against them, they were fighting for survival, for their lives and for their freedom. When that immediate threat receded, the exaltation of defiance wore off and a gradual weariness set in. Retribution and vengeance were not enough to fight for; people needed a new motive. Many of them found it in visions of a new and better world that would dawn at home, a land fit, not for 'heroes' but for ordinary, decent people.

CHAPTER TEN

LEFTWARD, LOOK,
THE LAND IS BRIGHT

AS EARLY AS 4 JANUARY 1941 *Picture Post*, the popular news-picture
magazine which began shortly before the war and quickly won itself over
a million readers, published a special issue entitled 'A Plan For Britain'. The
great fire-raid on the City of London had only just taken place and the Blitz
was being carried nightly to cities all over the country, yet here were pictures
of the pre-war slums and unemployed contrasted with visions of a prosperous
future of planned cities of glass and grass, with articles by distinguished
names on Work for All, Health for All and Better Education for All. The
editorial recalled the failure to build the promised 'land fit for heroes' after the
First World War. 'This time we can be better prepared if we think now. . . .
The new Britain is the country we are fighting for.'

This was optimistic talk when Britain still had no allies and every prospect
of being invaded the following spring, though it was not the first time that
people had heard talk of fighting for a better world. In the invasion-haunted
white-hot weeks of summer 1940 J. B. Priestley's *Postscripts* had invited his
listeners to consider what they were risking their necks for:

> There are two ways of looking at this war. First, as a terrible interrup-
> tion. . . . As soon as we decently can, let's go back to where we started the
> day before war was declared. All wrong, it isn't true. There's nothing that
> really worked that we can go back to. My view, for what it's worth, is that
> we must stop thinking in terms of property and power and begin thinking
> in terms of community and creation.

He also reminded them of what happened after 1918 to many of the
'heroes' to whom Lloyd George had made promises. 'After a year or two,
there were a lot of shabby young-oldish men who tried to sell second-hand
cars or trailed round the suburbs asking to demonstrate a vacuum-cleaner.'
Of that betrayal people needed little reminding. Those who had not fought in
the first war had fathers or husbands or uncles who had – and who had also

lived through the Depression. When people looked back to life before the war, what most of them saw was dole queues, hunger marches and appeasement – for all of which they had the 'Guilty Men', mainly Conservative politicians, to thank.

It was not surprising, therefore, that *Picture Post* found itself inundated with sacks of mail from its readers responding positively to the vision of a new Britain. But *Picture Post* was not a lone voice. There was the *Daily Mirror* with its capacity for putting its views in simple dramatic language, its hard-hitting columnist Cassandra (William Connor) and cartoonist Zec, not forgetting the scantily-pantied strip-cartoon heroine, Jane. The favourite target of the *Mirror* was the outdated class-ridden mentality summed up in the person of 'Colonel Blimp', the pre-war invention of cartoonist David Low, who still drew him in the London *Evening Standard*. By this time a good many Blimpish generals, like Ironside, had been removed from active posts but the *Mirror* campaigned against 'brass-hatted boneheads' in high places and the government ministers such as Sir John Anderson 'whose hearts are not in the war'. Churchill wrote an infuriated letter to the paper's proprietor, Cecil King: 'There is a spirit of hatred and malice against the government which surpasses anything I have ever seen in English journalism. One would

100 David Low's cartoon character, 'Colonel Blimp', whom he introduced before the war, symbolised for many people the obsolete class structure and mentality of the Baldwin Thirties. Here he is trying to put his spoke into post-war planning for a more equal society

"DAMMIT, YOUNG MAN, WE MUSTN'T PUT THE CART BEFORE THE HORSE!"

have thought that in these hard times some hatred might be kept for the enemy.' It was the anti-Conservative line that had caused this over-reaction. Churchill pursued a vendetta against the paper for the rest of his time in office, demanding at one point that it should be suppressed because of a Zec cartoon (see page 175). There may have been justification for suppressing the *Daily Worker* for eighteen months in 1941, when it was claiming that people were dying needlessly in the Blitz for imperialism and generally fomenting agitation for 'a people's government', but there was never a case for calling the *Mirror* unpatriotic. Churchill, Bevin and Morrison had to be content with giving it a Cabinet-backed warning.

It was not only the left-of-centre newspapers like the *Mirror*, *News Chronicle* (Liberal) and *Daily Herald* (Labour) which talked of a change in the old order, however. *The Times* itself employed as one of its leader-writers the historian E. H. Carr, who differed from the élitist views which it more usually advocated: 'The New Order cannot be based on the preservation of privilege, whether of a country, of a class or of an individual,' it declared. If *The Times* was on the side of reform, even more so was the Archbishop of Canterbury. William Temple, a scholarly, unworldly man by upbringing, had surprised Anglicans by joining the Labour Party for some years because it was 'based on moral ideals'. In December 1940, a letter to *The Times* from the Archbishops of Canterbury, York and Westminster and the Free Church moderator had demanded that 'extreme inequality in wealth and possessions' should be abolished and 'every child given an equal opportunity, regardless of race or class'. Temple signed as the then Archbishop of York and the following year called a conference of 400 clergy to consider 'how Christian thought can be shaped to play a leading part in the reconstruction after the war'. In 1942, when he succeeded as Archbishop of Canterbury, 'the people's archbishop' published a little best-seller called *Christianity and the Social Order*, which advocated better housing, holidays with pay and family allowances as part of a Christian social order.

Pocket-sized Penguin books, price sixpence, had led the pre-war paperback publishing revolution and during the war there was a series of topical 'Penguin Specials'. Temple's book was one of them (it sold 140,000), and another (150,000 copies sold in three months) was the oddly named *Unser Kampf* (a mocking variation of Hitler's *Mein Kampf*) by Sir Richard Acland. Acland was a Liberal MP who had become a Christian Socialist and advocated the common ownership of all major resources, including the land; he himself had given his considerable family estates in Devonshire to the National Trust. The enthusiastic response to his book led him to launch an organisation called Forward March. Meanwhile J. B. Priestley, after being taken off the air at home, was touring the country as a speaker and had taken on the chairmanship of the '1941 Committee', consisting mainly of editors of progressive papers and reformist politicians, including Acland. In the summer of 1942 the two groups merged to form a new political party, Common

101 Archbishop William Temple, well know for his Socialist views (and past membership of the Labour Party), argued for a 'Christian social order' after the war, including equal opportunity for every child, better housing and family allowances

Wealth (Priestley soon resigned and left the leadership to Acland). There was a by-election truce between the three main parties which formed the wartime coalition, which meant that when a by-election occurred, the party that already held the seat would nominate a candidate who would not be opposed by the other two parties: the only competition came from independents. Common Wealth candidates immediately made serious inroads into the Conservative vote in many constituencies and overturned it to win three of the 'safest' Conservative seats. This was in spite of the fact that Common Wealth policies were radical. Acland, an earnest man who preached his doctrines with religious fervour as if politics were a form of personal salvation, called for the building of a new Jerusalem in England's green and pleasant, or dark and noisome, land, according to which part of it you inhabited. His appeal was very much to the middle-class voter with an uneasy social conscience. 'If you could conjure up and photograph our members, they would look very much like the sort of people who would today be members of the Liberal–SDP alliance,' he said recently, 'with the difference that we were attracting these people for a programme which was way out to the left of the Labour Party. The common ownership of the great productive resources was not advocated with the idea of making people richer in a material sense. It was the necessary foundation for a more morally based society.'

There were, then, plenty of influential voices to be heard, all agreeing pretty closely that the war was being fought – or ought to be being fought – to bring about a much more equal society than existed before it began. This soon became a commonplace among speakers of many political hues, including Conservatives. Witness R. A. Butler, President of the Board of Education: 'Britain will emerge from the war as one single society or community in which all careers will be open to talent.' Or Sir James Grigg, top civil servant, who became War Minister: 'It is Britain's mission to build out of the wreck of the old world a better and juster one with equality of opportunity for all.' And Captain Quintin Hogg, MP (later Lord Hailsham), founding member of the Tory Reform Committee: 'We are rapidly producing, whether we desire it or not, a classless society – the marks of respect that went to wealth or privilege in the past are going to education and technical skill in the present.'

Even the Prime Minister made such a pronouncement, not to the nation as a whole, it is true, but to the boys of his old school, Harrow, in December 1940: 'When this war is won, it must be one of our aims to establish a state of society where the advantages and privileges hitherto enjoyed only by the few shall be far more widely shared by the many.' But the key words here for Churchill were 'when this war is won'. The Cabinet had been urged to make a statement of war aims on several occasions but Churchill always opposed this – beating Hitler was, in his eyes, the only war aim needed. He liked to end his speeches with vague, rhetorical promises of advancing into 'broad, sunlit uplands', wherever they might be. But he vetoed the issue of a statement of war aims because 'precise aims would be compromising' (and would probably divide the coalition). By 1941 public demand was pressing for one. Within a few weeks of *Picture Post* publishing its plan for post-war Britain, a new Cabinet committee was set up on 'reconstruction problems', chaired at first by Arthur Greenwood, one of the Labour Party's elder statesmen.

A Home Intelligence Survey on 'Public Feeling on Postwar Reconstruction' in 1942 found that 'In all classes of the community, unemployment is thought to be the outstanding post-war problem. It is, indeed, more than a problem, it is a personal and individual fear.' Interestingly enough, the second most urgent problem was thought to be 'the replacement of private profit by service to the community' – the very ideal that Archbishop Temple, Acland, Priestley and their like were urging. It does not follow that it was *because* of their influence that people reacted against the ugly side of capitalism; they had only to consult their own memories of it to decide that they did not want to return to Baldwin's and Chamberlain's Britain. By 1942 there had been plenty of opportunity for these feelings to be expressed and discussed; war brought everyone long periods of waiting – in shelters and queues, ARP posts and on fire-watching duty and, above all, in the services.

From August 1941 the Army positively encouraged discussion of post-war problems by the troops through the weekly (compulsory) briefing session of the Army Bureau of Current Affairs, known as ABCA, which was directed by W. E. Williams of the Workers' Educational Association. It supplied lecturers and booklets with the title *Current Affairs* to guide the discussions, which were usually led by a platoon commander or some other officer of the unit. 'We are fighting not to win, but to win *something*: the more we clear our minds here and now about the world we want after the war, the more likely we are to attain it,' ran a typical sentence from one of the booklets. These general discussion groups were intended as a form of adult education and political enlightenment on non-controversial lines, to improve morale and motivation to fight. Whether they remained uncontroversial depended on who was leading the discussion – a well-informed political activist in the ranks could have a field day wiping the floor with the opposition. On the other hand many of the troops were bored or treated the discussions as a welcome break from 'square-bashing' and the assault course, a chance for a smoke or a discreet 'kip'. Opinions differ about the effect of these discussions, but what effect there was was bound to have led to questioning of the status quo.

On to this fertile soil, ripe for new visions, longing to be rid of Yesterday's Men and their discredited policies, the Beveridge Report fell like manna in the desert on 1 December 1942. It almost coincided with the Battle of Alamein, and it transformed the Home Front as completely as the Alamein victory transformed the fighting war. The man who now stepped forward on to the stage was in some ways a 'Montgomery' of welfare. Beveridge was sixty-two, five years younger than Churchill but, like him, a Victorian Liberal by background. As a young man laden with the honours of Oxford scholarship, he had awakened his social conscience by serving at Toynbee Hall, the East End social mission, which showed him the scale of unemployment and poverty in Edwardian England. In 1908 Churchill, President of the Board of Trade in the Liberal government, invited Beveridge to become a civil servant in his Ministry, where he introduced the new Labour Exchanges for the unemployed. Beveridge had already published a study of unemployment and left the civil service after the First World War with the top rank of Permanent Secretary. After directing the London School of Economics he returned to Whitehall as adviser to Ernest Bevin (who didn't like him) on manpower requirements. He was everything it was possible to be in the corridors of Whitehall, short of actually being a minister. A thin, reedy, scholarly man, with a profile that puckered at the chin like a sage ostrich, he also had all the arrogance of a Victorian rationalist, a certain belief in social progress and a conviction that he knew best how to attain it.

The Beveridge Report was the report of a committee of over twenty civil servants on 'Social Insurance and Allied Services', but in practice Beveridge himself laid down its principles, drafted it, signed it as his own and publicised it in meetings, speeches and broadcasts. One of the people whose backs he put up thereby was Churchill. When, to his surprise, he was not invited to join the government as 'Minister of Social Insurance' to carry out his recommendations, he set up a new unofficial Beveridge inquiry into unemployment with private backing. This report, which was published with the title *Full Employment in a Free Society* in 1944, was as famous and possibly more controversial than his first. So there were really *two* Beveridge reports and his name dominated the thinking about reconstruction for the last four years of the war. 'He knew everybody, he was clever, he was a very good social scientist but I don't think he was a lovable man,' said Sir Norman Chester, who was the Beveridge Committee's secretary. 'He did not go out to get your love but he had boundless energy at sixty-three and he was one of those rare people you were glad to have worked with. He was a big man in his thinking.'

The 1942 Report described itself as 'a plan for social security to abolish physical want by ensuring for all citizens at all times a subsistence income and the means of meeting exceptional expenditure at birth, marriage and death'. This 'cradle-to-grave' insurance was to be achieved by flat-rate contributions and flat-rate payments which would be the same for everybody, irrespective of their income. The brief had been to tidy up all the existing schemes of partial insurance, public and private, against sickness, unemployment and industrial accident, and to provide pensions for old age, disability and widowhood. The former were a tangle which included some people and excluded others; for example, a man's wife and family were not covered by his health insurance. There were great numbers of private insurance schemes, societies and clubs to which people paid pennies a week to ensure that they got some inadequate sum for sickness or their funeral expenses. Beveridge's scheme rationalised all this and substituted for the idea of getting only what you paid for, the right of anyone unable to work to draw a subsistence income from the state. This would ensure that no one would fall below a 'national minimum' to the level of poverty. Sir Norman Chester explained Beveridge's thinking: 'He saw that by using the insurance scheme he could, in his words, "abolish want". He developed his idea that insurance could be used to redistribute income, not between the rich and poor, but between those who were working and those who weren't, because they were sick or unemployed or old.'

On top of this basic minimum there were to be child allowances and maternity, marriage and death grants, to allow the exceptional expenses of normal life to be met without hardship (or means-testing). This was thinking in big and simple principles but Beveridge went much further:

> Organisation of social insurance should be treated as one part only of a comprehensive policy for social progress. Social insurance, fully developed, may provide ncome security; it is an attack on Want. But Want is one only of five giants on the road of reconstruction and in some ways the easiest to attack. The others are Disease, Ignorance, Squalor and Idleness.

102 Sir William Beveridge, whose 'Report on Social Insurance' in 1942 showed how to 'abolish want', was hailed as the prophet of a Utopian new Britain. He followed it with an investigation of how to maintain full employment after the war

[227]

This was language which all could understand and it chimed in with the national mood. Britain's money and manpower were by now fully mobilised to destroy Hitler – could they not slay a few giants nearer home as well? The giant Disease, said Beveridge, was to be slain by a new comprehensive National Health Service, and Idleness by a scheme to prevent mass unemployment ever returning. These were the assumptions on which social security depended. As objectives they appealed to the public even more strongly. Here was the road to Utopia indeed, and here was a man who had worked out in detail how to get there.

The Report came out to an overwhelming welcome. The Stationery Office was besieged: 635,000 copies were sold, a record for White Papers. The Labour Party, the Liberal Party, the TUC and the British Council of Churches welcomed it unreservedly. Even the younger Conservatives of the Tory Reform Committee, a group of some forty-five MPs led by Quintin Hogg, hailed it as 'a flag to nail to the mast, a rallying point for men of goodwill, above all an opportunity to establish a social conscience in the Tory party'. Beveridge was invited to introduce his Report in a broadcast *Postscript*. It was, he told the audience, 'a means of redistributing national income so as to put first things first, to ensure the abolition of want before the enjoyment of comforts'. Shortly afterwards he spoke again: 'One of the discoveries of 1942 is the deep and vivid interest of the people of Britain in the kind of Britain which is to emerge when the floods of war subside. . . . One cannot make a people's war except for a people's peace.' The press was uniformly welcoming. The BBC broadcast summaries of his proposals in twenty-two languages. It was powerful propaganda for British leadership in social questions, eclipsing the Nazis' claims for the achievements of National Socialism. Dr Schmidt, German state propagandist, was moved to try to discredit it. 'Beveridge has feet of clay. The wine of enthusiasm of British Leftists has been watered down. Nothing will be left but a state grant for veterinary treatment for cats and dogs,' he jeered.

Apart from the Nazi party, the only people to give the Report a surly, if not hostile reception, were the traditional Conservatives. For three months the coalition government simply remained silent and Beveridge's request to see Churchill went unanswered. An ABCA pamphlet by Beveridge himself explaining his recommendations was issued for discussion in mid-December and then hurriedly withdrawn two days later. Beveridge's plans, it was explained, were too controversial for Army discussion. But it was too late to undo the initial publicity and the spontaneous effect the Report had had.

Home Intelligence at the Ministry of Information reported 'almost universal approval by people of all shades of opinion and by all sections of the community'. A public opinion poll taken in the first fortnight after publication of the Report found that 95 per cent of those questioned had heard of it and 86 per cent believed it should be put into effect. Even employers (73 per cent), upper-income groups (76 per cent) and the professions (91 per cent), who had least to gain personally, were strongly in favour. Mass Observation found its interviewees were inspired by Beveridge – 'A grand thing if it means what it says.' . . .'A lovely thing in its entirety but it will be a hard fight to get it.' . . . 'Exhilarating to hear it read out on the news.' But quite a large number were sceptical about whether it would come to pass – 'They'll promise us the moon while the war's on but as soon as it's over they'll find some excuse for sliding out of it' was a typical reaction.

Churchill was away at the Casablanca conference when the Report was published, but he directed that any decision on implementing Beveridge should be left for a newly elected government to make after the war. The chief opponent in the Cabinet was Sir Kingsley Wood, Chancellor of the Exchequer and a last survivor of Chamberlain's government, which was notorious for parsimony. In the time-honoured Treasury tradition he argued that the country could not afford Beveridge's proposals. Beveridge had already argued out the practicable cost with J. M. Keynes, the economic guru who was then at the Treasury, and got his blessing, but Kingsley Wood wrote to Churchill that the scheme 'is ambitious and involves an impracticable financial commitment, which would greatly increase taxation because insurance contributions would only pay for part of it'. He added sardonically – 'the weekly progress of the millionaire to the Post Office for his old age pension would have an element of farce but for the fact that it is to be provided in large measure by the taxpayer'. Beveridge had estimated the cost at £700 million in 1945 and £850 million, twenty years later. This was on the basis of £2 a week (£27 today) for the unemployed and the pensioner.

When the House of Commons at last debated the Beveridge Report in February 1943 the government's line was to accept many of the proposals of the Report but avoid any commitment to realising them until the war was over. Sir John Anderson, exhibiting a weary lack of enthusiasm, warned them: 'It has been my duty to point out that there can be at present no binding commitment.' Kingsley Wood emphasised the government's lack of commitment to the point of almost total apathy. Only Herbert Morrison, himself an enthusiast for the Report, promised that the government would do its best to carry through two-thirds of the proposals. Promises were not enough. The Tory Reform Committee called for the immediate setting up of a Ministry of Social Security. When it came to the vote they toed the line, but 97 Labour MPs rebelled *en masse* with 9 Liberals, including Lloyd George, the pioneer of state welfare. There were 121 votes against the government. One result was that Ernest Bevin, treating the revolt as a personal criticism of himself, refused to attend any more Labour Party meetings.

So battle was joined on the question of what post-war Britain's priorities were to be. It was a fateful battle, one which, more than anything else, would decide the post-war general election. It would hardly be too much to claim that the Conservatives lost that election two years before it was held by their half-hearted response to Beveridge. Barbara Davies, for example, remembered the effect of Beveridge on her and her fellow-workers who used to discuss politics in the Armstrong–Whitworth factory at Baginton, Coventry:

> Having been the eldest daughter of a widow, I knew very well about the means test, the ten-shillings-a-week widow's pension, and I knew the poverty before the war. I can actually remember children at school with no shoes, I really can, because they were so hard up. This was in the Depression and even in those days it seemed appalling. So when the Beveridge Report came out, talking of giving us a welfare state where there would be no poverty, no one starving, and free health care, it just seemed the sort of world we were all looking for.

Even cricket clubs discussed the Report. 'I remember playing with a club known as "The Bowden Gentlemen" and when I arrived, knowing that I had some knowledge about it, the team wanted to discuss it,' said John Beavan, then a well-known Fleet Street journalist. In a clutch of 1943 by-elections, the Report was the major issue. Left-wing candidates, especially those of the Common Wealth party, demanded 'Beveridge in full – Now' and the Conservative vote in general fell by 8 per cent. Home Intelligence reports found 'a large disappointed majority' after the Commons debate, who were 'cynical, disappointed or angry'. Most people thought that the government was trying to kill or shelve the Report, or whittle down its benefits: 'the government's attitude has crystallised people's worst fears for the post-war period.' *Picture Post*, whose post-war plan had in some ways anticipated Beveridge, ran an editorial signed by its editor Tom Hopkinson: 'The House of Commons has not quite killed the Report. It has filleted it. It has taken out the backbone. . . . Opponents of the Report spoke as though it were an attempt to cadge money off the rich on behalf of the not entirely deserving poor.'

'The mood of the country was distinctly to the left of the government,' recalled Hopkinson. 'There was no question of changing government in mid-stream. But the idea grew that there must be quite a different society when the war was over.' By now it was becoming obvious which party was not likely to engineer that new society. 'I knew, because they told me, that a lot of people were fighting the war to keep Britain exactly as it had been,' wrote J. B. Priestley. 'But none of them lived in back-to-back houses, mostly on tea, bread and margarine.'

The lessons of the by-elections were not lost on the government. Churchill himself was persuaded to broadcast on post-war prospects in an attempt to restore the government's lost credit. In March 1943 he 'peered through the mists of the future' and offered the prospect of a four-year reconstruction plan, to be put to the voters after the war and carried out, if approved, by a new government. He suggested that he, too, was a Beveridge fan. 'I and my colleagues must be ranked as strong partisans of national compulsory

insurance for all purposes from the cradle to the grave.' He talked of the abolition of unemployment. He even mentioned 'a broadening field for State enterprise and ownership' as well as a housing drive, educational reform and improved health services. In short, in a vague, sweeping way he proposed to deal with Beveridge's five evil giants – but not until later.

In the same month Beveridge announced that he was going to conduct his own inquiry into the question of full employment as a private citizen, funded by well-wishers such as Sir Edward Hulton, proprietor of *Picture Post*, and David Astor, heir to the *Observer*. This caused dismay and panic in government circles. Another Beveridge report! No doubt there would be another great popular outcry to adopt the Sage's findings on this hot potato. There then ensued what Beveridge called 'the White Paper Chase'. The government hastily appointed its own inquiry. 'They put everything possible into an attempt to deal with employment before the new Beveridge report should be published,' he said. Both reports were ready by May 1944 but it was six months before Beveridge's *Full Employment in a Free Society* could be produced and put on sale. Although he lost the race, there was no doubt which of the two documents was the more radical and influential. Beveridge declared: 'Twice depression and falling employment have been reversed by

103 A poster issued by the Army Bureau of Current Affairs contrasted the clean lines of the modern Finsbury Health Centre (with implications of a future National Health Service) with the bad old days of insanitary slum conditions and children with rickets. The poster was withdrawn by government order

world wars. . . . We ought to decide to cure unemployment without war.' His solution was that future Budgets should be balanced in human rather than financial terms to ensure that there was enough public expenditure, on top of private expenditure, to employ the whole of the manpower of the country. This was the Keynesian concept of deficit budgeting ('priming the pump') to increase demand, which was relatively untried.

Beveridge's main contention, however, went further than economic measures to increase employment. His social philosophy, the bedrock belief on which the future welfare state rested, was stated like this: 'We should regard Want, Disease, Ignorance and Squalor as common enemies, not as enemies with whom each individual may seek a separate peace, escaping to personal prosperity while leaving his fellows in their clutches. That is the meaning of social conscience – that one should refuse to make a separate peace with social evil.' Shorn of its somewhat old-fashioned turns of phrase, it boiled down to something close to John Donne's 'No man is an island'. Such was the spirit of those optimistic times. And yet within ten years, the prevailing climate had turned right round and could be summed up by the catchphrase, 'I'm all right, Jack.'

Beveridge left a great deal of detail out of his account – there is little mention of wage levels and the effect of collective bargaining on employment, for instance, or of the need for post-war industry to be competitive in cost. But in concentrating on ethical goals, Beveridge was reflecting the feelings of a great section of the British people in wartime. They had discovered concern for one another through common danger, they had accepted fair shares under common privations, and by gigantic common effort the war economy had produced the tools to finish the job of beating a more powerful enemy. The war economy, where everything was planned to serve one purpose, was of course a much simpler economy, whose resources were nationalised in all but name. The economist Sir Alec Cairncross, who spent the war administering aircraft production, explained:

> It was rather like a Communist economy – they have much in common. You work on the basis of programmes and the government has a hand in practically everything. . . . When things became scarce, you did not let prices rise, as normally happens, you tried to ration or license or use quotas. You could compel people to join the armed forces or you could direct them to industry. In wartime, control of industry was possible because the government was paymaster, the government was the employer, the government controlled all the new materials, sites, factories, machine tools, everything that the firms making munitions wanted. Firms could concentrate on production. They need not worry about marketing. Their profits were assured. The government was going to buy the stuff. But in peacetime you are manufacturing for the average consumer. It's a very different story.

By 1943 there was full employment to an unprecedented degree – even the majority of disabled people were doing war-work. The contrast with pre-war mass unemployment was obvious. 'People felt that if they could plan the war economy so successfully, they should be capable of planning the peace. If the government could get rid of unemployment in wartime, they should be able to do it in peacetime,' said Cairncross. When Bevin went down to the south coast with Churchill just before D-Day, to inspect the troops who were about to embark, they called out to him: 'When we've done this job for you, Ernie, are we going back on the dole?' He told the story often. 'Both the Prime Minister and I answered: "No, you are not."' It was the issue on which people felt most anxiety about the future. But the other giants demanded attention too.

A National Health Service was not a new idea and it was common ground between the parties. The British Medical Association back in 1938 had suggested that the two parallel systems of hospitals should be integrated – one run by local authorities, the other voluntary, relying on charity, legacies and flag days and usually struggling with debt. The war brought into being the Emergency Medical Service for various categories of war injury, which functioned in both types of hospital, staffed by doctors and nurses whose salaries were paid by the state. People saw this as a model on which to build a National Health Service for all and a commission of medical authorities proposed one in 1942. In 1944 the Ministry of Health produced a White Paper on what form a free, comprehensive service should take. It visualised that doctors would mainly work in local authority health centres, not private practices, and be paid salaries by the state, like teachers, instead of fees. These proposals proved too radical for the BMA, and right up until the passing of the NHS Act in 1948 it fought doggedly against the idea of doctors on salaries, although some private practice was still to be allowed. But at least the principle that everyone – irrespective of means, age, sex or occupation – should have equal access to the best and most up-to-date medical treatment was clearly stated as the object of a National Health Service in the White Paper. Once stated, it could not be withdrawn, whatever the BMA said.

This was only the first of many White Papers on social policy to appear in 1944. Reconstruction was the watchword of the time. Lord Woolton had been given the title of Minister of Reconstruction in November 1943, and a Reconstruction Priorities Committee sat in review of the plans which poured out. In May there was the White Paper on employment policy and in September the government's proposals on national insurance, a watered-down version of the Beveridge plan. There was a housing White Paper which promised a large house-building programme as soon as the war ended, together with half a million 'pre-fabs' as a stop-gap (a Ministry of Town and Country Planning had already been set up in 1943). If plans and White Papers and the deliberations of committees had had any real substance, the wartime coalition would rank as one of the great reforming administrations, like the

Liberals of 1906. In fact only two proposals did become reality – family allowances were introduced in February 1945, for all children under school-leaving age except the first, and in August 1944 the Education Act was passed.

This reform is always known as the Butler Education Act, in honour of that unorthodox, subtle and wily politician who was president of the Board of Education (under the act he became Minister of Education). R. A. Butler ('Rab', later Lord) had one important advantage in getting his reforms on the statute book: he was *not* Sir William Beveridge. Churchill would not have the Beveridge proposals passed in wartime but the House of Commons had to have something to keep it busy. As his chief whip pointed out, 'This bill will not create divisions against the government. It is splendid to have it available.' Nevertheless, the Education Act was a radical reform of an undemocratic school system, under which five children out of six had received no more than an elementary school education to the age of fourteen.

Now there was to be free secondary schooling to the age of fifteen, which would one day be raised to sixteen. There would be 'equality' of opportunity through examinations at eleven-plus to get into grammar schools, for the bright scholars, and technical schools, for the bright but less academic pupils. 'Secondary modern' schools catered for the rest. It was still a caste system and left a further élite class – at the fee-paying public schools – untouched; it was suggested that 25 per cent of their pupils should come from state schools, paid for by their local authorities. Direct grant schools were also mixed: they could give 50 per cent of their places to fee-paying pupils. The act even visualised nursery schools to be provided by Local Education Authorities.

Butler showed great energy, touring the country to explain the proposals, and there was remarkable unanimity of support – except from the churches, which provided a third of the existing schools and jealously guarded their sectarian religious teaching. Most of these schools were in antiquated buildings – 10,000 Church of England schools had been built before the twentieth century began – and many needed rebuilding. Butler skilfully undermined church opposition by offering the church schools a choice of becoming 'aided' (in which case the state would meet only half the cost of repair and rebuilding) or 'controlled' (in which case the church gave up much of its control of the curriculum but did not have to pay for building costs). All schools were to give compulsory non-sectarian religious education. The debate on this, the biggest measure of reform passed during the war, went smoothly except when the government was defeated on an amendment calling for equal pay for women teachers – the only substantial defeat on a vote which it ever suffered. Churchill demanded another vote, of confidence. 'You knocked me off my perch. You have got to put me back on my perch, otherwise I won't sing,' he said.

Butler emerged with credit as the foremost Tory reformer of them all, one

104 The one major social reform of the war years was the Education Act of 1944, which introduced secondary schooling for all to the age of fifteen. It was the work of R.A. Butler, one of the few reforming Conservatives who could get on with Churchill, and who shared many ideas with the Labour ministers

who had the rare gift among reformers of getting along with Churchill. He sat
on the Reconstruction Committee opposite Attlee, Bevin and Morrison and
claimed that on post-war proposals such as the health service, social
insurance, housing and unemployment there was little division between the
parties. 'There is no doubt that Bevin and I were thinking along similar lines,
except for nationalisation,' he wrote, 'but we all felt we must create a more
equable peacetime world.' Five years of working together had made for a
great deal of understanding and common outlook between the ministers. For
some of them it was hard, even distasteful, to imagine a return to party strife,
but this was not the feeling of the Labour party rank and file, which
demanded that Labour should fight the next election as an independent party.
The leading Labour rebel, Emmanuel Shinwell (who had refused minoi office
under Churchill) told them: 'Some gentlemen in power have not the least
intention of giving the workers any more in the future than they had in the
past. There will be a thin time for them if they do not use their power to
enforce their just claims.'

Germany surrendered on 7 May 1945. The V-for-Victory signs that had
been painted and chalked on walls for four years had at last been fulfilled. The
ships in harbour ushered in VE Day, 8 May, with three short blasts and one
long one, the morse code V-sign. Churchill gave his personal version of the
two-fingered V-sign as his car was swept along Whitehall to the House of
Commons in the midst of a sea of celebration. After standing on the
Buckingham Palace balcony with the King and Queen, he later appeared on a
balcony in Whitehall to a rapturous reception from the crowds. 'This is *your*
victory,' he told them. 'No – it is yours,' some of them roared back. They
sang 'Land of Hope and Glory' together. Bonfires were lighted, bells pealed
out, bands played and fireworks (such as could be found after so many years
without Guy Fawkes Days) were let off. It was a day of mixed feelings, not
only of relief and joy but of somewhat dazed bewilderment. One of the first
proofs of peace returning was that the BBC broadcast the first weather
forecast since September 1939. It promised 'bright intervals' and gave
warning of a large depression approaching.

Fred Barnes summed up the odd mixture of contradictory feelings which
many people experienced that day: 'There came a peculiar sense of relief and
yet almost a sense of regret because we were living on a razor's edge during
the war. It was living with a capital L and there was a feeling of loss. You were
glad it had finished but there was still that feeling that you'd lost something.'

One of the Mass Observers who kept diaries, remembering that Japan
had still to be defeated, wrote with prophetic inspiration: 'After the storm I
went to join the longest fish-queue that I can remember. Several people with
relations in the Far East said they couldn't really celebrate. Believe me, there's
going to be more fighting, more dying, more monstrosities still to come.'

Churchill proposed that the coalition government should remain in being
until the war with Japan was over. Attlee, the Labour leader, and Ernest Bevin

argued for accepting the invitation, but the National Executive of the party voted decisively against it. Churchill and his ministers resigned on 23 May, and a 'caretaker' government of Conservatives and a few non-party ministers took over to see the country through until it had a new government after the election announced for 5 July. The new, temporary Minister of Labour was R. A. Butler, who described going to the Ministry to ask his outgoing predecessor, Bevin, if he would show him round and introduce him to the senior officials. 'I won't on any account,' Bevin retorted. 'Churchill ought not to have broken up the coalition, he should have run at any rate till the end of the Japanese war and then we should not be in this position.' Then he turned to his secretary and said, with finality, 'Fetch me my 'at.'

Bevin did not expect, and neither did most of the Labour Ministers, that they stood any serious chance in the election against the immense authority and prestige which victory had conferred on Churchill. Most people believed the result to be a foregone conclusion – especially the Conservative Party, which expected to ride to an easy victory on Churchill's coat-tails. The party's election campaign seemed to consist of one long triumphant tour of the country by Churchill, greeted everywhere his car travelled with shouts and applause and banners. Julian Amery, Conservative candidate for Preston, described Churchill's reception in his open car.

> In towns and villages the pavements were three and four deep with people; even in the country lanes people had come out. I've never seen such an emotional reception in Britain for any politician. Cripples came out with Union Jacks tied to their crutches and waved them. . . . He was cheered to the echo and there was a sort of wave of gratitude went out towards the man – though many of those who were cheering must have voted against him a matter of days later.

There was one flaw in his performance that needs to be put into the balance. Acclaimed though he was, this was for most people their first close-up view of 'Winston', the embodiment of the voice they knew so well, and many were disconcerted by what they saw. He sat immobile in the back of an open car, pink from too much make-up (for make-up was thought essential even for men's public appearances at that date) but in spite of that looking a spent and very tired man. He would acknowledge the cheers with a flip of his famous V-sign, or a tip of his out-moded, high-crowned bowler hat. But he seemed to stare at the crowds as if in a trance, scarcely aware of them. The effect was like looking at a waxwork figure of a statesman from a bygone era, scarcely the man to deal competently with modern social problems of which he had no personal experience.

On the other side of the hustings the political ranks were alive with new faces in uniform. Major Denis Healey or Squadron Leader Aidan Crawley were typical of the Labour Party's 120 services candidates. Never before had

105 (Facing page) Churchill gives his well-known version of the V-sign on VE Day as he is cheered and chaired by the crowd in Whitehall. Two months later they would vote him out of power

106 Election, 1945: the Labour posters go up. The parties' programmes did not differ so much as their credibility with regard to being ready to carry out radical social reforms

so many officers called on their audiences to vote Labour; they were more remarkable than the Conservative officer candidates, especially to middle-class voters. Conservative candidates were often safe, unexciting local bigwigs.

Lord Beaverbrook played the role of Svengali in Churchill's shadow, thanks to their long-standing friendship, although he was detested among the Tory Party. When Churchill made his first election broadcast on 4 June he declared that if the Labour Party won and introduced socialism into Britain, they would require 'some form of Gestapo' to silence criticism. This was a terrible blunder. After the high patriotic tone of Churchill's wartime speeches, to accuse the men he had worked with for five years – Attlee, Bevin, Morrison and the rest – of being no better than the Nazis, was an unwarranted smear and plainly ridiculous. 'The voice we heard was that of Mr Churchill but the mind was that of Lord Beaverbrook,' commented Attlee, though the words were Churchill's own. He once referred to his audience, unfortunately, as 'you listening to me in your cottages'. Some said that Churchill cost his party a million voters by convincing them that he was out of touch with the mood of the country. Another factor was that Labour had come of age. For the first time the Labour Party leaders were seasoned in office and well experienced in directing the energies of the nation as ministers in major departments. Ultimately the election, in which the party programmes ostensibly had much in common, turned on the question of credibility. Which of them was most likely to fulfil the general promises of wide-ranging social reforms? Ever since Churchill turned down Beveridge there had been only one answer.

The night before the result was declared, he recorded, he went to bed in the belief that the British people would summon him to continue leading them. 'Just before dawn I woke suddenly with a sharp stab of almost physical pain' and 'a hitherto subconscious conviction that we were beaten'. His premonition was impressive. The next day the arithmetic stared him and everyone in the face. Nearly 12 million people had voted Labour (47.8 per cent of the votes cast), giving the party 393 seats, while nearly 10 million had voted for the Conservatives (39.8 per cent), giving them only 213 seats. Five members of Churchill's Cabinet and thirty-two members of his government were voted out. While the Conservatives were savaged, the Liberals were almost annihilated: only 12 of their 306 candidates made it to the House of Commons. Two of the defeated Liberals were Sir William Beveridge and Sir Archibald Sinclair, the party leader.

'Let's face it, whoever imagined such a result?' asked the commentator's voice on the newsreel, showing the newspapers being delivered with their huge headlines, 'Labour Landslide'. Tom Hopkinson was at Lord Rothermere's Conservative party at the Dorchester on the night the poll was declared. 'The results were flashed up on a big screen and as they came up "Labour Victory" … "Labour Victory" … "Labour Victory" … an indignant Conservative came up to me and said, "It's your bloody *Picture Post* that's responsible for this!" I said I thought the bloody *Daily Mirror* was just as responsible for it.'

107 26 July: the poll result is declared. Clement Attlee, Labour Party leader and Churchill's deputy premier throughout the war, now steps into his shoes

A change had come over Fleet Street during the war years which made the political balance between the national papers almost even. 'In the 1945 election for the first time the anti-Conservative press, with 6 million copies a day, was almost as big as the pro-Conservative press with 6.5 million. This was largely due to the increase in circulation of the *Daily Mirror* to something like 2.4 million,' said John Beavan, former editor of the *Daily Herald* and later Lord Ardwick. 'The Labour party had a certain amount of sympathy from *The Times* and the *Observer* as well, and this was a new factor. But the *Daily Mirror* had established itself as the friend of the forces and its campaign was a subtle one. Instead of saying "Vote Labour" it said "Vote for Them", the servicemen – meaning "See they are not cheated again". It meant vote Labour, without actually saying so.'

Afterwards the service vote was credited with having clinched the result for Labour. 'Among the servicemen, there was the feeling that they were as good as anybody else, and they wanted the right to tell their officers off once the war was over,' said Denis Healey. 'There was this theory that there was a Socialist plot to influence people through the ABCA discussion groups, but the importance of ABCA, I think, has been exaggerated.' The truth was that it did not need an ABCA, any more than it needed *Picture Post* or the *Daily Mirror* itself, to tell those who had been fighting, or the civilians who had been enduring, that they wanted total change, a new world. But the shock to the Colonel Blimps was severe. Albert Levine, who was serving in the Army in Cairo, described how the election result was received among senior officers there:

> Some of them were very sullen, making openly nasty remarks about mob rule. One or two were almost hysterical. The ordinary soldiers on the whole were tremendously enthusiastic about it. I remember being in a room where both officers and other ranks were listening to the results coming through. The officers were far from poker-faced. There was fear on some faces, there was resentment on others and the physical movement between the two groups was most interesting. The other ranks clustered round the radio eagerly and the officers withdrew to the other end of the room, listening from a distance, physically distancing themselves from these would-be rebels. You could imagine they almost felt that the tumbrils were going to come out and the lamp-posts were going to be dangling with ropes.

Sam Bardell, who was a sergeant major serving in Cairo, remembered the election result having a very visible effect on Army behaviour:

> For three days no officer was saluted. We really thought that the revolution had come, a new dawn had dawned. They had to start introducing saluting patrols to get it back. I think most people had a great

deal of contempt for the officers. The regulars were having a very soft time of it and in many cases were very stupid men. And there was also a tremendous class feeling, that they were a superior race. Large numbers of hotels and clubs were out of bounds to us. There was still that feeling of animosity, that it was Them and Us. So 1945 was a grand time to be alive. We really felt that things were going to be done.

'The basic thing about the Second World War,' reflected ex-Major Denis Healey,' was that it didn't kill, but it wounded the tradition of deference which had played a very big part in British elections up to the end of the Thirties. It ended the habit of deferential voting. It was a genuine political watershed.' But to the newly politically-conscious people in factories and homes, who had just voted for the first time (there had not been an election for ten years), it was a time for apocalyptic feelings. Barbara Davies spoke for her discussion groups at the aircraft factory:

All my colleagues, all my peer group, could think of nothing else, because this was the new world, this was a fresh start. We didn't know that Britain would be so badly in debt, we didn't consider who was going to pay for the war. All we knew was that it was the end of an ill regime and the start of something new and we looked forward with great hopes.

Whether those great hopes of a new world and a fresh start were to be fulfilled rather than disappointed, or disappointed rather than fulfilled, is a matter of interpretation beyond the scope of this book. But it is important to remember what the hopes were. The British people did not emerge from the traumatic experience of the Second World War the same people as went into it in 1939. And the chief difference that was made to the vast majority was in their expectations, in what they asked from life in the future. After all, they had won. And if they had managed to destroy the enemy together, then surely a small instalment of Utopia was not beyond their means to create? The would-be builders of the New Jerusalem did not paralyse their hopes with sceptical questions. They did not reflect that Britain was no longer a world power – though this was demonstrated at Hiroshima and Nagasaki within a couple of weeks. They did not pause to consider that Britain was virtually bankrupt, though this was soon demonstrated when the American lend–lease agreement was withdrawn abruptly and the debts were called in. For the time being there was still enough of a feeling of national unity and shared sacrifice to make these ideal aims seem attainable.

So, gradually, nearly 2 million soldiers, sailors and airmen came home, were issued with 'demob' suits and fitted themselves back into their civilian lives and domestic hearths. Many of them were coming home to children who did not recognise them – who asked 'Who's that man, Mummy?' – and some who were not specially pleased to see them, at first. J. B. Priestley wrote a

108 *Home again: these RAF 'boys' – none of them in the first flush of youth – emerge from the demobilisation centre, half in their 'demob' suits, the other half carrying them in parcels*

novel about these bewildered returned servicemen, *Three Men in New Suits*, in which one of them argues that people at home 'are not very different now than they were before the war. But we are – and that's the point. We don't try to return to the muddle of the pre-war time. We don't want the same kind of men looking after our affairs. We don't keep shouting "That's mine – clear off." We don't try to make our little corner safe and to hell with anybody else! Instead of grabbing, we plan. Instead of competing we co-operate.' Of course, Priestley could see as well as anyone that this mood would not last. He wrote later: 'The British were absolutely at their best in the Second World War. They were never as good, certainly in my lifetime, before it, and I'm sorry to say they've never been so good after it.'

For the people whose memories have illuminated this book the war altered life in a great variety of ways. For some it brought a legacy of ill-health – like Vi Maxwell who had the horrifying experience of being trapped in an underground shelter with her baby as the water level gradually rose around her: 'You relive it over and over again – and through that, I now have a phobia of being in a confined space.' To some families it brought divorce, like that of Patricia McCann, who said of her parents: 'If it hadn't been for the war, they possibly would have stayed together and things would have been a lot different for me.' Some were changed in unexpected ways, like Emma Kitching who, before the bomb reduced her home to rubble, was so houseproud that everything in it had to match: 'I hadn't been married long and I wouldn't have put a cup and saucer on the table without the teapot to match. After I saw my home gone, and all my wedding presents, I vowed then I would never be so houseproud again – and I never was.'

Some still miss the childhood pleasures they never knew, like Jean Carberry who was told she was too grown-up to expect her toys to be replaced after the bombing. 'We had to share a doll and at Christmas time we never got toys. They said once, there isn't a Father Christmas, so when I was about nine, that was it, that was my childhood.' People who were slightly older felt they had missed their youth. 'I was nearly twenty by the time all the rationing and everything stopped,' said land girl Joan Shakesheff, 'We'd been without things, we'd been deprived of things, we'd been deprived of our youth.' Others were deprived of their young married life. 'Our husbands went off to fight,' said Mickey Lewis, 'and although some of it was exciting, I should have liked to have children earlier than I did and a decent home and I didn't have it. But I don't think at the time we saw it as a sacrifice, because goodness knows what would have happened if we'd lost.' 'We were the lucky ones,' said Doris White. 'I used to think about all the RAF fellows and Americans who got killed and what a waste it was. Even now I can cry if I think too much about it.'

But alongside the sense of what was lost, there was also a memory of something that was gained in wartime – and which seemed to get lost when it was over. Tom Hopkinson reflected: 'Peace-time society always tends to be a battle for oneself – a me-first situation. In the war this was blessedly different. Everybody felt they should do what they could for someone else. If they were bombed out, the nearest families took them in. If you were travelling by car in the country, you gave lifts to people who were walking.'

'There was this general feeling that we were one nation – a feeling of equality, that everybody was valuable, that everybody's effort counted,' said John Beavan, 'It was a much more equal society than we had before and some of it remains.'

'The big thing about the war was that it mixed people up, it broke down the class and occupational barriers that existed before,' said Denis Healey, 'Everybody had a value and in that sense all men and all women were equal. This had a profound effect on people's attitude to social and political problems.'

'There are a large number of people who will tell you that in spite of all the fear, the loss, the suffering, the privation and so on, the war years were the happiest years of their life,' said Sir Richard Acland. 'By and large we ate the same rations, we wore the same clothes and we shared a common purpose and there was a sense that this kind of spirit had got to continue after the war.'

ZEC

"Thank you for light in the darkest hours." *Britain showed by an overwhelming Labour vote that it had had enough of Tory rule. But Churchill's personal war leadership will never be forgotten.* **(August 16, 1945)**

109 The Daily Mirror *cartoonist, Zec, who had often angered Churchill, offers him a farewell salute as a setting sun. Ahead, a new dawn beckoned without him*

'My most lasting memory is funnily enough not of unrelieved gloom, bombs, black-outs, food rationing and the rest,' said Fred Barnes. 'It is rather of what nice people we all were then – kindly, friendly people.'

'It was something you would never forget, seeing people come together like that,' said Bert Sparling. 'It was a great community spirit. I wouldn't have missed it for the world. I went straight overseas for two or three years at the end of the war and when I came back, it had gone.'

SELECT BIBLIOGRAPHY

Paul Addison, *The Road to 1945* (Cape, 1975)

Earl of Avon, *The Eden Memoirs* (Cassell, 1965)

Michael Balfour, *Propaganda in War* (Routledge and Kegan Paul, 1979)

Corelli Barnett, *The Audit of War* (Macmillan, 1983)

Cecil Beaton, *Self-Portrait with Friends*, ed. Richard Buckle (Weidenfeld and Nicolson, 1979)

Sir William Beveridge, *Power and Influence* (Hodder and Stoughton, 1953); *Report on National Insurance and Allied Services* (HMSO, 1942); *Full Employment in a Free Society* (Allen and Unwin, 1944)

Peter Black, *The Biggest Aspidistra in the World* (BBC Publications, 1972)

Asa Briggs, *History of Broadcasting, Vol 3: War of Words* (OUP, 1970)

Susan Briggs, *Keep Smiling Through*, (Weidenfeld and Nicolson, 1975)

Vera Brittain, *England's Hour* (Macmillan, 1941)

Alan Bullock, *Life and Times of Ernest Bevin*, vol 2 (Heinemann, 1967)

R. A. (Lord) Butler, *The Art of Memory* (Hodder and Stoughton, 1982)

Chips – The Diaries of Sir Henry Channon, ed. Robert Rhodes James (Weidenfeld and Nicolson, 1967)

Winston Churchill, *The Second World War*, 6 vols (Cassell, 1948–54); *The War Speeches*, ed. Charles Eade, 3 vols (Cassell, 1951–2)

J. A. Cole, *William Joyce, Lord Haw-Haw* (Faber, 1964)

John Colville, *The Fringes of Power: Downing Street Diaries* (Hodder and Stoughton, 1985)

Noel Coward, *The Noel Coward Diaries* (Weidenfeld and Nicolson, 1982)

Basil Dean, *The Theatre at War* (Harrap, 1956)

Peter Fleming, *Invasion 1940* (Hart Davis, 1957)

Martin Gilbert, *Winston Churchill, Finest Hour* (Heinemann, 1983)

Sir Arthur Harris, *Bomber Offensive* (Collins, 1947)

Tom Harrisson, *Living Through the Blitz* (Collins, 1976)

A. P. Herbert, *Independent Member* (Methuen, 1950)

Tom Hopkinson, *In This Our Time* (Hutchinson, 1982)

Sir Brian Horrocks, *A Full Life* (Collins, 1960)

Frank Huggett, *Goodnight Sweetheart: Memories of the Second World War* (W. H. Allen, 1979)

Bernard Kops, *The World is a Wedding* (Granada, 1963)

John Lehmann, *I Am My Brother* (Longmans, 1960)

Norman Longmate, *How We Lived Then* (Hutchinson, 1971)

Rose Macaulay, *Letters to a Sister* (Collins, 1964)

Arthur Marwick, *The Home Front* (Thames and Hudson, 1976)

W. R. Matthews, *St Paul's in Wartime* (Hutchinson, 1946)

Rayne, Minns, *Bombers and Mash* (Virago, 1981)

Guy Morgan, *Red Roses Every Night* (London Quality Press, 1948)

Leonard Mosley, *Backs to the Wall* (Weidenfeld and Nicolson, 1971)

Sir Harold Nicolson, *Diaries and Letters, 1939–45*, ed. Nigel Nicolson (Collins, 1967)

Barbara Nixon, *Raiders Overhead* (Scolar Press/Gulliver Publishing, 1943)

George Orwell, *The Collected Essays, Letters and Journalism* ed. Sonia Orwell and Ian Angus, 4 vols (Secker and Warburg, 1968)

J. B. Priestley, *Postscripts* (Heinemann, 1940) *Margin Released* (Heinemann, 1962) *Three Men in New Suits* (Heinemann, 1945)

Charles Reid, *Malcolm Sargent: A Biography* (Hamish Hamilton, 1969)

Victoria Sackville-West, *Country Notes in Wartime* (Hogarth Press, 1941)

Sir Harold Scott, *Your Obedient Servant* (André Deutsch, 1959)

John Strachey, *Post D* (Gollancz, 1941)

A. G. Street, *From Dusk Till Dawn* (Harrap, 1942)

Penny Summerfield, *Women Workers in the Second World War* (Croom Helm, 1984)

Christopher Sykes, *Nancy – The Life of Lady Astor* (Collins, 1972)

A. J. P. Taylor, *Essays in British History* (Hamish Hamilton, 1976)

H. M. Tomlinson, *The Wind is Rising* (Hodder and Stoughton, 1941)

John Wadsworth, *Counter Defensive* (Hodder and Stoughton, 1946)

Sir John Wheeler-Bennett, *King George VI* (Macmillan, 1958)

Jerome Willis, *It Stopped at London* (Hurst and Blackett, 1944)

H. A. Wilson, *Death Over Haggerston* (A. R. Mowbray, 1941)

John Gilbert Winant, *Letter from Grosvenor Square* (Hodder and Stoughton, 1947)

Lord Woolton, *Memoirs* (Cassell, 1959)

Poems quoted

Leon Atkins, 'Dunkirk' from *The Oasis Selection* (Everyman, Dent, 1985)

John Betjeman, 'Westminster Abbey' from *Collected Poems* (John Murray, 1979)

Noel Coward, 'Don't Let's be Beastly to the Germans' from *The Lyrics* (Heinemann, 1965)

Cecil Day Lewis, 'The Stand-To' from *Word All Over* (Jonathan Cape, 1943)

A. P. Herbert, 'Invasion', 'Top Wop' and 'Brown Bread' from *Siren Song* (Methuen, 1940) and *Bring back the Bells* (Methuen, 1943)

Laurie Lee, 'Sea Front' from *The Sun My Monument* (Hogarth Press, 1944)

Stephen Spender, 'Epilogue to a Human Drama' from *Collected Poems 1928–85* (Faber, 1985)

Ruthven Todd, 'These are Facts' from *These are Facts* (Dent)

INDEX

Numbers in *italics* refer to illustrations